Guardianship
Court of Last Resort for the Elderly and Disabled

Guardianship
Court of Last Resort for the
Elderly and Disabled

Winsor C. Schmidt, Jr.

*Professor of Political Science
and
Director, Center for Health
Services Research
The University of Memphis*

CAROLINA ACADEMIC PRESS
Durham, North Carolina

KF
553
.S36
1995

© Copyright 1995 Winsor C. Schmidt, Jr.
All Rights Reserved

ISBN: 0-89089-925-8
LCCN: 94-073845

Carolina Academic Press
700 Kent Street
Durham, North Carolina 27701
Tel. (919) 489-7486
Fax (919) 493-5668

Printed in the United States of America

This book is dedicated to my mother and father,
Miriam Tebbetts Schmidt and Winsor Chase Schmidt
who accomplish a family,
an aspiration of guardianship.

Contents

Acknowledgments	ix
Introduction	xiii

Part I: An Overview Case Study of Guardianship and the Need for Reform — 1

    Chapter 1 Guardianship of the Elderly in Florida: Social Bankruptcy and the Need for Reform — 3

Part II: The Extent of Unmet Need for Guardian Services — 17

    Chapter 2 Legal Incompetents' Need for Guardians in Florida — 19

    Chapter 3 Elderly Nursing Home Residents' Need for Public Guardianship Services in Tennessee — 37

Part III: Findings from a National Study of Public Guardianship and the Elderly — 51

    Chapter 4 Issues in Public Guardianship — 53

    Chapter 5 Summary and Discussion of Major Findings from a National Study of Public Guardianship and the Elderly — 69

    Chapter 6 Alternatives to Public Guardianship — 79

Part IV: The Functioning of Guardianship Court: What Happens to People in the Court of Last Resort — 89

    Chapter 7 Guardianship of the Elderly in Tallahassee, Florida — 91

    Chapter 8 Accountability of Lawyers in Serving Vulnerable, Elderly Clients — 107

    Chapter 9 Recommended Judicial Practices in Guardianship Proceedings for the Elderly — 119

Part V: The Functioning of Guardian Programs and Services: What Happens to People after the Court of Last Resort — 133

    Chapter 10 The Evolution of a Public Guardianship Program — 135

Chapter 11   A Descriptive Analysis of Professional and
             Volunteer Programs for the Delivery of
             Guardianship Services   145

Part VI: A Summary of What is Known, and Unknown,
          About Guardianship   179
    Chapter 12   Quantitative Information About the Quality
                 of the Guardianship System: Toward a Next
                 Generation of Guardianship Research   181

Part VII: Beyond the Court of Last Resort: Involuntary
          Adult Protective Services   203
    Chapter 13   Improving the Social Treatment Model in
                 Protective Services for the Elderly:
                 False Needs in the Therapeutic State   205
    Chapter 14   Adult Protective Services and the
                 Therapeutic State   217

Part VIII: Conclusions and Recommendations   237
    Chapter 15   Model Public Guardianship Statute   239

Contributors   263
Index   265

Acknowledgments

The idea and encouragement to compile these essays in book form come from my colleague, Bill Marty (University of Memphis).

My co-author on several of the essays, the late William Bell, took the initiative of interesting several of us at Florida State University to begin what has become a guardianship research agenda. Another co-author, mentor, and friend, Kent Miller, is singularly responsible for introducing me to a great and delightful institution and career, the university. Another co-author and friend, Elaine New, acted as at least de facto project director in the early research.

I am grateful for permission to use the essays, which come from the following sources:

Chapter 1 (Schmidt)—*Guardianship of the Elderly in Florida: Social Bankruptcy and the Need for Reform*, 55 Florida Bar Journal 189 (March 1981).

Chapter 2 (Schmidt and Peters)—*Legal Incompetents' Need for Guardians in Florida*, 15 Bulletin of the American Academy of Psychiatry and the Law 69 (1987).

Chapter 3 (Hightower, Heckert, and Schmidt)—*Elderly Nursing Home Residents' Need for Public Guardianship Services in Tennessee*, 2 (3/4) Journal of Elder Abuse and Neglect 105 (1990). © By The Haworth Press, Inc. All rights reserved. Reprinted with permission. For copies of this work, contact Marianne Arnold at The Haworth Document Delivery Service (Telephone 1-800-3-HAWORTH; 10 Alice Street, Binghampton, N.Y. 13904). For other questions concerning rights and permissions contact Wanda Latour at the above address.

Chapter 4 (Schmidt, Bickel, Bell, Miller, and New)—*Issues in Public Guardianship*, 15 The Urban and Social Change Review 21 (Winter 1982).

Chapter 5 (Schmidt, Miller, Bell, and New)—*Summary and Discussion of Major Findings*, in Public Guardianship and the Elderly, Cambridge, Mass.: Ballinger Publishing Co., pp. 167–177 (1981). Copyright © (1981). Reprinted with permission of HarperCollins Publishers.

Chapter 6—Winsor C. Schmidt, Kent S. Miller, William G. Bell, and Elaine S. New, "Alternatives to Public Guardianship," STATE AND LOCAL GOVERNMENT REVIEW, Vol. 14, No. 3 (September 1982): 128–131. Reprinted by permission of the Carl Vinson Institute of Government, University of Georgia.

Chapter 7 (Peters, Schmidt, and Miller)—*Guardianship of the Elderly in Tallahassee, Florida*, 25 THE GERONTOLOGIST 532 (Oct. 1985). Copyright © The Gerontological Society of America. Reprinted with permission.

Chapter 8 (Schmidt)—*Accountability of Lawyers in Serving Vulnerable, Elderly Clients*, 5 (3) Journal of Elder Abuse and Neglect 39 (1983). © By The Haworth Press, Inc. All rights reserved. Reprinted with permission. For copies of this work, contact Marianne Arnold at The Haworth Document Delivery Service (Telephone 1-800-3-HAWORTH; 10 Alice Street, Binghampton, N.Y. 13904). For other questions concerning rights and permissions contact Wanda Latour at the above address.

Chapter 9 (Schmidt)—*Recommended Judicial Practices in Guardianship Proceedings for the Elderly*, 61 Florida Bar Journal 35 (May 1987).

Chapter 10 (Schmidt)—*The Evolution of a Public Guardianship Program*, 12 Journal of Psychiatry and Law 349 (1984).

Chapter 11 (Schmidt, Miller, Peters, and Loewenstein)—*A Descriptive Analysis of Professional and Volunteer Programs for the Delivery of Guardianship Services*, 8 (2) Probate Law Journal 125 (1988). National College of Probate Judges and Boston University School of Law. Copyright © 1988 by the Trustees of Boston University. Reprinted with permission.

Chapter 12 (Schmidt)—*Quantitative Information About the Quality of the Guardianship System: Toward a Next Generation of Guardianship Research*, 10 (1) Probate Law Journal 61 (1990). National College of Probate Judges and Boston University School of Law. Copyright © 1990 by the Trustees of Boston University. Reprinted with permission.

Chapter 13 (Schmidt and Miller)—*Improving the Social Treatment Model in Protective Services for the Elderly: False Needs in the Therapeutic State*, 1 Journal of International and Comparative Social Welfare 90 (Fall 1984).

Chapter 14 (Schmidt)—*Adult Protective Services and the Therapeutic State*, 10 Law and Psychology Review 101 (1986).

Chapter 15 (Schmidt, Miller, Bell, and New)—*Model Public Guardianship Statute*, in Public Guardianship and the Elderly, Cambridge, Mass.: Ballinger Publishing Co., pp. 179–203). Copyright © (1981). Reprinted with permission of HarperCollins Publishers.

I thank Sharon Beasley for her excellent secretarial services, and Heather Donahue, Rochelle Luster, Caryn Cloud, and Stine Moss-Cooperwood for their proofreading assistance. Robin Quinn, Research Associate for the Center for Health Services Research, consulted and assisted with preparation of the manuscript. I thank Shirley Amitrano for her excellent research assistance.

I very much appreciate the good humor of my teenage son, Winsor, who has taken great glee in reciprocally identifying any and all procrastination and tardiness in the preparation of this book. I also thank my wife, Lenore, for her work outside and inside the home in making this project easier.

Finally, I thank Mayapriya Long, Andrew Wilson, and the staff at Carolina Academic Press.

The chapters are slightly edited from the original form, but significant material is not deleted. Some overlap occurs, but this allows each chapter to stand on its own in addition to constituting part of a whole. Bracketed material consists of the most significant references since the essay was first published.

Introduction

The purpose of this book is to inform health, gerontological, social service, and legal professionals and students, as well as state and federal judges, legislators, and the attentive public about the findings, analyses, conclusions, and implications from over a decade of personal national and state research on guardianship and protective services for the elderly and disabled.

Approximately half a million people are under guardianship in the United States. Guardianship is intended as a last resort, but this court of last resort is an institutional fiefdom that has historically received little scrutiny. As the national population ages, and the lifespan increases, more people are potentially subject to being adjudicated incompetent in court and appointed a guardian as a substitute decisionmaker.

People get involved with the guardianship system as a last resort for a variety of reasons. Failure to execute a "living will" concerning the management of their property and person if incapacitated means the court must decide. Failure to execute a "durable power of attorney" concerning who a person chooses to act as decisionmaker if the person becomes incompetent means the court chooses a surrogate. The absence of willing and responsible family members and friends, or resources to hire a professional guardian, results in appointment of a public employee guardian by the court. Limited social and protective services can turn guardianship into a dumping ground.

There are more legal procedures and criteria protecting an accused criminal than there are procedures and criteria protecting persons who are allegedly incompetent. Most guardianship courts operate locally with paper files rather than computers. The courts and their offices are frequently understaffed and underfunded. Court reviews of how well a guardianship manages a person and the person's property are generally sporadic. Few appeals or restorations of competence occur. Little centralized state or national oversight is available. Most guardianships last for the remainder of one's life, or until the money runs out.

One of the biggest problems with guardianship is the unmet need of people who are functionally incompetent, but have no willing and responsible family members or friends to act as guardians, or no resources to hire one. The extent of this need is specifically documented for the state of Florida (America's demographic future with the its high percentage of elderly), and in the nursing homes in the state of Tennessee.

A national study of public guardianship documents the extent to which this safety net institution assists and hinders the elderly in securing access to their rights, benefits, and entitlements. There is considerable evidence that public and private guardianship serves third party interests (family members, hospitals, nursing homes, social service agencies) rather than the interests of the incompetent ward. There is some evidence that guardianship services increase the rate of institutionalization, and of death. Alternatives to guardianship, and prevention services, are considered.

The workings of a specific guardianship court are explored. The need for greater accountability of lawyers in the guardianship process is assessed. This provides a foundation for an elaboration of recommended judicial practice reforms.

The disposition of persons adjudicated incompetent, and how well their person and property are managed, are covered. Both professional and volunteer programs for the delivery of guardian services are analyzed.

An overview of quantitative information about the quality of the guardianship system is provided.

Finally, an assessment of involuntary adult protective services is presented. Protective services are represented to the public as a preventive or diversionary device for guardianship. But involuntary protective services operate in more shadow with less legal protection and accountability than guardianship. As light is shed on guardianship, involuntary protective services may become the last resort of the next decade.

Guardianship

Court of Last Resort for the Elderly and Disabled

Part I

An Overview Case Study of Guardianship and the Need for Reform

Chapter 1

Guardianship of the Elderly in Florida: Social Bankruptcy and the Need for Reform

Winsor C. Schmidt, Jr.

Guardianship is the authority of a guardian, and the relation between guardian and ward.[1] A guardian manages the person and property of another, the "ward," who is considered incapable of self-administration.[2] Guardianship in Florida is governed by the Florida Guardianship Law.[3] The historical purpose of guardianship is care of another, but closer examination reveals an alternative function:

> Recognize guardianship for what it really is: the most intrusive, non-interest serving, impersonal legal device known and available to us and as such, one which minimizes personal autonomy and respect for the individual, has a high potential for doing harm and raises at best a questionable benefit/burden ratio. As such, it is a device to be studiously avoided.[4]

Guardianship is avoided, statistically. A guardianship study of six states (Delaware, Minnesota, North Carolina, Ohio, Washington and Wisconsin), with a total population of 29 million, found that 17,000 guardian-

---

1. Black's Law Dictionary 636 (5th ed. 1979).
2. *Id.* at 635.
3. Fla. Stat. ch. 744 (1979), *as amended*. Detailed information on the Florida Guardianship Law is available in several sources. See, *e.g.*, Fla. Bar C.L.E., Florida Guardianship Practice (1978); Florida Justice Institute and the Florida Bar, Older Floridians Handbook: Laws and Programs Affecting Older Floridians, (1980); Florida State Hospital, Guardianship Manual, Chattahoochee, Fla: Model Legal Services (1980).

[*Cf.* Fla. Stat. ch. 744 (1989), as amended; Barnes, *Beyond Guardianship Reform: A Reevaluation of Autonomy and Beneficence for a System of Principled Decision-making in Long Term Care*, 41 Emory L.J. 633 (1992).]

4. E.S. Cohen, Protective Services and Public Guardianship: A Dissenting View (address at 31st Annual Meeting of the Gerontological Society, Dallas, Texas, November 20, 1978).

ship petitions were filed in one year.[5] This filing rate of .059 percent (one of every 1,706) corresponds interestingly with the filing rate of .056 percent (one of every 1,785) for Florida in 1977 (4,724 guardianships opened in a population of 8,432,927).[6] Involuntary civil commitment for mental treatment and for alcohol treatment are more frequent events, for example. However, these data do not reflect the growing and potential impact of guardianship, especially from the perspective of individual wards.

Older persons are an at-risk group according to both the legal[7] and functional criteria for guardianship. Guardianship law emphasizes mental incapacity in justifying the adjudication of incompetence, with the consequence that "anyone, especially an older person, who needs a guardian is popularly assumed to be mentally ill. The aged person with a few of the symptoms of chronic brain syndrome, such as forgetfulness, is more likely to be judged mentally ill and therefore to be declared incompetent."[8] The aging of the population bulge can bring proportionately increased numbers of persons into the guardianship process.

There is also evidence that as deinstitutionalization proceeds, and where involuntary civil commitment criteria and procedures become more restrictive, use of guardianship increases.[9] This tendency may combine with a

---

5. M. Axilbund, Exercising Judgment for the Disabled: Report of an Inquiry into Limited Guardianship, Public Guardianship and Adult Protective Services in Six States (Executive Summary), Washington, D.C.: ABA Commission on the Mentally Disabled (1979), p. 21.

6. W. Schmidt, K. Miller, W. Bell, & E. New, Public Guardianship and the Elderly (1981), p. 148; Older Americans, 1977, U.S. Department of Health, Education, and Welfare, Pub. No. (OHD) 78-20006 (1978).

7. E.g., "senility" has been a triggering criterion in Florida. Fla. Stat. § 744.102(5) (1979). *But see* In re Asa B. Brown, 45 Mich. 326, 7 N.W. 899 (1881) (mere allegation of age or senility is insufficient to support guardianship petition); McGuigan's Estate, 349 Pa. 581, 37 A.2d 717 (1944).

8. J. Regan & G. Springer, Protective Services for the Elderly, p. 36, a working paper prepared for the Special Committee on Aging, U.S. Senate (1977), *citing* Lehman, Guardianship, in Social Welfare of the Aging 312 (Kaplan & Aldridge eds. 1962). *See also* Cohen, Old Age and the Law, 53 Women's L.J. 96 (1967).

9. *See* W. Schmidt et al., *supra* note 6 (California, Maryland, and Missouri are three states where this phenomenon is allegedly occurring).

This may be part of a larger social control continuum whereby decriminalization of alcohol and drug offenses in the criminal justice system leads to enhanced use of civil commitment, at which point "criminalization" of civil commitment (tightening criteria and procedures) leads to enhanced use of guardianship. I predict that reform of guardianship (tightening criteria and procedures) will result in enhanced use of adult protective services (see Fla. Stat. §§ 410.10–410.11). Society tolerates only a certain amount of deviance before calling into play certain incapacitative devices, usually in the name of "rehabilitation", benevolence, and paternalism. *See generally,* N. Kittrie, The Right to be Different: Deviance and Enforced Therapy (1971).

growing number of poor people to verify one commentator's conclusion: "When examined in the larger context of social programming through which we purport to help the less advantaged, involuntary guardianship emerges as an official initiation rite for the entry of the poor and the inept into the managed society."[10]

Furthermore, annual per capita filing rates do not take into consideration the net annual addition to guardianship rolls (1,400 to 1,500 in Florida[11]—guardianships opened, minus guardianships closed through death, exhaustion of the estate, and restoration of legal competence), the number of people who could be adjudicated incompetent but are not,[12] and the number of people for whom some alternative, or moral equivalent of guardianship, suffices. Guardianship is much more frequent than judicial utterances of acquittal by reason of insanity (an event "rarer than the annual incidence of poisonous snake bites in Manhattan"[13]), yet scholarly and case law attention to guardianship does not even approach the mountain of literature and litigation on the insanity defense.

Personal Consequences

The personal consequences of guardianship are substantial. The subject of guardianship "may be subject to greater control of his or her life than one convicted of a crime."[14] In Florida, a person adjudicated incompetent has been statutorily "presumed to be incapable of managing his own affairs or of making any gift, contract, or instrument in writing that is binding on him or his estate."[15] In most states, a finding of legal incompetence restricts or takes away "the right to: make contracts; sell, purchase, mortgage, or lease property; make gifts; travel, or decide where to live; vote, or hold elected office; initiate or defend against suits; make a will, or revoke one; engage in certain professions; lend or borrow money; appoint agents; divorce, or marry; refuse medical treatment; keep and care

---

10. Mitchell, *Involuntary Guardianship for Incompetents: A Strategy for Legal Services Advocates*, 12 Clearinghouse Rev. 451, 466 (1978).
11. W. Schmidt, *et al., supra* note 6, at 148.
12. State social workers in Florida in 1977 claimed that 2,700 people, 1,700 age 60 and over, identifiable by name and address, needed to be adjudicated legally incompetent and have a guardian appointed. Memorandum from the Aging and Adult Services Program Office, Department of Health and Rehabilitative Services, Tallahassee (1977), table reprinted in W. Schmidt, *et al., supra* note 6, at 147.
13. A. Stone, Mental Health and Law: A System in Transition, Rockville, MD: NIMH (1975), p. 218 *citing* Cohen, *Review of A. Goldstein, Insanity Defense*, 13 Contemp. Psych. 386 (1968).
14. Heap v. Roulet, 590 P.2d 1, 3 (Cal. 1979).
15. Fla. Stat. § 744.331(8) (1979).

for children; serve on a jury; be a witness to any legal document; drive a car; pay or collect debts; manage or run a business."[16] The loss of any one of these rights can have a disastrous result, but taken together, their effect is to reduce the status of an individual to that of a child, or a nonperson. The process can be characterized as legal infantilization.

These consequences might be mitigated, at least on a *quid pro quo* basis, if guardianship services were beneficial. Unfortunately, there is evidence that guardianship is beneficial only to persons other than the ward. In their landmark study of over 400 guardianships, Alexander and Lewin found that wards ended up worse in every case:[17]

> Under the present system of "Estate Management by Preemption" we divest the incompetent of control of his property upon the finding of the existence of serious mental illness whenever divestiture is in the interest of some third person or institution. The theory of incompetency is to protect the debilitated from their own financial foolishness or from the fraud of others who would prey upon their mental weaknesses. In practice, however, we seek to protect the interests of others. The state hospital commences incompetency proceedings to facilitate reimbursement for costs incurred in the care, treatment and maintenance of its patients. Dependents institute proceedings to secure their needs. Co-owners of property find incompetency proceedings convenient ways to secure the sale of realty. Heirs institute actions to preserve their dwindling inheritances. Beneficiaries of trusts or estates seek incompetency as an expedient method of removing as trustee one who is managing the trust or estate in a manner adverse to their interests. All of these motives may be honest and without any intent to cheat the aged, but none of the proceedings are commenced to assist the debilitated.[18]

Or, as a psychiatrist more succinctly put it, "'for every $100,000 in a given estate a lawyer shows up, for every $25,000 a family member shows up.'"[19]

Another study illustrating the high risks of intervention involved a quasi-experimental design carried out by Blenkner and associates through the Benjamin Rose Institute in Cleveland.[20] The provision of enriched, protective services (including guardianships) to the experimental group not

---

16. R. Brown, The Rights of Older Persons (1979), p. 286.
17. G. Alexander & T. Lewin, The Aged and the Need for Surrogate Management (1972), p. 136.
18. *Id.* at 135.
19. W. Schmidt, *et al., supra* note 6, at 109.
20. M. Blenkner, M. Bloom, M. Nielson, & R. Weber, Final Report: Protective Services for Older People, Findings from the Benjamin Rose Institute Study, Cleveland (1974); Blenkner, Bloom, and Nielson, *A Research and Demonstration Project of Protective Services*, 52 Soc. Case Work 483 (1971).

only failed to prevent or slow deterioration or death, but the experimental group actually had a higher rate of institutionalization and death than did the control group who received nothing.

Guardianship has sometimes been used for an individual who is "likely to...inflict harm on himself,"[21] despite some other evidence that involuntary treatment for dangerousness to self increases the rate of suicide.[22] Thus, empirical questions about guardianship elicit suggestions that guardianship serves third party interests, fails to make the ward better off than before appointment of a guardian, increases the chances of institutionalization and probably of death, results in more negative outcomes as the time of the guardianship relationship increases, and constitutes a most restrictive alternative that is inevitably overutilized.

Alternatives to Guardianship

There are less restrictive[23] alternatives to guardianship. Appropriate utilization of such alternatives should make guardianship even more of a last resort. These alternatives[24] include power of attorney; durable family power

---

21. Fla. Stat. § 744.331(1) (1979).

22. Greenburg, *Involuntary Psychiatric Commitments to Prevent Suicide*, 49 N.Y.U.L. Rev. 227, 236, 250, 256–59 (1974).

In analogous areas, a long term major delinquency program found no significant difference between treatment and control groups; in fact, the longer and more intense the treatment, the more negative were eventual outcomes. *See* McCord, *A Thirty-Year Follow-Up of Treatment Effects*, 33 Am. Psychologist 284 (1978); McCord and McCord, *A Follow-Up Report on the Cambridge Somerville Youth Study*, 322 Annals 89 (1959); McCord, Consideration of Some Effects of a Counseling Program (Unpublished Draft 1979).

A study of mental patients released from Alabama mental institutions by court order concluded that "family members adjusted expectations and accepted the patient home" when the state did not provide the alternative of a mental hospital. Leaf, *Patients Released After "Wyatt": Where Did They Go?*, 28 Hospital & Community Psych. 366 (1977).

23. *See, e.g.*, Shelton v. Tucker, 364 U.S. 479, 488 (1960) ("In a series of decisions this Court has held that, even though the governmental purpose be legitimate and substantial, that purpose cannot be pursued by means that broadly stifle personal liberties when the end can be more narrowly achieved. The breadth of legislative abridgement must be viewed in the light of less drastic means for achieving the same basic purpose.")

24. *See generally* R. Brown, *supra* note 16, at 343–347; Older Floridians Handbook, *supra* note 8, at 42–46; W. Schmidt, *et al.*, *supra* note 6, at 182; E. Wadleigh, Aging and the Law—Protective Services, (1979); Horstman, *Protective Services for the Elderly: The Limits of Parens Patriae*, 40 Mo. L. Rev. 215 (1975); Regan, *Protective Services for the Elderly: Commitment, Guardianship and Alternatives*, 13 William & Mary L. Rev. 569 (1972).

of attorney;[25] single transaction court ratification of a particular action; joint tenancy; inter vivos transfers of property; deeds of guardianship;[26] trusts; substitute or representative payee;[27] protective services;[28] and civil commitment.

When the less restrictive alternatives are exhausted, the last resort of guardianship can be considered. Important concerns at this time are the criteria and procedures for guardianship.

An important study undertaken by the National Law Center of George Washington University indicated that statutory definitions for incompetence are vague and contribute to an erroneous belief that individual capabilities are well reflected in generalizations about age, mental or physical health, and the like.[29] Attorneys and physicians who participated frequently in guardianship cases could not agree on the meaning of such criteria, frequently with such observations as "has no psychiatric meaning," or "ambiguous as hell."[30]

A reform alternative to such criteria as Florida's[31] could restrict guardianship eligibility to "gravely disabled"[32] persons who lack the capacity to make informed decisions about proposed care, treatment, or management services.[33] "Gravely disabled" is adopted from the California conserva-

---

25. See Fla. Stat. § 709.08 (1979); Alexander, *Premature Probate: A Different Perspective on Guardianship for the Elderly*, 31 Stan. L. Rev. 1003 (1979); *Legal Problems of the Aged and Infirm—The Durable Power of Attorney—Planned Protective Services and the Living Will*, 13 Real Prop. Prob & Tr. J. 1–87 (1978). [*Cf.* J. Federman & M. Reed, *Abuse and the Durable Power of Attorney: Options for Reform*, Albany, NY: Gov't Law Center of Albany Law School (1984) (national survey of 410 responding attorneys, social service providers, and NY surrogate court judges, of 7,000 surveys distributed, found that 94% believed durable power of attorney abuse occurs at least occasionally; provides 15 legislative reform options.)]

26. *See, e.g.*, Schlesinger, *Deeds of Guardianship*, 8 Prob. & Prop. 4 (1978).

27. Recipients of funds from several government agencies (Civil Service, Department of Defense, Railroad Retirement Board, Social Security Administration, Veterans Administration) can have substitute payees appointed if an individual meets a test of incapacity that varies from agency to agency. See Regan, *supra* note 24, at 612–13.

28. See Fla, Stat. §§ 410.10–410.11 (1979).

29. R. Allen, E. Ferster, & H. Weihofen, Mental Impairment and Legal Incompetency (1968).

30. *Id.* at 39–40.

31. Fla. Stat. § 744.102(5), *as amended* (1980), and § 744.331(1) (1979).

32. "Gravely disabled" is recommended by the Suggested Statute on Guardianship. *Legal Issues in State Mental Health Care: Proposals for Change—Guardianship*, 2 Mental Disability L. Rep. 444 (1978).

33. For definition of "lack the capacity...," *see Proposals for Change—Guardianship*, *supra* note 32, at 450, and W. Schmidt, *et al.*, *supra* note 6, at 191. Arguably, this criterion is a "constitutional precondition" to intervention in an individual's life by court order. *See Legal Issues in State Mental Health Care: Proposals for Change—Civil Commitment*, 2 Mental Disability L. Rep. 77, 89–93 (1977).

torship law[34] that, along with New York's, has been commended as a model.[35] "Gravely disabled" could be defined as "unable to meet essential requirements for one's physical health or safety or to manage one's financial resources as a result of a severe mental disorder."[36]

"Severe mental disorder", in turn, could be defined as "a severe impairment of emotional processes, ability to exercise conscious control of one's actions, or ability to perceive reality or to reason or understand, which impairment is manifested by instances of grossly disturbed behavior."[37] This definition includes the emotional, volitional, and cognitive components of mental functioning in terms understandable to physicians, attorneys, judges, and laypersons alike. Persons suffering from such casual or categorical generalities as "advanced age", epilepsy, mental retardation, and acute addiction or alcoholism would qualify if the disability produced a functionally severe mental disorder.

Guardianship procedures nationally do not seem to decrease the risk of erroneous deprivation of the liberty and property interests noted above. Presence of the proposed ward at the incompetency hearing is frequently waived,[38] often on the ironic ground that presence at one's own hearing will be harmful.[39] Other due process issues include inade-

---

34. Cal. Welf. & Inst. Code §§ 5008(h), 5350 (West 1972).

35. R. Brown, *supra* note 16, at 287.

36. *See Proposals for Change—Guardianship*, *supra* note 32, at 450; W. Schmidt, *et al.*, *supra* note 6, at 191.

37. *Proposals for Change—Guardianship*, *supra* note 32, at 450, 133; W. Schmidt, *et al.*, *supra* note 6, at 192.

38. A Los Angeles study involving over 1,000 guardianship and conservatorship filings found that in 84 percent of the cases, the only persons present at the hearing were the judge, petitioner, and petitioner's attorney. National Senior Citizens Law Center, untitled, unpublished study, *cited* by Horstman, *supra* note 24, at 235. Alexander and Lewin found that the alleged incompetent is frequently not brought to court, and only 16 percent had guardians ad litem appearing for them at the hearing. G. Alexander & T. Lewin, *supra* note 27, at 25.

39. Fla. Stat. § 744.331(4) (1979) stated: "The hearings shall be conducted in as informal a manner as may be consistent with orderly procedure and in a physical setting not likely to have a harmful effect on the mental health of the alleged incompetent."

There may be anecdotal evidence for such a policy, but I know of no empirical basis. On the other hand, the deleterious effects of long-term institutionalization and transfer shock as a result of such mechanisms as guardianship are well known.

[Procedure research suggests that adversary procedure produces greater satisfaction and perception of fairness by the child in the analogous area of child custody disputes. Melton & Lind, *Procedural Justice in Family Court: Does the Adversarial Model Make Sense?*, 5 Children & Youth Services 65 (1982). Adversary procedure may also be therapeutic. *See, e.g.*, Ensminger & Liguori, *The Therapeutic Significance of the Civil Commitment Hearing: An Unexplored Potential*, 6 J. Psychiatry & L. 5 (1978); Perlin, *An Invitation to the Dance: An Empirical Response to Chief Justice Warren Burger's "Time-Consuming Pro-*

quate notice;[40] the absence of counsel or essentially symbolic rather than aggressive representation in all but a very few cases;[41] the absence of court review;[42] the fact that appeals are nonexistent or usually waived;[43] that the vague legal standard is arbitrarily applied;[44] that dismissals of petitions are rare;[45] and that hearings are cursory, with most only taking several minutes.[46] Given the importance of counsel for the exercise of procedural rights, any ineffective assistance of counsel is a particularly disturbing development. More than one commentator has noted that counsel in such mental disability cases as guardianship functioned "'as no more than a clerk, ratifying the events that transpire[d], rather than influencing them.'"[47] Examples of such procedural practices were specifically identified in Florida.[48]

---

cedural Minuets" Theory in Parham v. J.R., 9 Bull. Am. Acad. Psychiatry & L. 149 (1976); Tyler, *The Psychological Consequences of Judicial Procedures: Implications for Civil Commitment Hearings*, 46 S. Methodist U. L. Rev. 433 (1992); Wexler, *Grave Disability and Family Therapy: The Therapeutic Potential of Civil Libertarian Commitment Codes*, 9 Int'l. J. L. & Psychiatry 39 (1986). The preference for adversary procedure may have a cultural bias. Leung & Lind, *Procedural Justice and Culture: Effects of Culture, Gender and Investigator Status on Procedural Preferences*. 50 J. Personality & Soc. Psychology 1134 (1986).]

40. Horstman, *supra* note 38, at 235.

41. See G. Alexander & T. Lewin, *supra* note 17; Horstman, *supra* note 24, at 236, 245; Solender, *The Guardian Ad Litem: A Valuable Representative or an Illusory Safeguard?*, 7 Texas Tech. L. Rev. 619 (1976).

42. See Alexander, *Forward: Life, Liberty, and Property Rights for the Elderly*, 17 Ariz. L. Rev. 267 (1975).

43. See Horstman, *supra* note 38, at 260; Mitchell, *supra* note 10, at 459.

44. Mitchell, *supra* note 10, at 456.59.

45. See, e.g., Levy, *Protecting the Mentally Retarded: An Empirical Survey and Evaluation of the Establishment of State Guardianship in Minnesota*, 49 Minn. L. Rev. 821 (1965).

46. *Id.* at 881; Mitchell, *supra* note 10, at 454.

47. Perlin, *Representing Individuals in the Commitment and Guardianship Process* in Legal Rights of Mental Disabled Persons, 501 (1979) *citing, e.g.*, Van Ness & Perlin, Mental Health Advocacy—The New Jersey Experience (N.L. Kopolow & H. Bloom eds.), Mental Health Advocacy: An Emerging Force in Consumers' Rights 63, 68–69 nn. 31–39 (1977).

Such practice in mental disability cases is not only unprofessional, but also probably unconstitutional. State *ex rel.* Memmel v. Mundy, No. 441–417 (Wis. Cir. Ct., Milwaukee Cty, Aug. 18, 1976) [1 Mental Disability L. Rep. 183 (1976)], aff'd, 75 Wis. 2d 276, 249 N.W. 2d 573 (1977). A vigorous and sophisticated public defender reduced the involuntary commitment rate to two percent following this litigation. T. Zander, The Mental Commitment Law as Scapegoat (Aug. 1979).

See also In re Paunack, 355 So. 2d 1195 (Fla. 1978).

48. *See* W. Schmidt *et al.*, *supra* note 6, at 149–64.

Statutory Remedies

In addition to the Uniform Probate Code,[49] suggested statutory remedies to procedural, and substantive, guardianship deficiencies abound.[50] A suggested Model Public Guardianship Statute contains guardianship procedure and criteria that attempt to combine the best of all the suggestions, in addition to reflecting a survey of the guardianship statutes in the fifty states.[51]

Highlights of the reform proposal include: functional, rather than causal or categorical, eligibility; partial or limited guardianship;[52] specified purpose of restoration, or development, of capacity; monitoring of private guardianships by public guardians; voluntary guardianship; determinant guardianship terms of no more than one year per term; precondition

---

49. At least eleven states have adopted the Code in significant part: Alaska, Arizona, Colorado, Idaho, Maine, Minnesota, Montana, Nebraska, New Mexico, North Dakota, and Utah.

50. *See* ABA Commission on the Mentally Disabled State Legislative Project, Guardianship and Conservatorship (1979), pp. 75–167; *Guardianship and Conservatorship Act*, 3 Mental Disability L. Rep. 266 (1979); *Legal Issues in State Mental Health Care: Proposals for Change—Guardianship*, 2 Mental Disability L. Rep. 444 (1978); Legal Research and Services for the Elderly, National Council of Senior Citizens, Inc., Guardianship and Conservatorship in Legislative Approaches to the Problems of the Elderly: A Handbook of Model State Statutes 119 (1971); J. Regan & G. Springer, Model Guardianship Conservatorship and Power of Attorney Legislation, *supra* note 8, at 75.

51. *See* W. Schmidt, et al., *supra* note 6, at 179–203, *infra* chap. 15.

This model statute was introduced by Representative Kirkwood during the 1980 Florida legislative session as House Bill 539. [*Cf.* Fla. Stat. ch. 744 (1989), as amended.]

One review of the model statute, while complimenting the provision of due process protection, suggests that it does not go far enough. National Senior Citizens Law Center Washington Weekly (April 18, 1980), pp. 4–5.

52. The American Bar Association (Aug. 1980) adopted as policy a resolution (Report No. 111) urging states to enact laws calling for limited guardianship, where appropriate, to help persons with diminished capacity to live in the general community with maximum self-sufficiency. *See* Fla. Stat. section 343.12(2), as amended (1980). *But see* M. Axilbund, *supra* note 5 (indicating infrequent use of limited guardianship in the 12 to 16 limited guardian states).

To the extent all-or-nothing guardianship is a deterrent to adjudication of incompetence in cases of partial incapacity, limited guardianship enhances the necessity for increased procedural protections because the risk of erroneous incompetence increases. Also, despite a presumption of competence, partial incompetence may taint, both legally and practically, those capacities that are not adjudicated.

The Florida Bar's Committee on the Mentally Disabled engaged in extensive preparation of a partial guardianship bill that enjoyed widespread support, except from the Real Property, Probate, and Trust Law Section.

of the availability of beneficial services; "clear, unequivocal, and convincing" as the standard of proof; required presence of the proposed ward at the hearing except when medically incapable; right to counsel including minimum required duties; right to jury trial;[53] right to independent medical and psychological evaluation; qualified right to remain silent at any evaluation;[54] right to present evidence and confront and cross-examine witnesses; applicability of formal civil rules of evidence; qualified prohibition of opinion testimony regarding diagnosis;[55] right to instruction of jury or court regarding the influence of any psychotropic medication on the proposed ward; right to appeal and appellate counsel; required application of the least restrictive alternative principle; physician immunity for emergency treatment without consent, instead of temporary guardianship, emergency guardianship, and the like; qualified right to services; and, provision for public guardianship.

The Supply of Guardians

Public guardianship is an aspect of the area of guardianship most in need of reform—the supply of guardians.[56] An incompetent with a sizeable estate, or with willing and responsible family members or friends, has little difficulty in having someone serve as guardian. A proposed ward without such resources,[57] however, has a very different situation.

In April 1977, Florida's Office of Aging and Adult Services found in a statewide survey of its social workers that 2,700 identifiable people (1,700 were over age 60) had an unsatisfied need for a guardian. Almost 1,000 of these had been adjudicated incompetent, but no guardian appointed.[58] The balance needed to be adjudicated incompetent and have a guardian appointed, in the opinion of the social workers, but for most of them no guardian was available.

---

53. At least twenty-two states offer the proposed ward the right to a jury of peers. Developmental Disabilities State Legislative Project, *supra* note 50, at 5.

54. *See* Lessard v. Schmidt, 349 F. Supp. 1078, 1101 n. 33, 1102 (E.D. Wis. 1972) *vacated*, 414 U.S. 473 (1974), *on remand*, 379 F. Supp. 1376 (E.D. Wis. 1974), *vacated*, 421 U.S. 957 (1975), *on remand*, 413 F. Supp. 1318 (E.D. Wis. 1976).

55. *See* Ennis & Litwack, *Psychiatry and the Presumption of Expertise: Flipping Coins in the Courtroom*, 62 Cal. L. Rev. 693, 708–11 (1974).

56. *See generally* W. Schmidt, *et al.*, *supra* note 6.

57. Florida contains a disproportionate number of older persons who are geographically separated from family and friends.

58. This group consists primarily of people who had been involuntarily committed, but released without the simple restoration of competency. Fla. Stat. § 744.464 (1979).

Another vacuum in the provision of guardianship services exists for institutionalized persons, especially the elderly in nursing facilities and the state mental hospitals. At Florida State Hospital, for example, there are at least 600 patients who are legally incompetent, without guardians, but classified as "voluntary" patients.[59] Most are elderly people who were institutionalized under the pre-Baker Act civil commitment statute with criteria of mental (legal) incompetence, never appointed a guardian,[60] and administratively transferred in summary fashion without a hearing away from the protections allowed involuntaries under the Baker Act. A proportionate number of incompetent "voluntaries" without guardians (almost one-third of the Florida State Hospital resident population) probably exists at Florida's other mental institutions.

The consequences of guardianship may be serious, but the effect of legal incompetence without a guardian, or of functional incapacity without guardianship assistance, is total lack of protection. In thirty-four other states, there is some statutory provision for public guardianship to address the need for guardians.

Problems of Public Guardianship

Public guardianship, the appointment and responsibility of a public official to serve as legal guardian, is not without its own problems. In Los Angeles the public guardian has been sued for inappropriate institutionalization of wards, and in Chicago the former public guardian was found to have looted estates of personal property, failed to seek entitlements, consented to experimental medical treatment on mental patients, and noted visits to wards who in fact were dead at the time of the alleged visits.[61] However, the public guardian experience in Arizona and Delaware

---

59. *See In re* Gamble, 394 A.2d 308 (N.H. 1978) (state's responsibility to provide guardians for indigent incompetent residents of state mental hospitals). *See also* Vecchione v. Wohlgemuth 377 F. Supp. 1361 (E.D. Pa. 1974), 426 F. Supp. 1297 (E.D. Pa. 1977), *aff'd* 558, F.2d 150 (3rd Cir. 1977), *cert. den. sub. nom.* Beal v. Vecchione, 434 U.S. 943 (1977) ($9.1 million in Social Security benefits ordered returned to incompetent mental patients through state compensated guardian officers where benefits were taken without a hearing).

60. The current statute requires a guardian advocate to be appointed upon any finding of incompetence to consent to treatment. *See* Fla. Stat. §§ 394.459(3)(a), 394.467(3)(a), 394.467(4)(h). There is difficulty finding willing and responsible persons to serve as guardian advocate where there are no family, friends, or compensation.

Fla. Stat. § 393.12(2), as amended (1980), creates a mandate for guardian advocates of the retarded.

61. *See* W. Schmidt, *et al.*, *supra* note 6.

is generally favorable: nonintrusive professional guardianship service that assists persons without family, friends, or resources to secure access to rights, benefits, and entitlements.

The success of public guardianship is dependent upon several clear considerations. The public guardian must be independent of any service providing agency (no conflict of interest), and the public guardian must not be responsible for both serving as guardian, and petitioning for adjudication of incompetence (no self-aggrandizement). The public guardian must be adequately staffed and funded to the extent that no office is responsible for more than 500 wards, and each professional in the office is responsible for no more than thirty wards.[62] A public guardian is also only as good as the guardianship statute[63] governing adjudication of incompetence and appointment. Failure in any of these considerations will tip the benefit burden ratio against the individual ward, and the ward would be better off with no guardian at all.

Florida's Approaches

Florida has several approaches to the need for guardians that is met in other states by public guardianship. These approaches include: benign neglect; informal guardianship by neighbors, nursing homes, and the like without legal process or authority; civil commitment to a mental institution ("poor man's guardianship"); private attorneys on a pro bono or nominal fee basis (sometimes with dozens of wards each); banks or trust companies (for modest estates);[64] nonprofit corporations,[65] usually with a religious affiliation; county social service programs utilizing volunteers; and, citizen groups serving as guardian banks.[66]

These approaches are not meeting Florida's needs, but the best alternatives to public guardianship may be dramatic enhancement of the last three. The Cathedral Foundation in Jacksonville, for example, seems to perform an excellent service. The keys to such approaches are willingness to work oneself out of a job; resistance to the social service starvation that sees any service, even guardianship, as better than none; and avoidance

---

62. *Id.*
63. A model public guardianship statute is available for guidance. *Supra* note 51; *infra* chap. 15.
64. In other parts of the country, some banks will profitably service small estates that are grouped together. Another idea is such service as a required public contribution.
65. *See* Fla. Stat. § 744.305.
66. *See* W. Schmidt, et al., *supra* note 6, 149–56.

of being both guardian and applicant for adjudication of incompetence (a point worth repeating.)

Guardianship is a comparatively unheralded device that can be expected to grow in use as the country, and state, population's average age increases. The purpose of guardianship is assistance, the *parens patriae* responsibilities of the state made manifest. Unfortunately, more than cursory consideration of guardianship in practice yields fairly negative results.

The literature relating to guardianship contains little that endorses general guardianship practice or argues forcefully for guardianship.[67] Numerous individual professionals cite a large need for guardianship, but positive results for individual wards are so far no more than anecdotal at best, and disappointing in the aggregate.

There are less restrictive, and more appropriate, alternatives to guardianship. Several models now exist for guardianship criteria, procedures, public guardianship, and alternatives to public guardianship. Guardianship

---

67. In addition to the sources noted above, *see, e.g.*, National Center for Law and the Handicapped, Guardianship of the Mentally Impaired: A Critical Analysis (1977); Alexander, *On Being Imposed Upon by Artful or Designing Persons—The California Experience with the Involuntary Placement of the Aged*, 14 San Diego L. Rev. 1083 1977); Alexander, *Who Benefits from Conservatorship?*, Trial Magazine (May, 1977); Coleman & Soloman, *Parens Patriae "Treatment" Legal Punishment in Disguise*, 3 Hastings L.Q. 345 (1976); Effland, *Caring for the Elderly Under the Uniform Probate Code*, 17 Ariz. L. Rev. 373 (1975); Frachter, *Toward Uniform Guardianship Legislation*, 64 Mich. L. Rev. 983 (1966); Hodgson, *Guardianship of Mentally Retarded Persons: Three Approaches to a Long Neglected Problem*, 37 Albany L. Rev. 407 (1973); Kart & Backham, *Black-White Differentials in the Institutionalization of the Elderly*, 54 Soc. Forces 901 (1976); McDougal, Lasswell, & Chen, *The Human Rights of the Aged: An Application of the Norm of Non-Discrimination*, 28 U. Fla. L. Rev. 639 (1976); Morris, *Conservatorship for the Gravely Disabled: California's Nondeclaration of Nonindependence*, 15 San Diego L. Rev. 201 (1978); Pickering, *Limitations on Individual Rights in California Incompetency Proceedings*, 7 U. Cal. Davis L. Rev. 457 (1974); *Report of ABA Committee on Legal Incapacity, Guardianship of Property of Incompetents*, 9 Real Prop. Prob. & Tr. J. 535 (1974); *Report of Committee on Problems Relating to Persons Under Disability, Conservatorship: Present Practice and Uniform Probate Code Compared*, 5 Real Prop. Prob. & Tr. J. 507 (1970); Rohan, *Caring for Persons Under a Disability: A Critique of the Role of the Conservator and the Substitution of Judgment Doctrine*, 52 St. John's L. Rev. 1 (1977); Comment, *An Assessment of the Pennsylvania Estate Guardianship Incompetency Standard*, 124 U. Pa. L. Rev. 1048 (1976); Comment, *North Carolina Guardianship Laws—The Need for Change*, 54 N.C. L. Rev. 389 (1976); Comment, *Probate Code Conservatorship: A Legislative Grant of New Procedural Protections*, 8 Pac. L. J. 73 (1977); Note, *The Disguised Oppression of Involuntary Guardianship: Have the Elderly Freedom to Spend?*, 73 Yale L.J. 676 (1964); Conservatee Rights Committee, The Status of Conservatees in Santa Clara County [California] (February 1979) (unpublished).

should presume an exhaustion of all alternatives. Guardianship in any event may reflect individual, professional, and social service bankruptcy. The need for guardianship reform seems great, and should proceed.

Part II

The Extent of Unmet Need for Guardian Services

Chapter 2

Legal Incompetents' Need for Guardianship in Florida

Winsor C. Schmidt, Jr.
Roger Peters

> *Abstract.* This study assesses the alleged need for guardians in Florida. A survey of the state's seventy-four public receiving facilities, community mental health centers, and clinics; thirty private receiving facilities; eleven Aging and Adult district offices; Developmental Services institutional and residential placements; and six state mental hospitals revealed that 11,147 persons in Florida reportedly need a legal guardian. The limitations, implications, and possible policy responses to this alleged need are discussed.

Although there is growing discussion about guardianship as a sociolegal disposition for the incompetent mentally ill, developmentally disabled, and elderly, there has been no systematic effort to assess the extent of need for guardianship. This chapter reports an assessment of the alleged need for guardians in the state of Florida, a state said to reflect the demographic future of the United States. This chapter does not document the actual need for guardianship, but rather the need perceived by the significant, accessible, legal, psychiatric, and social institutions in the state. The need, and means for reducing the perceived need for guardianship, will be discussed.

Background

In 1982 the Florida Legislature appropriated $160,000 to the Office of the State Courts Administrator for the purpose of developing a Public Guardianship Pilot Program. Florida, unlike thirty-four other states, does not have a statutory provision for "public guardianship."[1] "Public guardian-

---

1. W. Schmidt, K. Miller, W. Bell, & E. New, Public Guardianship and the Elderly (1981) [hereinafter Public Guardianship].

ship" is the judicial appointment and responsibility of a public official in a state or local government agency or court (compared with a private individual in private guardianship) to serve a legal incompetent, the "ward," who does not have willing or responsible family members or friends to serve as guardian.[2] Public guardianship is capable of such abuse that it should be done correctly, or it should not be done at all.[3]

One purpose of the Florida Public Guardianship Pilot Program is to assess the need for public guardians in Florida. Past guardian needs assessments include:

1. An April 1977 statewide survey by the Florida Aging and Adult Services Program Office of state social workers' caseloads identifying 1,399 legally incompetent persons without guardians and 910 functional incompetents needing adjudication and appointment of a guardian.

2. A 1978 identification by the Department of Health and Rehabilitative Services (HRS) Human Rights Advocacy Committee for Florida State Hospital of one third of the institution's population as legally incompetent and without a guardian.

3. A 1979 U.S. Administration on Aging national study[4] of public guardianship uncovering: (1) a 1977 Tampa survey of medical opinions indicating 700 local citizens needing adjudication and appointment of a guardian, (2) a 1978 Broward County Social Services Division questionnaire finding twenty of twenty-one respondents citing need for guardianship program, and (3) 1979 Hillsborough County (Tampa) Mental Health Association estimate of 600 people in need of guardianship.

4. A February 1981 survey of three District Four (Jacksonville, Florida) community mental health centers finding .06% of that area's population legally incompetent but with no guardian, projected as 5,000 people on a statewide basis.

5. A 1979 study[5] of six states (Delaware, Minnesota, North Carolina, Ohio, Washington, and Wisconsin), with a total population of twenty-nine million, where seventeen thousand guardianship peti-

---

2. *Id.*; Bell, Schmidt & Miller, *Public Guardianship and the Elderly: Findings from a National Study*, 21 Gerontologist 194 (1981).

3. Public Guardianship, *supra* note 1.

4. Public Guardianship, *supra* note 1.

5. M. Axilbund, Exercising Judgment for the Disabled: Report of an Inquiry into Limited Guardianship, Public Guardianship and Adult Protective Services in Six States (Executive Summary), Washington, D.C.: American Bar Association Commission on the Mentally Disabled (1979).

tions were filed in one year. This filing rate of .059 percent (one of every 1,706) corresponded interestingly with the filing rate of .056 percent (one of every 1,785) for Florida in 1977 (4,724 guardianships opened in a population of 8,432,927).
6. A 1981 Florida HRS Aging and Adult Services caseload survey by judicial circuit showing 542 persons adjudicated incompetent but with no guardian.
7. A June 1982 Florida HRS Developmental Services Program Office assessment (3.77% error rate) identifying: 1,643 Sunland clients in need of a guardian and 606 "community" (foster care, group home, residential rehabilitation centers, intermediate care facilities for the mentally retarded) clients in need of a guardian, for a total of 2,249.
8. A July 1982 Florida "institutionalized" (state hospital) population survey showing 802 legal incompetents with no guardians, an apparent decline from a similar May 1981 institution survey.
9. A Summer 1982 Florida State University Institute for Social Research review of all Leon County Probate Court guardianship files since January 1977 showing that people without potential guardians do not reach formal adjudication.[6]
10. A November 1982 assessment by the Dade County Grand Jury identifying the need for public guardianship in Dade County.[7]

Definitions

Unless otherwise provided, "legal incompetent," "incompetent," and derivations refer to persons who are legally incompetent by operation of law. "Functional incompetent" and derivations refer to persons who are alleged to meet legal criteria for incompetence but have not been formally adjudicated incompetent. Functional incompetents allegedly need guardianship services, whether private or public. "Guardian advocate" and derivations are legal terms of art originating in Florida Statutes sections 394.459(3)(a) (1982) and 393.12(2)(a) (1981). A guardian advocate under Chapter 394 relating to mental health is not the same as a guardian advocate under Chapter 393 relating to mental retardation. A mental health guardian advocate is appointed upon a finding of incompetence to consent to treatment, whereas a Chapter 393 guardian advocate is a limited

---

6. Peters, Schmidt, & Miller, *Guardianship of the Elderly in Tallahassee, Florida*, 25 Gerontologist 532 (1985) [hereinafter Peters].

7. Dade County Grand Jury: Final Report of the Grand Jury, Miami: Office of the State Attorney (1982).

"guardian" appointed without any adjudication of incompetence. Some literature suggests that guardianship is an illusory solution to incompetence to consent to treatment.[8]

Methodology

This needs assessment was conducted via a February 1983 telephone survey of 121 Florida facilities and agencies. Of these sources of data, seventy-four were public receiving facilities, community mental health centers, or clinics: thirty were private receiving facilities, eleven were HRS Aging and Adult Services district offices, and six were state hospitals. Information solicited from all sources included the number of legally incompetent clients without guardians served by the particular facility/agency as well as the number of functionally incompetent clients. All sources except HRS district offices were asked to disclose information regarding the number of clients incompetent to consent to treatment and without guardian advocates (Florida Statutes section 394.459(3)a) and to describe the degree of overlap between clients who are legally incompetent and those incompetent to consent to treatment. These sources were also asked to supply information concerning demographic characteristics of legally incompetent clients without guardians (age, race, sex, amount of assets, and extent of physical/psychiatric disabilities), although only state hospitals and public receiving/community facilities maintained sufficient client populations to warrant this search.

State hospital staff were asked to provide the most extensive information, including (in addition to the above data): (1) the number of clients maintained who were eligible for guardian advocates under the "retardation" statute (Florida Statutes section 393.12(2)a), (2) the number of legally incompetent clients who could be discharged but for the absence of a guardian, and (3) reasons or explanations for the decrease in the number of legal incompetents without guardians between May 1981 and July 1982. Information gathered from HRS Aging and Adult Service district offices pertains to clients legally or functionally incompetent and reasons for changes in the population of legal incompetents without guardians from 1981 to 1983.

For the larger agencies and facilities surveyed by telephone, information was solicited from caseworkers, case managers, or social workers. These staff tended to have the most direct client contact and were most

---

8. Gutheil, Shapiro & St. Clair, *Legal Guardianship in Drug Refusal: An Illusory Solution*, 13 Am. J. Psychiatry 347 (1980).

aware of both the legal status of clients and of recent fluctuations in agency caseloads. In most agencies, a single caseworker acted as research coordinator, polling colleagues to assess the particular client population served. An initial call to such caseworkers indicated the request, with follow-up calls several days later. Identification of relevant client populations at several hospitals required assessment at various levels—usually of inpatient, outpatient, and aftercare units. For smaller agencies, a single administrative staff person often was able to provide client information without consulting others.

For about 75% of agencies and facilities sampled, information consisted of estimates made by caseworkers. Estimates were sometimes reported to be only ballpark figures and were necessary due to the reported absence of legal status information in client files. For smaller facilities, and for such larger facilities as Florida State Hospital and Peach River Center, information represents a case-by-case review. The vast majority of staff contacted were cooperative and eager to assist in the needs assessment.

Nonjudicial assessments of legal incompetence are of course suspect but, in the absence of better information, must necessarily suffice. The absence of legal status information in client files is probably not unusual in public bureaucracies nationally. The lack of centralized (versus county level) information about legal incompetence and guardianship status is also problematic.[9]

The telephone survey was chosen as the methodology in order to assure a high response rate, to minimize costs, and to facilitate follow-up questions. Telephone surveys present certain methodologic difficulties, but such a survey seemed appropriate under the economic circumstances of this needs assessment.

The 1983–1985 Department of Health and Rehabilitation Services budget issue was also reviewed for purposes of obtaining a count of developmental services clients. Developmental services clients are listed in a Client Information System and are therefore more amenable to reliable estimates.

Public Receiving and Community Facilities

Public receiving facilities, clinics, and community mental health centers in Florida maintain the largest number of clients eligible for public guardianship services. A state total of 1,036 legal incompetents without guardians was identified, as well as 2,770 functionally incompetent clients.

---

9. Dade County Grand Jury, *supra* note 7.

Of the legally incompetent clients without guardians, fewer than 10% require guardians solely for medical consent purposes. The majority of clients require supervision of both financial and personal (daily living, self-care) needs. Most legally incompetent clients from public or community agencies reportedly suffer from senility or organic brain syndrome. (This, of course, does not suggest that all persons suffering from senility or organic brain syndrome are incompetent. In fact, such labels as "senility" and "organic brain syndrome" are too readily used in the incompetency and guardianship process in lieu of more useful functional and behavioral descriptions.[10]) To a lesser extent, these clients are also afflicted with other psychiatric conditions.

Fully two-thirds of this legally incompetent population is female, 85% is Caucasian, and the average age of such clients is 63. In comparison to the legally incompetent hospitalized population, incompetent clients without guardians served by public/community agencies tend to represent a broader age range. Administrators from several community facilities claim that two distinct patient populations are being served: one group of younger (lower age) psychotic patients and one group of older patients (over 65) having medical disorders with psychiatric disability. Most clients are eligible for Social Security Insurance (SSI)/Medicaid, and a few have other types of assets.

Administrative staff indicate a larger overlap between clients identified as incompetent to consent to treatment (without guardian advocates) and those identified as functionally incompetent. Although incompetence to consent is not as widespread a problem with public and community agencies as is legal incompetence under Florida Statutes Chapter 744, relating to guardianship, lack of guardian advocates appears to be a persistent dilemma facing public receiving facility administrators. Several courts do not appoint guardian advocates on a regular basis, apparently because of policies by clerks or judges, or ignoring of statutory provisions requiring client consent by various facilities. When guardian advocates are appointed, the responsibility is often reportedly assumed by public defenders, public receiving facility administrators, or family members. Questions about guardian advocate liability and immunity apparently deter some persons from serving as guardian advocates.[11] These individuals may be ill-equipped to review treatment needs of clients or may have particular vested interests in choice of treatment that may conflict with those of the client.

---

10. Peters, *supra* note 6.
11. [*See also* M. Kapp & J. Detzel, Alternatives to Guardianship for the Elderly: Legal Liability Disincentives and Impediments, Dayton, Ohio: Wright State University School of Medicine (1992).]

In comparison to state hospitals, community mental health centers or other outpatient facilities have relatively little contact with clients who are incompetent to consent. Administrators and staff are uneasy in offering treatment when clients are incompetent to consent, and often circumvent difficulties concerning the lack of guardian advocates by referring clients to state hospitals for treatment. At several community mental health centers, however, staff report that they always have a handful of these clients to deal with and need a part-time staff just to locate guardian advocates. Public receiving facilities that operate significant inpatient operations are more profoundly affected by the lack of guardian advocates. Staff of the University Hospital Community Mental Health Center (Jacksonville), for example, face over thirty crisis incidents per month involving incompetency to consent issues. The University Center may be finessing consent requirements, however, because the Fourth Circuit (three counties around Jacksonville) reports only twelve requests for appointment of a guardian advocate in March 1983.

According to staff reports, legally incompetent clients without guardians from public/community agencies are primarily in need of financial supervision. A subset of this group requires "comprehensive care," including management of personal needs. Staff identified several major flaws inherent in the guardian recruitment process. In many jurisdictions, staff could not find guardians capable of providing supervisory care for indigent clients who are without family members. Often the courts, whether clerks or judges, discourage initiation of incompetency proceedings for these clients if no guardians are available and willing to serve.

Although the vast majority of incompetents without guardians live in the more densely populated districts in Florida, failure to provide adequate guardian services in rural communities may have more severe consequences. This problem is perhaps most acute with deinstitutionalized but legally incompetent hospital patients. Public receiving facility staff in rural districts claim that the lack of community mental health facilities and personnel creates a situation in which deinstitutionalized legally incompetent patients are often left unsupervised. Left to their own resources, they become involved in drinking, illicit drugs, and sale, abuse, or neglect of medications and frequently are the victims of criminal activities. This creates a "revolving door" syndrome: without intermediate (inpatient) care facilities in which to place these clients when they decompensate, and without guardians to protect and perform surrogate functions for the legal incompetents, they are sent back to state hospitals for treatment.

Conversely, there are reports that, when guardians are available, social workers sometimes find the guardians to not always serve the best interests of clients. In some instances, guardians reportedly attempt to appropriate funds from the ward's estate. In other cases, guardians will not agree to have wards released from state hospitals or do not live in the vicinity of the state hospital, rendering the guardians unable to provide supervisor care for the ward. Faced with the lack of conscientious guardianship alternatives, social workers must often choose between lesser evils: in one district, a client reportedly spent $7,000 from her checking account in a single month, yet staff were reluctant to allow family members to assume guardianship responsibilities and "plunder" the estate. Reported irregularities in guardianship are no longer new phenomena.[12]

A common concern voiced by public/community mental health staff is the lack of centralized recordkeeping in the state regarding legal incompetency, and guardianship. Staff report that they are often unaware (sometimes for years) that clients are legally incompetent or may have guardians assigned. When clients are transferred from state hospitals to public/community agencies, information about legal status remains at the hospital. This is a particular problem with long-term (chronic) clients who have been transferred many times between hospitals and less restrictive facilities. Thus, the public/community statistics here compiled on incompetents without guardians may not include a sizeable number of these unidentified incompetents. In several cases, staff at public receiving facilities are able to "track down" information on clients' legal status, although this is not kept in active agency files. The staff often express surprise at discovering the number of legally incompetent clients (with or without guardians) being served by their agency. Although lacking legal authority, incompetent clients are sometimes allowed to manage personal finances and to make treatment decisions without assistance of a guardian.

State Hospitals

Over 30% (853) of the non-developmentally disabled legal incompetents (2,842) without guardians in Florida and about 10% (624) of functionally incompetent clients (6, 054) reside in state hospitals. Of all hospitals, Florida State Hospital, the largest, maintains the majority of such clients. Within this hospital, two units (geriatric and long-term care) account for about 60% of the Florida State Hospital population in need of guardianship services.

---

12. *See, e.g.*, G. Alexander & T. Lewin, The Aged and the Need for Surrogate Management (1972); Public Guardianship, *supra* note 1; Regan, *Adult Protective Services: An Appraisal and a Prospectus* in Improving Protective Services for Older Americans, National Law and Social Work Seminar Proceedings and Prospects, Portland, M.E.: University of Southern Maine Center for Research and Advanced Study (1982); Dade County Grand Jury, *supra* note 7.

Of the 853 incompetent hospital clients without guardians, about half could reportedly be discharged immediately if guardianship services were available in the community. The remainder would benefit from supervision of both their estates and treatment while institutionalized. Florida State Hospital and Northeast Florida State Hospital (Macclenny) appear to be the most likely beneficiaries of public guardianship services. Of 553 incompetent clients without guardians at Florida State Hospital, almost half could reportedly be discharged if guardians were available. At Macclenny, of 158 clients said to be eligible for guardianship services, about 90% could reportedly be released were guardians present.

Relative to the nonhospital population, hospitalized incompetents are slightly older (average age, 67), are less often female (58%) and Caucasian (60%), have fewer resources (including only about 40% who are eligible for SSI), and are more often characterized by primarily psychiatric disabilities (55%). This group appears to present a particular challenge to public guardians or other potential guardian service providers. Most hospitalized incompetents without guardians have lived as inpatients for many years and do not have immediate access to vocational training or halfway house experiences. It would be incumbent upon public guardians to provide this population with a good deal of reorientation to community activities and resources. The presence of both psychiatric and medical disorders in the hospital population indicates the need for guardians to periodically assess the need for outpatient psychiatric care and to be aware of existing medical facilities in the community. Of course, good hospital and nonhospital health and social services could vitiate the need for continued legal incompetence and guardianship in many cases.

Two hospitals report difficulties in securing guardian advocates for clients incompetent to consent, or eligible for advocate services under the retardation statute (Florida Statutes section 393.12). Florida State Hospital maintains 308 incompetent to consent clients without guardian advocates, and forty retarded clients eligible for section 393.12 advocate services. At Macclenny, 125 clients need guardian advocates, and ninety-five are eligible for section 393.12 advocacy. Hospital staff report a large overlap between clients who are incompetent and clients who are incompetent to consent. Lack of guardian advocates sometimes delays treatment required before a client may be discharged. At Florida State Hospital, one client was held custodially for four months due to difficulty in locating a guardian advocate. Despite mandatory provisions in mental health legislation, several jurisdictions are not appointing guardian advocates on a regular basis. This appears to pose a particular problem for Macclenny. The absence of private or nonprofit guardianship agencies in the northeast Florida community provides additional difficulties for administrators at Macclenny in soliciting guardian advocates. Also, courts may discourage hospital administrators from petitioning for guardian advocates. At G. Pierce Wood Memorial (state) Hospital, for example, a $10 fee is required for each request. Instead of waiting for the hospital finance office to process such requests, administrators reportedly resort to full involuntary placement proceedings to facilitate implementation of treatment programs. South Florida State Hospital administrators claim to circumvent problems with incompetence to consent by actively reviewing such clients and referring them to local courts.

Hospital staff offer several explanations for the recent decrease (especially from 1981 to 1982) in hospitalized legal incompetents without guardians. Systematic causes for this decline include: more frequent use of restoration to competency (apparently influenced by aggressive six-month competency evaluations); location of family members to serve as guardians or the willingness of nursing homes to accept clients without guardians; and reluctance of staff to initiate incompetency proceedings. The decline in incompetents without guardians also might be explained in part by external changes that affect the hospital population, such as: increased efforts at deinstitutionalization of psychiatric inpatients, greater numbers of voluntary (and competent) patients, and death of clients (especially those adjudicated incompetent before 1972). It might be expected that the number of hospitalized incompetent patients without guardians will continue to register a marked decline in years to come, although deinstitutionalized clients will still require guardianship services.

Private Receiving Facilities

Private receiving facilities maintain relatively few clients (579) who might be eligible for public guardian services. These facilities tend to serve acute psychiatric patients and do not typically have well-established aftercare units for long-term outpatient care. Only the facilities in Districts 5, 7, 10, and 11 (nine counties surrounding Clearwater, Orlando, Fort Lauderdale, and Miami), respectively serve more than 100 functionally or legally incompetent clients without guardians. Also, these districts each report maintaining ten to twenty clients who are incompetent to consent and without guardian advocates. Although private receiving facilities serve a small minority of incompetent clients without guardians, expansion of guardian services would probably provide relief for what one staff termed a "perpetual problem." Due to the lack of guardians in the community and the lack of community outreach staff at private receiving facilities, many incompetents in these facilities do not receive optimal supervision of their estates and treatment programs. At one facility, staff report recurrent difficulties in assisting acutely psychotic patients who face eviction from apartments, foreclosures on mortgages, and the like because of the absence of available guardians and the inability to assign representative payees on short notice.

HRS Aging and Adult Services

In HRS Aging and Adult Services caseloads, some 3,034 clients would reportedly benefit from guardianship. Of these, 878 are legally incompetent (without guardians) and 2,156 are functionally incompetent. Aging and Adult Services cases are distributed fairly evenly throughout the state, although Districts 3,7,10, and 11 (twenty-three counties in north central and south Florida) report a disproportionate number of such cases. It should be noted that data collected do not represent a case-by-case analysis of Aging and Adult Services files. Instead, figures are based on February 1983 estimates by district case managers. Case managers report confidence that estimates are within a 5% margin of error. Three districts (twenty-three counties surrounding Tallahassee, Jacksonville, and Tampa) still cite evidence gathered for a similar survey conducted in 1981. Data compiled from these three districts have not been updated.

Aging and Adult Services staff give several reasons for fluctuations in the number of clients needing guardians. In districts registering increases in this population since 1981 (especially in central Florida), staff claim that caseloads expanded due to an influx of elderly population coming from the Miami area and from northern counties. In several districts registering decreases in the population eligible for guardianship services, staff reason that more aggressive attempts have been made to locate (private) guardians and to utilize community groups such as the Suncoast Lutheran agency. Analysis of ten district reports comparing the number of legal incompetents in 181 and 1983 indicates that HRS now handles about 20% more of this client population.

Developmental Services

According to the 1983–1985 Department of Health and Rehabilitative Services budget issue and count obtained from the Client Information System, Developmental Services has 1,643 institutionalized clients and 608 residential placements who qualify for guardianship services. Guardianship services for developmental services would facilitate: corrective non-emergency treatment; maintenance in the least restrictive environment commensurate with client capabilities; and arranging medical care, management of property and other assets, physical and emotional supports, legal assistance, and payment of bills.

Summary

Quantitative

A substantial number (11,147) of persons appear to be eligible for public guardianship services in Florida. From a nonhospital population, including clients from public and private facilities, and HRS Aging and Adult Services, 5,430 are functionally incompetent and 1,989 are legally incompetent and without guardians. From the state hospital population, 624 clients are functionally incompetent and 853 are legally incompetent without guardians. From both populations (combined), 6,054 functional incompetents and 2,842 legal incompetents appear to be eligible for public guardianship services. From Developmental Services, 1,643 institutionalized clients and 608 residential placements reportedly qualify for guardianship service.

These figures may actually underestimate the potential clientele of a public guardianship agency. Two groups of clients not included in the present assessment are those private clients residing in nursing homes[13] and adult congregate living facilities. Accurate information concerning intellectual/physical functioning and legal status of nursing home clients is extremely difficult to ascertain. Several nursing home ombudsman committee staff claim that such information is currently unavailable or that nursing homes are unwilling to disclose this type of data. However, several other staff involved with integrated medical/psychiatric/long-term care facilities suggest that at least 10% of all nursing home clients in south Florida are legally incompetent and without guardians. A large percentage of the nursing home population might also be functionally incompetent. Private clients needing guardians in adult congregate living facilities are similarly difficult to estimate. An important responsibility of a public guardianship agency would be to establish liaison with nursing homes and adult congregate living facilities in order to assess the need for guardians and guardian advocates within this population.

Another group of clients not identified by the present survey are those living outside the domain of state mental health services (hospitals, public and private facilities, HRS agencies). HRS Aging and Adult Services staff from several districts express confidence that a large number of potential clients have not been located, or identified to protective services, but

---

13. *Cf.* chap. 3, *infra*.

might benefit from public guardianship. This population might include transients or others who are at "high risk" of physical or financial loss without provision of public guardianship. The present survey also probably underrepresents the need for public guardianship to the extent that the listings of state public and private mental health facilities provided by the HRS Mental Health Program Office may not include recently opened facilities or those reopening in new locations throughout the state.

Location

Clients legally incompetent and without guardians are serviced by public receiving and community facilities (1,036 total), HRS Aging and Adult Services (878 total), and state hospitals (853) total). Functional incompetents are primarily serviced by public receiving and community facilities (2,770 total) and by HRS Aging and Adult Services (2,156). Legally or functionally, incompetent clients served by nonhospital agencies and facilities are distributed fairly evenly throughout several geographic districts. Districts 7 (903), 8 (1,025), and 11 (1,503) (sixteen counties around Orlando, southwest Florida, and Miami) report the greatest number of eligible clients. Of state hospitals, Florida State Hospital reports by far the greatest number of clients in need of guardianship services (553 legal incompetents, 220 functional incompetents). Three other hospitals (Macclenny, South Florida, and G. Pierce Wood) also report significant numbers of such clients.

Diagnostic

According to information gathered from state hospitals, and from public receiving/community facilities, those in need of guardianship services are typically female (62%), elderly (average age, 65), and predominantly white (74%). Eligible clients are about as likely to be diagnosed with organic brain syndrome and senility as with schizophrenia, and often manifest both medical and psychiatric conditions that contribute to their need for supervision. Clients often receive, or are eligible to receive, Medicaid, and SSI benefits. Few have additional resources beyond public assistance. A large majority of clients assessed as potential recipients of guardianship services need more than just a surrogate decisionmaker for medical consent purposes. The most urgent need expressed is for supervision of client finances, although a substantial number of clients may require comprehensive guardianship services (for both person and property). Plenary guardianships reportedly may be most appropriate for clients residing in state hospitals or other inpatient facilities. About half of hospital inpatients without guardians, for example, would not be considered for discharge were guardians available due to severity of deficits in self-care and daily living skills.

Advocacy Services

Over 1,000 clients were identified who are incompetent to consent to treatment but are without guardian advocates. These clients are located in public receiving/community facilities (674 total), state hospitals (457 total), and, to a lesser extent, in private receiving facilities (75 total). Of all facilities in the state, Florida State Hospital appears to maintain the largest number (308) of clients who are incompetent to consent and without a guardian advocate. About 145 clients at state hospitals are eligible for guardian advocacy under the retardation statute. Most of these clients are maintained at Macclenny (95 total) and at Florida State Hospital (40 total).

Subjective Reports

Over 90% of facilities and agencies during the course of the assessment provide unsolicited reports affirming the need for public (or other auxiliary) guardianship services to supplement or replace existing resources. Most staff contacted report a significant shortage of private guardians and guardian advocates. Consequences of this shortage include delay of patient release from inpatient facilities, lack of aftercare supervision in the event that clients are released without guardians, inadequate monitoring of client treatment programs and finances, and diversion of social worker/case managers' attention from treatment and service delivery issues. According to staff reports, current mechanisms to assess the need for guardians and to assign guardians lack "process consolidation." Administrators are concerned with the absence of a centralized record-keeping agency that would allow determination of clients' legal status. Further, probate courts are not presently equipped to provide guardians for indigent clients due to the inability to identify potential guardians and because of the absence of available community resources to serve in this capacity. As a result, the guardianship process currently appears to discriminate between indigent and nonindigent populations and serves to exclude a number of indigent clients from guardianship care.

Consequences of Being Legally Incompetent and without a Guardian

Despite a contrary consensus in the law and in social science literature and research, the argument is still heard in Florida that public guardianship is a superfluous, redundant service already being performed generally by the Department of Health and Rehabilitation Services, and specifically by HRS social workers, nurses, physicians, and the like. Why, after all, does a legally incompetent resident of a state mental institution, for example, need a legal guardian when the resident's every need (e.g., food clothing, shelter, health care, etc.) is taken care of by the institution and its staff? This, of course, is an articulation of the *parens patriae* (literally "parent of the country"; the role of the state as sovereign and functional guardian of legally disabled persons) responsibility of the state to care for persons who are unable to care for themselves.

The argument, however, is spurious in at least two significant ways. First, it fails to recognize the harmful aspects of state paternalism:[14] in exercising its *parens patriae* role, the state is not infrequently, if understandably (insufficient resources for example), the problem for its clients. Second, the argument reflects ignorance of the arguably clear legal mandate. Florida Statutes section 744.331(c)(9)(1981) provides; "When a person is adjudicated mentally or physically incompetent, a guardian of the person shall be appointed..." Florida Statutes section 394.459(3)(a) (1982) provides, "If the court finds that the patient is incompetent to consent to treatment, it shall appoint a guardian advocate." Florida Statutes section 393.12(2)(a) (1981) provides, "If a retarded person needs protection for his property or person, the court, without an adjudication of incompetency but using the procedures established in chapter 744, shall appoint a guardian advocate..." The issue of whether a state has a responsibility to provide guardians for legal incompetents is also clearly addressed in *In re Gamble*, 394 A.2d 308 (N.H. 1978), in which a state supreme court held that the state must obtain, nominate, and compensate guardians of indigent residents of state institutions.

Essentially, a public guardian is necessary to provide individual protection and surrogate decisionmaking to legal incompetents who have no other protection or sympathetic guidance.

Without a guardian, a legal incompetent in Florida faces a statutory presumption "to be incapable of managing his own affairs or of making any gift, contract, or instrument in writing that is binding on his estate"

---

14. *See, e.g.,* Horstman, *Adult Protective Services for the Elderly: The Limits of Parens Patriae,* 40 Mo. L. Rev. 215 (1975).

[Florida Statutes section 744.331(8)]. In most states legal incompetence restricts or takes away the right to:

    Make contracts

    Sell, purchase, mortgage, or lease property

    Make gifts

    Travel or decide where to live

    Vote, or hold elected office

    Initiate or defend against [law] suits

    Make a will, or revoke one

    Engage in certain professions

    Lend or borrow money

    Appoint agents

    Divorce or marry

    Refuse [or consent to] medical treatment

    Keep and care for children

    Serve on a jury

    Be a witness to any legal document

    Drive a car

    Pay or collect debts

    Manage or run a business[15]

Without a legal guardian, 421 legally incompetent residents of Florida's state mental hospitals cannot be discharged (although they are otherwise eligible) to less restrictive, and generally less expensive, care.

Conclusion and Recommendations

The documented statistical, legal, and human need of legal incompetents for guardians in Florida is considerable. To the extent that Florida represents the demographic future of an aging America, this case study documents a current and prospective national need. Guardians also serve such third party interests as state and private hospitals and other agencies seeking reimbursement for costs, discharge of inappropriate admissions, and admission to more appropriate services. (The legitimacy of such third-party interests, compared to incompetents' interests, is debatable, of course.[16]) In any case, the unmet need for guardians justifies statewide

---

15. R. Brown, The Rights of Older Persons (1979), p. 286.
16. Alexander & Lewin, *supra* note 12.

implementation of a public guardianship program in Florida and other states.

At the same time, in a cutback environment and period of revenue shortfalls, it would be unrealistic to blithely proceed attaching program to need. There are several ways in which the rather substantial statistical need can be softened and programming then concentrated on the problem core.

First, an aggressive, systematic, and comprehensive effort should be undertaken by state social service departments to restore the legal competence of those who are inappropriately incompetent. Successful efforts have recurred in District Four (Jacksonville) and at Florida State Hospital, but there has not been a comprehensive effort throughout the Florida system. Restoration is a comparatively simple and inexpensive legal process and is certainly less costly than inappropriate service from a public guardian.

Second, there is a statutory cause for many of Florida's (and other states', e.g., Virginia) legal incompetents without guardians. Florida Statutes section 394.471 (1981) grandfathers the legal incompetence of hundreds of people involuntarily committed before July 1, 1972. Before July 1, 1972, one of the criteria for involuntary commitment was legal incompetence [Florida Statute section 394.20 et seq. (1949)]. Also there was no requirement, as there is now, that a guardian must be appointed for someone declared legally incompetent. Section 394.471 provided for review of pre-1972 commitments from July 1, 1972 until July 1, 1973, but made no provision for review of incompetence: "Nothing in this part invalidates any order appointing a guardian or determining incompetency." Another recommendation, therefore, is that the grandfathered legal incompetence produced by section 394.471 (and similar provisions in other states) be remedied by statutory revision. Alternatively, public guardianship programs could have sufficient independence, expertise, and programmatic obligation to seek judicial relief, as in New Hampshire, for legal incompetents without guardians.

A third way in which the demand for public guardianship can be reduced and made more realistic is through the use of less restrictive alternatives to guardianship.[17] These alternatives include: power of attorney, durable family power of attorney;[18] single transaction court ratification of a particular action, like medical consent; substitute or representative payee; protective services (Florida Statute sections 410.10–410.11); trusts; joint

---

17. See, e.g., Regan, *Protective Services for the Elderly: Commitment, Guardianship and Alternatives*, 13 Wm. & Mary L. Rev. 569 (1972).

18. *Legal Problems of the Aged and Infirm: The Durable Power of Attorney, Planned Protective Services and the Living Will*, 13 Real Prop. Prob. Tr. J. 1 (1978).

tenancy; *inter vivos* transfers of property; deeds of guardianship;[19] and even civil commitment. HRS District One (four counties of the western Florida panhandle) reports success in avoiding incompetency through the use of representative payees.

Florida has joined thirty-four states in public guardianship efforts. The current and future need for public guardians is particularly great given Florida's high and growing proportion of elderly citizens and position as the destination for Sunbelt migration away from Snowbelt family and friends. A similar need should be evident in other such states. Limited resources are being spent inefficiently on inappropriate institutionalization for lack of a guardian. The need for guardians can be reduced, but statewide implementation of public guardianship programs should proceed.

---

19. Schlesinger, *Deeds of Guardianship*, 8 Prob. Prop. 4–6, 14–15 (1979).

Chapter 3

Elderly Nursing Home Residents' Need for Public Guardianship Services in Tennessee

David Hightower
Alex Heckert
Winsor C. Schmidt, Jr.

Abstract. This study assesses the need for public limited guardian, conservator, representative payee, and power of attorney services among elderly nursing home residents in Tennessee in the Summer and Fall of 1988. Of the 295 licensed nursing homes in Tennessee, 123 responded that 32% of their residents were receiving one of the services, and 10% of their residents (1,044 of 10,555) needed one of the services. As many as 3,003 residents in Tennessee may need one of the services. The effects of size and location of nursing homes are measurable but minimal. The problems of recordkeeping and conflict of interest are cited.

Background

In July 1986, the Tennessee legislature established a program of public guardianship for the elderly to be administered by the Tennessee Commission on Aging. Section 34-7-101 of the Tennessee Code Annotated (TCA), entitled "Public Guardianship for the Elderly Law," was created with the intent to establish a statewide program of public guardianship for those disabled persons sixty years of age or older. The program was designed for those who are unable to meet the essential requirements for their physical health or to manage essential aspects of their financial resources. Many elderly have no willing and responsible family member or friend to serve as guardian, or resources to compensate a private guardian. For those who qualify as indigent under SSI guidelines, the state imposes no fees or costs of any kind against the ward's estate.

Recent data obtained from the Tennessee Commission on Aging public guardianship program show that 215 clients were served by the program during the quarter of October-December 1988.[1] Of these 215 clients, 117 required full guardianships. Ninety-eight clients required alternatives services: limited guardianship (18), representative payee/legal custodian (54), guardian ad litem (13), and power of attorney (13). Potential wards are referred to the public guardian program district agencies from various sources, including family members, nursing home staff, hospital staff, adult protection services, attorneys, and other interested persons.

For a state the size of Tennessee, with a population of approximately 517,588 individuals over the age of sixty-five in 1980, it seems likely that some dysfunctional, socially isolated elderly are falling through the gaps in the system. The purpose of this study is to assess the extent of need for public guardianship among elderly nursing home residents in Tennessee. Is there substantial unmet need for public guardianship among elderly nursing home residents in Tennessee? No such assessment has been made to date by the state or by the Commission on Aging which administers the program.

Definitions

As used in this study, the term "ward" is defined from the Tennessee statute as a disabled person sixty years of age or older who has been placed under the protection of a public guardian by the court due to the person's inability to meet the essential requirements for personal physical health, or to manage the essential aspects of personal financial resources, and who has no willing and responsible family member or friend to serve as a guardian, or resources to compensate a private guardian. A "disabled person" means any person determined by the court to be in need of partial or full supervision, protection and assistance by reason of mental illness, physical illness or injury, advanced age, developmental disability or other mental or physical incapacity. "Public guardian" in Tennessee is defined as an employee of the state appointed by the court to serve as limited guardian, guardian ad litem, or conservator, or authorized by statute to serve as representative payee or to accept power of attorney. "Limited guardian" means any person appointed by the court to manage, supervise or protect a disabled person, to the extent ordered by the court. A "guardian ad litem" is any person appointed by the court to represent the ward during court proceedings. It is not necessary that the guardian ad litem be an attorney. A "conservator" is anyone appointed by the court

---

1. W. Schmidt & A. Heckert, National Guardianship Census and Empirical Comparison of Guardianship and Alternatives to Guardianship (1989) (unpublished manuscript).

to have charge and management of the property of a disabled person, and if the court deems it advisable, also to have custody of the person subject to the direction of the court. It should be noted that in the language of the conservatorship statute, section 34-4-202 of the TCA,"...no person will be penalized for choosing to proceed under one law [conservatorship] as opposed to the other [limited guardianship]." The Tennessee legislature specifically intended the Conservatorship Law of 1980 as an alternative method to the limited guardianship law that deals with estates of incompetents and disabled persons.

Review of Literature

Guardianship is a concept that has been recognized since the time of Cicero and Plutarch. Current perspectives have evolved from English common law. The responsibility for administering the property of a person judged to be "incompetent" is entrusted to a relative or willing friend until such time as the disabled person recovers. Guardianship is based upon the doctrine of "parens patriae" (literally, "father of his country") which attributes to the state (or sovereign) both the right, and the duty, to protect the persons and property of those unable to care for themselves. Guardianship confers upon one individual the right and authority to make decisions regarding the management of another person's estate, material possessions, or personal affairs.[2]

As a protective intervention, guardianship is receiving increasing attention as a strategy for protecting persons at risk from exploitation, abuse, and neglect. However, since the autonomy of the ward is so greatly affected, often resulting in the deprivation of many, if not all, decision-making powers, the mechanism is viewed by many professionals as the intervention of last resort. Guardianship of the elderly has become a topic of much concern in the past decade due to the growing numbers of elderly in our population.

Data presented to the Senate Special Committee on Aging state that by the year 2030, twenty-one percent of the U.S. population will be age sixty-five or over. Of that 64.5 million Americans, thirty million will be over the age of seventy-five. At the beginning of this century, less than one in ten Americans was fifty-five or older, and one in twenty-five was sixty-five

---

2. *See, e.g.*, Alexander, *Foreward: Life, Liberty and Property Rights for the Elderly*, 17 Ariz. L. Rev. 267 (1975); Alexander, *On Being Imposed Upon by Artful or Designing Persons—The California Experience with the Involuntary Placement of the Aged*, 14 San Diego L. Rev. 1083 (1977); Langen, *Protecting the Interests of the Ward*, 2 L. & Hum. Behav. 267 (1978); Schmidt, *The Evolution of a Public Guardianship Program*, 12 J. Psychiatry & L. 349 (1984).

or older. By 1985, the population over fifty-five was twenty-one percent and those sixty-five or older was twelve percent. Those Americans eighty-five or older comprise one of the fastest growing age groups in this nation. Between 1980 and 2020, this group will triple in size and by 2050 will be seven times as large, constituting over sixteen million Americans.[3]

How our system will judge who is not competent, where they will be domiciled, who will manage their assets, and who will make consenting decisions on their behalf are issues of great import and scholarly debate. Even a preliminary review of current literature on the subject of guardianship (public or private) reveals a variety of themes that have generated professional concern. Among them are the issues of: involuntary commitment and civil rights,[4] due process and judicial reform,[5] competency evaluation,[6] role of the guardian,[7] the psychological effects of guardianship,[8] and the extent of need for guardians.

In 1983, one of the first published guardianship needs studies was conducted in Florida by Schmidt and Peters.[9] The Florida study assessed the alleged need for public guardianship via a telephone survey of the state's seventy-four public receiving facilities, community mental health centers, and clinics; thirty private receiving facilities; eleven Aging and Adult district officers; Developmental Services institutional and residential placements; and six state mental hospitals. Along with basic demographic characteristics and data concerning the extent of physical and psychiatric disability, the survey requested the number of legally incompetent clients

---

3. U.S. Senate Special Committee on Aging, *Developments in Aging*, 100th Cong., 1st Sess. (1987).

4. *See, e.g.*, Alexander (1975, 1977), *supra* note 2; Schmidt, *supra* note 2; Schmidt, *Guardianship of the Elderly in Florida: Social Bankruptcy and the Need for Reform*, 55 Fla. B. J. 189 (1981).

5. *See, e.g.*, Atkinson, *Towards a Due Process Perspective in Conservatorship Proceedings for the Aged*, 18 J. Fam. L. 819 (1980); Mitchell, *Involuntary Guardianship for Incompetents: A Strategy for Legal Services Advocates*, 12 Clearinghouse Rev. 451 (1978); Schmidt, *Adult Protective Services and the Therapeutic State*, 10 L. & Psychology Rev. 101 (1986); Schmidt, *Recommended Judicial Practices in Guardianship Proceedings for the Elderly*, 61 Fla. B. J. 35 (1987).

6. *See, e.g.*, Baker, *Competent for What?*, 79 J. Nat'l Med. A. 715 (1987); Nolan, *Functional Evaluation of the Elderly in Guardianship Proceedings*, 12 Med. & Health Care 210 (1984).

7. *See, e.g.*, Schmidt, *supra* note 2; Schmidt (1987), *supra* note 5; Schmidt, Miller, Peters & Loewenstein, *A Descriptive Analysis of Professional and Volunteer Programs for the Delivery of Public Guardianship Services*, 8 Prob. L. J. 125 (1988).

8. *See, e.g.*, Parmalee, *Protective Services for the Elderly: Do We Deal Competently with Incompetency?*, L. & Pol. Q. 397 (Oct. 1980).

9. Schmidt & Peters, *Legal Incompetents' Need for Guardians in Florida*, 15 Bull. Am. Acad. Psychiatry & L. 69 (1987).

with and without guardians served by the facility, and the number of functionally incompetent clients. The latter category was defined as those clients "...alleged to meet legal criteria for incompetence, but have not yet been formally adjudicated incompetent".[10]

The study found that nearly 3,000 legal incompetents as well as 6,000 functional incompetents, were in need of guardianship services. Another group of 2,250 clients from Developmental Services was alleged to be in need of guardianship services for a combined total of more than 11,000 clients. Further, Schmidt and Peters reported that these numbers probably undercounted the overall need in Florida. Absent from their survey were data concerning private clients residing in nursing homes and adult congregate living facilities, and those outside of the state service system. Some examples of the latter would include transient groups, clients served by the federal government (e.g., the Department of Veterans Affairs), clients who never sought any form of public assistance, and those housed in unlicensed facilities, or those who never applied for social services benefits. This Tennessee study is the only assessment conducted statewide in Tennessee, or in any other state, of the need for guardians in the private nursing home population.

Methodology

This need assessment survey was developed in order to document the existing level of need for guardianship services among the elderly residents of Tennessee nursing homes. Originally, homes for the aged and residential homes were included in the survey, but the latter were excluded from the analysis for reasons described below. A list prepared by the State of Tennessee of all licensed facilities was utilized as a mailing list. Unlicensed facilities were excluded for obvious reasons: no means of securing addresses or telephone numbers was available, and unlicensed facilities would be unlikely to respond given the possibility of exposing themselves to possible litigation or closing.

Since the entire "licensed-facility" population was approximately 500 facilities, the whole population was surveyed rather than a sample of those facilities. This decision was made for two reasons. First, it was suspected that return rates would be low since the survey was entirely voluntary. Second, a survey of the entire population was financially feasible.

The survey was conducted in two phases. First, a questionnaire was constructed that solicited information about the number of residents; the number of residents in the age groupings of sixty and under, 61–64, 65–74, and seventy-five and over; the number of white and nonwhite residents;

---

10. *Id.* at 70.

the number of male and female residents; the number of Medicaid eligible residents; the number of residents having only mental disabilities, only physical disabilities, and some combination of physical and mental disabilities; the number of current residents that have already been appointed some form of guardianship services; and the number of current residents perceived to need each of the following but for whom there was not a willing and able family member or friend to serve: limited guardian, conservator of property, conservator of person, representative payee, and power of attorney. Respondents were also asked to rate the degree of difficulty in completing the survey ("much," "some," and "no"), as well as how confident they were regarding the accuracy of the information supplied ("not confident," "doubtful," "hard to say," "somewhat confident," and "very confident"). The questionnaire also included statutory definitions of the type of guardianship services to aid administrators in completing the needs assessment.

Questionnaires were mailed in the Summer of 1988 to each licensed facility appearing in the 1987 state guide, along with a cover letter explaining the purposes of the survey and a self-addressed postage-paid envelope. To facilitate higher response rates, the survey was intentionally designed to obtain only aggregate quantitative data with the unit of analysis being the nursing home. Thus, completing the survey did not violate any confidentiality regulations of the residents or their records, and data could be easily entered into a data base management system (DBASE III).

The second phase of the study involved a follow-up telephone survey in the Summer and Fall of 1988. Any facility that provided incomplete or contradictory information or that did not promptly return the survey was telephoned to solicit the necessary information. At most facilities, the respondent was the social services director, but in some cases, administrators, social workers, nursing directors, or records managers completed the survey and/or received the follow-up telephone calls. In some instances, figures obtained were estimates that represented the respondents' best judgment because relevant information was not contained in client files. Lack of computerized records also prohibited some respondents from reporting precise information regarding clients' legal status since assembling such data would be too time consuming.

With reference to the number of clients with perceived need, as Schmidt and Peters point out, "...nonjudicial assessments of legal incompetence are of course suspect but, in the absence of better information, must necessarily suffice."[11] As stated, statutory definitions of various legal statuses were provided to assist respondents. It should be pointed out that

---

11. *Id.* at 72.

although perceptions of incompetency by nursing home staff may not be valid and reliable indicators of actual need of public guardianship services, they are good measures of "need for referral". The role of nursing home staff in the system is not to make legal decisions regarding incompetency and need for public guardianship services, but instead, on a subjective basis, to make referrals to public guardian district agencies for further processing. Of course, if reliable and valid measures of incompetency were available, it would make everyone's job easier. Perhaps one set of measures should be developed for referring agencies (such as nursing homes) that err on the side of referring clients (i.e., have a higher number of false positive ratings of incompetency), and another set of more precise measures should be developed for judges who make formal guardianship decisions. Nevertheless, it is important that residents who are perceived by nursing home staff to be in need of public guardianship services actually be referred to district agencies for evaluation. In this study, it is those residents that should be referred, but have not been, who constitute unmet need.

A mail survey with telephone follow-up was chosen as the methodology to increase the response rate, minimize costs, to facilitate follow-up questions, and answer any questions administrators might have about the survey, its objectives, or any legal ramifications. Although such methodology has inherent difficulties, the economic circumstances of this needs assessment warranted its usage.

After the first phase of the study (mail survey), residential homes were excluded from the study because it was discovered that almost all licensed residential homes require their residents to be competent and able. Most do not supply medical services or skilled care services. Most residential home administrators contacted stated that their regulations excluded anyone who was adjudicated or later became adjudicated by the court as incompetent.

One hundred and ninety-four residential homes were eligible at the beginning of the study; thirty-one responded to the initial mail survey. Of these, only eight indicated that a public guardian could be utilized in some capacity, generally as a representative payee. And of these eight homes, six homes had six residents or less. An additional seven homes contended that family members were acting "unofficially" as guardians. The remainder insisted that they would not accept anyone who was incompetent. Telephone inquiries to another twenty-five residential homes that had not responded to the survey revealed that applicants who needed skilled care or who were incompetent were not accepted. Overall, of the fifty-six homes with which contact was made, none of the larger homes (twenty residents or more) would accept residents needing guardianship services of any kind. Therefore, the administrators themselves indicated that residential homes should not be included in the survey. The researchers concurred with this opinion; consequently these facilities were omitted from the analysis.

Data from the surveys were entered into a data base management system (DBASE III) and transferred to SPSS/PC for statistical analysis. Because the entire population of nursing homes were surveyed, the analysis is descriptive, with frequency distributions, measures of central tendency, and crosstabulations constituting the analysis techniques. The unit of analysis is the nursing home.

Findings

From the time the study was initiated, fourteen facilities that were on the original list of eligible facilities closed. With the exclusion of the residential homes as described above, 295 facilities remained eligible for the study. One hundred and twenty-three surveys were received for a response rate of 41.7%. As Table 1 demonstrates, of the 123 valid cases, a total of 12,226 residents are reported as domiciled within the various facilities.

Given that the total number of beds available in these homes is 12,894 according to the state guide of licensed nursing homes, the occupancy rate

Table 1. Mean Number and Percentage of Nursing Home Residents with Particular Demographic Characteristics

Variable	mean proportion	(st. dev.)	Absolute Totals Number*	(%)
Number of Females	72	(.59)	8785	(73%)
Number of Males	27	(.24)	3250	(27%)
Number of Whites	87	(.61)	10331	(88%)
Number of Nonwhites	12	(.33)	1426	(12%)
Aged 64 and Under	12	(.09)	1361	(12%)
Aged 65–74	15	(.16)	1756	(15%)
Aged 75 and Above	72	(.61)	8622	(73%)
Medicaid Eligible	73	(.76)	8725	(74%)
Total # of Residents	99	(.80)	12226	(100%)

*Absolute numbers for sets of characteristics do not sum to the total 12,226 because of missing data.

is 94.8%. The average number of residents per facility is around ninety-nine, the median is seventy-nine, the mode twelve, and the standard deviation .80, which reflects the wide distribution of size of nursing homes in Tennessee. Females constitute 73% of the reported population with an average of nearly seventy-two female residents per facility. Conversely, males represent 27% of the reported population. Further, the data reveal that nearly 88% of the residents are white.

The older elderly are substantially represented in Tennessee nursing homes. Around 73% of the total reported population is seventy-five years of age or older; 15% are sixty-five to seventy-four years old; and the remaining 12% are under sixty-five years of age. Finally, approximately 74% of the residents were eligible for Medicaid reimbursement.

As shown in Table 2, 111 nursing homes provided complete data for the current legal status of their clients. In these homes, 238 out of a total of 10,513 residents, or 2.3%, were reported to have a limited guardian. One-hundred and two, or 1% were reported to have a conservator of property, and 190, or 1.8%, had a conservator of person. Six-hundred and eighty residents of the nursing homes surveyed, or 6.5%, used a power of attorney, whereas 2,136 residents, or 20.3%, used a representative payee. Thus, a total of 3,353 residents, or 31.9%, are currently represented by some form of Tennessee guardianship service.

Table 3 provides information pertaining to the amount of perceived need for public guardianship. There were a total 10,555 residents in the 113 nursing homes eligible for this section of the survey. Three-hundred and twenty-seven residents, or 3.1%, are perceived by nursing home staff to need a limited guardian. Forty-one, or 0.4% need a conservator

Table 2. Number of Nursing Home Residents Currently Receiving Guardianship Services in Tennessee.

Type of Service	Number	%
Limited Guardian	238	2.3%
Conservator of Property	102	1.0%
Conservator of Person	190	1.8%
Representative Payee	2136	20.3%
Power of Attorney	680	6.5%
Total Receiving Any Service	3353	31.9%
Total Number of Residents*	10513	100.0%

*Total number of residents in this table does not equal to 12,226 because twelve nursing homes had missing information on this section.

Table 3. Number of Nursing Home Residents with Unmet Need for Guardianship Services in Tennessee.

Type of Service	Number	(%)
Limited Guardian	327	(3.01%)
Conservator of Property	41	(0.40%)
Conservator of Person	80	(0.80%)
Representative Payee	417	(3.95%)
Power of Attorney	179	(1.70%)
Total Needing Any Service	1044	(9.90%)
Total Number of Residents*	10555	(100.00%)

*Total number of residents in this table do not equal to 12,226 because ten nursing homes had missing information on this section.

of property; eighty, or 0.8%, need a conservator of person; 417, or 3.95%, need a representative payee; and 179, or 1.7% are perceived to need someone to have power of attorney. This, a total of 1,044 residents, or 9.9%, are perceived to be in need of guardianship services but have no one to perform such duties. Interestingly, forty-nine facilities (43%) reported that no residents were in need of any form of public guardianship services.

To summarize the univariate data, over two-fifths of the residents of the responding Tennessee nursing homes (42%) were in need of Tennessee guardianship services; 32% were having their needs met at the time of the survey, and 10% had no one to assume such a role so public guardianship services were required. It should be noted that although 74% of the respondents indicated some degree of difficulty in completing the survey, fully 81% stated that they were "somewhat to very" confident that the information they provided was accurate.

Because of the 58% nonresponse rate, it is difficult to determine the overall level of unmet need for public guardianship services in Tennessee nursing homes. If the assumption is made that the nursing homes that returned the surveys are representative of all such homes and that, therefore, 9.9% accurately reflects the percentage of residents in need, then extrapolating to all nursing homes suggests that there are 3,003 out of 30,336 total nursing home residents in Tennessee who are in need of public guardianship services. This total also assumes that the occupancy rate for facilities that did not respond is the same 94.8% as for facilities that did respond.

To assess the degree of representativeness of the sample, all nursing homes were categorized by size (small = fifty beds or less; medium = fifty-

Table 4. Cross-Tabulation of Size of Facility by Location, with Associated Response Rates

	Location								
	Rural			Urban			Total		
Size	No.	%	Resp. Rate	No.	%	Resp. Rate	No.	%	Resp. Rate
Small (< 51 Beds)	12	19%	52.0%	13	21%	50.0%	25	20%	51.0%
Medium (51-149 Beds)	44	71%	43.6%	29	48%	35.4%	73	59%	39.9%
Large (150+ Beds)	6	10%	13.3%	19	31%	42.2%	25	20%	39.7%
Total	62	50%	43.7%	61	50%	39.9%	123	100%	41.7%

one to 149 beds; and large = 150 beds or more) and location (facilities were defined as urban if they were located in MSA counties; otherwise, they were considered as rural). Table 4 provides response rates by a cross-tabulation of these two variables. Large rural facilities and medium urban facilities had the lowest response rates (33.3% and 35.4% respectively), whereas small urban and small rural facilities had the highest response rates (50% and 52% respectively). Overall, then, the data demonstrate that the sample is reasonably representative of Tennessee nursing homes, at least as measured by these variables.

An additional clue that the responding facilities are reasonably representative of all nursing homes in Tennessee is that, according to the state guide, responding facilities have a total of 12,894 beds and nonresponding facilities, 19,099 beds. Thus, the responding facilities have 40.3% of the total available beds which closely matches the 41.7% response rate.

Breakdowns of mean levels of current guardianship usage and unmet need were also done by size and location to determine if there was more need in large, urban facilities. Literature on social networks of the elderly indicates that urban elderly are more likely to be socially isolated[12] and, hypothetically, they may be more likely to require public guardianship services. The cross-tabulation of size of facility by urban-rural status is shown in Table 4, along with associated response rates, whereas the breakdowns mentioned above are given in Table 5.

Sixty-one of the 123 homes that responded to the survey are urban, and sixty-two are rural. Twenty-five (20.3%) are categorized as small

---

12. *See, e.g.,* Coward & Smith, *Families in Rural Society* in D. Dillman & D. Hobbs (eds.), Rural Society in the U.S.: Issues for the 1980's, pp. 77–84 (1982); Youmans, *Rural Aged*, 429 Annals Am. Acad. Pol. & Soc. Sci. 81 (1977).

nursing homes, seventy-three (59.3%) as medium, and twenty-five (20.3%) as large. As Table 4 indicates, urban nursing homes are more likely to be large, with 31% of homes being so designated as compared to 10% of rural homes being categorized as large. Seventy-one percent of rural homes are designated as medium size as compared to 48% of urban nursing homes.

Table 5 shows by size and location of nursing home the percentage of residents that currently have someone serving in each of the five legal capacities, as well as the percentage of residents in need of the five Tennessee public guardianship alternatives. Because the entire population was surveyed, the sample is not a probability sample. Therefore, inferential statistics with significance testing are not supported by statistical theory. Accordingly, the reader should examine the mean percentage in a straightforward manner. Nevertheless, if the sample had been a probability sample, only one comparison (the percentage in urban and rural nursing homes having limited guardians) would be significant at the .05 significance level.

The overall patterns are as follow: urban nursing homes have slightly more residents currently using a guardian and also have slightly more residents in need of public guardianship services. Urban residents are slightly more likely to have a limited guardian, to have someone using

Table 5. Percentage of Residents Currently Served by a Guardian and Percentage in Need of a Public Guardian by Size and by Location.

# Residents with:	Size			Location		
	Small	Med.	Large	Rural	Urban	Total
Limited Guardian	10.4	1.4	1.6	1.3	8.3	4.6
Conserv. of Property	1.5	1.1	.7	1.2	1.0	1.1
Conserv. of Person	2.2	2.0	1.6	2.3	1.7	2.0
Rep. Payee	15.9	19.4	23.9	23.0	15.7	19.4
Power of Attorney	10.1	8.9	5.8	7.4	9.9	8.6
Total	40.1	34.8	33.6	35.3	36.6	35.6

# Residents in Need of:	Size			Location		
	Small	Med.	Large	Rural	Urban	Total
Limited Guardian	2.9	3.2	3.1	2.0	4.4	3.1
Conserv. of Property	2.1	.1	.7	.1	1.2	.6
Conserv. of Person	.2	.8	.6	.4	1.0	.7
Rep. Payee	2.4	3.6	5.2	4.0	3.2	3.6
Power of Attorney	.5	1.7	1.7	2.1	.8	1.5
Total	8.2	9.4	11.3	8.6	10.6	9.5

power of attorney, and to be in need of a limited guardian or a conservator of property or person. Rural residents are slightly more likely to have someone serving as representative payee and conservator of property or person, and to be in need of someone to serve as representative payee or to use a power of attorney.

Regarding the effects of size of facility, the data show that the smaller the facility the greater the percentage of current residents who have all forms of guardianship services, with the exception of representative payee. Large facilities are more likely to have larger percentages of residents using a representative payee. Pertaining to need for public guardianship, larger facilities appear to have more unmet need, primarily because their staff reported a greater need for public guardians to serve as representative payees and to accept power of attorney. All in all, then, the effects of size and location of nursing home were minimal.

Conclusion and Discussion

Even though the percentage of nursing home residents needing public guardianship services is seemingly small, this study has documented that al least 1,044 residents are perceived to require such services. This number is alarmingly high, even though it is an underestimate since 58% of the nursing homes did not respond to the survey. Those 1,044 potential clients, if provided with public guardianship program service, would immediately overload the statewide public guardianship program currently administered by the Tennessee Commission on Aging. As noted in the introduction, data obtained from the Commission indicate that 215 total clients were being served by the program during the quarter of October-December 1988. One-hundred and seventeen required full guardianship, the remaining ninety-eight required the following alternative services: limited guardianship (eighteen); representative payee/legal custodian (fifty-four); guardian ad litem (thirteen); and power of attorney (thirteen).[13] Since potential wards are referred to the public guardian program district agencies by various agents, including family members, nursing home staff, hospital staff, adult protective services, attorneys, and other interested persons, it is curious that so many nursing home residents with unmet need have not been referred to this program. At the least, those 1,044 residents with perceived need should be referred to the public guardianship district agencies.

Another interesting concern is the issue of conflict of interest. Many of the nursing homes responding to the survey indicated that the facility

---

13. W. Schmidt & A. Heckert, *supra* note 1.

or its administrator functioned as representative payee for a large number of its clients. In some cases, twenty-five or more residents were represented by the facility. Yet, many of the nursing home respondents did not perceive a need for an external monitor (such as a public guardian) to oversee or assume these responsibilities. In fact, many facilities that did not complete the survey frequently reported that workload and/or time constraints prevented them from doing so. Delegating these duties to someone outside the facility, appointed by the state, might serve both parties well. While this should not be construed as evidence of abuse or of intent to defraud clients of their funds, the introduction of a third party could at least reduce the potential and appearance of conflict of interest. None of the above residents were included in the category of residents with perceived need, but if they were included that figure would come closer to 1,500 clients. Reducing potential conflict of interest would appear to be in the best interests of both the facility and the governmental agencies that oversee licensure and disbursement of governmental funds.[14]

Finally, the state of record keeping that exists in many Tennessee nursing homes is a concern. The most frequently cited reasons for not completing the survey were time constraints, workload, and insufficient data. In the latter case, many facilities could not state if a client had or had not been adjudicated by a court, what form of guardianship had been imposed, or even who the legal guardian was. A common example reported would be "... a family member is acting 'unofficially' as a guardian but our records don't indicate who they are..." One can only surmise the confusion that must exist if that client should become acutely ill and require invasive medical/surgical intervention. Attempting to discover the proper party to sign a consent/release form could delay necessary treatment. Thus, computerization of client records would be valuable to both the client and the facility for reasons other than research. Over the last ten years, computers have become a staple of the small business community, as well as the patient care industry. While the state might be reluctant to mandate computerized management information systems for the nursing home industry, it might be appropriate for the state to mandate that facilities maintain records about the legal status of all residents of licensed facilities, along with the names and relationships of guardians and what form of protective services has been imposed. Further, nursing homes should report the names of any clients who need referral for assessing competency and/or protective services to public guardian agencies.

---

14. [*Cf.* Stiegel, *Proposed Solutions to Social Security Representative Payee Problems*, 24 Clearinghouse Rev. 570 (1990).]

Part III

Findings From a National Study of Public Guardianship and the Elderly

Chapter 4

Issues in Public Guardianship

Winsor Schmidt
Robert Bickel
William Bell
Kent Miller
Elaine New

Black's Law Dictionary[1] defines "guardian" as "a person lawfully invested with the power, and charged with the duty, of taking care of the person and managing the property and rights of another person, who, for some peculiarity of status, or defect of age, understanding, or self-control, is considered incapable of administering his own affairs." "Defect of age" clearly refers to incompetence by reason of being too young. Unfortunately, some guardianship statutes also include being old as eligibility criterion.

A "public" guardian is perhaps best defined in contrast to a private guardian. A guardian would be considered "public" where there is no private guardian. The reasons for there being no private guardian include such situations as those where there are no willing and responsible family members or friends to serve as guardian; and, where there is insufficient money in the estate, or *noblesse oblige* in the prospective guardian, to attract private attorneys, or banks, or other entities into guardianship service. A public guardian, then, may be conceptualized as the product of a failure in the private sector or market. Specifically, a public guardian is an agent of the government which has entered the guardianship market in response to a real or supposed demand and absence of supply.

This is not necessarily to suggest that the *parens patriae* (paternal) activities of government are inappropriate. *Black's Law Dictionary*, again, considers *"parens patriae"* to refer in the United States to the state as a sovereign, with "sovereign power of guardianship over persons under disability ... such as minors, and insane and incompetent persons."[2] Compare the

---

1. Black's Law Dictionary (rev. 4th ed. 1968).
2. *Id.* at 1269.

notion of *parens patriae* with the "police power" of the state "to prohibit all things inimical to comfort, safety, health, and welfare of society." Consider also the extent to which *parens patriae* is derivative of England where the *parens patriae*, or father or parent of his country, was the king. One might well inquire about the extent to which *parens patriae* is monarchical rather than democratic.

In short, police power enables the state to prohibit activity antagonistic to societal values; *parens patriae* seems to allow the state to require certain activity which the state has deemed consistent with societal values as the state interprets them. Attorneys especially should appreciate the analogous dilemma of being able to enjoin or prohibit certain activity in equity, but, because of enforcement difficulty, not being able to require a baseball player to play or ballerina to dance. Such a situation is remedied by awarding monetary damages. Perhaps such *parens patriae* activities as public guardianship can be most successfully accomplished through a similar award of money to the individual to make the individual as whole as the economy is able to accomplish.

The clientele for a public guardian seem to be primarily elderly persons.[3] It is estimated that two to three million elderly persons need some form of protective services,[4] public guardianship being one possible type. As the population bulge ages, the demand for such services can only intensify.

While guardianship was not originally intended to provide custody of the person, but rather preservation of economic resources,[5] the *parens patriae* power of the state has expanded to the point of potential and realized infringement upon liberty and individual autonomy, and entails stigma comparable to that of civil commitment.[6] Inasmuch as the costs of guardianship intervention have often far exceeded the benefits,[7] it is imper-

---

3. *See, e.g.*, Report of the Task Panel on Legal and Ethical Issues to President's Commission on Mental Health, Report to the President, Washington, D.C.: Superintendent of Documents, Volume IV Appendix, p. 1386 (1978) ("Very little research has been undertaken so far on the need for or effectiveness of a public guardian."). Recommendation 1(b) of the Task Panel is that "Public guardianship statutes should be reviewed for their effect in providing services to persons in need of but without guardianship." p. 1392.

4. J. Regan & G. Springer, Protective Services for the Elderly (July 1977) (a working paper prepared for the U.S. Senate Special Committee on Aging, 95th Cong., 1st Sess.).

5. *See, e.g.*, Developmentally Disabled Legislative Guide Project, A Review of State Guardianship Legislation, unpublished draft: American Bar Association Commission on the Mentally Disabled (1977), p. 1.

6. *See, e.g., Legal Issues in State Mental Health Care: Proposals for Change—Guardianship*, 2 Mental Disability L. Rep. 443 (1978). *See generally* W. Gaylin, I. Glasser, S. Marcus & D. Rothman, Doing Good: The Limits of Benevolence (1978). *See also* Horstman, *Protective Services for the Elderly: The Limits of Parens Patriae*, 40 Mo. L. Rev. 215 (1975).

7. J. Regan & G. Springer, *supra* note 4, at 24.

ative to determine whether the trend toward public guardianship is justified, given the short term public constraints of a "Proposition 13" atmosphere and the long term anticipation of a very large elderly population.

The purpose of our public guardianship research project was to assess the extent to which public guardianship assists or hinders older persons in securing access to their rights, benefits, and entitlements as a basis for public policy recommendations.

Conceptual Framework/Analytical Models

Some of the research activities were straightforward gathering and analysis of the relevant legal and social science literature, and a review and updating of existing public guardianship laws and proposed public guardianship bills. The conceptual effort concentrated on the extent to which public guardianship assists the elderly in securing "access" to rights, benefits, and entitlements. Should the research address "access" in the sense of "approach," i.e., the elderly being able to at least seek rights, benefits, and entitlements? Or should the research evaluate whether rights, benefits, and entitlements are actually obtained? As interesting and as important as the latter question may be, it became apparent that the level of funding for this project was not conducive to such an evaluation.

Instead the research will assess the "access," the opportunity provided to older persons by public guardianship to seek their rights, benefits, and entitlements. Does public guardianship enable older persons to enter the various affirmative government and social processes? Or does public guardianship itself constitute a negative, debilitative process? Is it the beginning of the end?[8] Is public guardianship the front door to constructive assistance, or is it the last door to oblivion?

There are several themes and tensions inherent to public guardianship and its administration. The tension between the state's inclination to be protective of the individual, and the individual's civil liberties, autonomy, and freedom from stigma has already been noted.

An historical perspective of past, present and future considerations contributes the past evolution of the "therapeutic state". Kittrie identified the therapeutic state as "the new hybrid system of social controls."[9] While

---

8. This concept, of course, is in sharp contrast to that of Robert Browning who wrote:
"Grow old with me!
The best is yet to be,
The last of life for which the first was made...."
quoted in Legal Research and Service for the Elderly, The Law & Aging Manual, Washington, D.C.: Legal Research and Services for the Elderly, p. 5 (1976).
9. N. Kittrie, The Right to be Different: Deviance and Enforced Therapy (1971).

the therapeutic state feeds upon the "*parens patriae* power and the state responsibility for public welfare," it is distinct from the "welfare state".[10] The welfare state makes services available to voluntary consumers; the therapeutic state assumes that its clients are too incompetent to be voluntary or to realize the beneficence of the proffered assistance, and therefore attempts to administer its services involuntarily.[11] The traditional clients of the therapeutic state have been the mentally ill and retarded, juvenile and defective delinquents, alcoholics, drug offenders, and sex offenders.[12] Older persons have been overrepresented in many of these so-called "deviant" populations, and one involuntary mechanism, in addition to civil commitment, has been guardianship:

> ....[A]nyone, especially an older person, who needs a guardian is popularly assumed to be mentally ill. The aged person with a few of the symptoms of chronic brain syndrome, such as forgetfulness, is more likely to be judged mentally ill and therefore to be declared incompetent.[13]

The danger of the therapeutic state lies in the conditioning of society to consider those with any label of deviance as "'different,' rarely considering the possibility that deviance could easily be broadened to encompass many unsuspecting candidates."[14] In short:

> The machinery by which the state responds to these individuals, and more fundamentally, the values of the general citizenry which encourage the establishment of such machinery is what is meant by "the therapeutic state."[15]

There is some opinion that the therapeutic state has not turned out to be the Orwellian monster anticipated. Kittrie himself has apparently recanted his former concern.[16] However, others have taken up where Kittrie left off and not only identify a currently healthy therapeutic state, but also anticipate a "1984" lamentable in its subtlety and sophistication.[17]

---

10. G. Myrdal, Beyond the Welfare State (1967).
11. N. Kittrie, *supra* note 9, at 41.
12. R. Singer & W. Statsky, Rights of the Imprisoned: Cases and Materials, p. 3 (1974). [*See* P. Conrad & J. Schneider, Deviance and Medicalization: From Badness to Sickness (1992).]
13. J. Regan & G. Springer, *supra* note 4, at 36, *citing* Lehmann, *Guardianship*, in Kaplan & Aldridge (eds.) Social Welfare of the Aging (1962).
14. N. Kittrie, *supra* note 9, at 361.
15. R. Singer & W. Statsky, *supra* note 12, at 15.
16. Address by Nicholas N. Kittrie, The Return of "Punishment" and the Decline of Therapy, The Second Annual Symposium on Mental Health and the Law, University of Richmond (March 6, 1978).
17. *See, e.g.*, K. Miller, Managing Madness: The Case Against Civil Commitment (1976). [P. Conrad & J. Schneider, *supra* note 12; K. Miller, The Criminal Justice and Mental Health Systems: Conflict and Collusion (1980).]

Thus, the attention formerly focused on civil commitment shifts to guardianship as commitment procedures are tightened and a legal model implemented. With the balancing of an informal, medical or therapeutic model in guardianship by a more formal legal model, it can be expected that the therapeutic model will prosper in newer areas, such as "protective" or "supportive" services generally. Given the past experience, legal balancing in protective services, too, will then occur.

Inherent in this historical conceptualization are not only the tensions between individual civil liberties and state paternalism, and between a medical-therapeutic model and a legal model, but also the stresses between public, private and quasi-public administration of such services as guardianship, between guardianship of the person and guardianship of property, between the alternative administration models for providing public guardianship,[18] and between the elderly and interest groups competing, or overlapping, for public guardianship services. [This multiple duality or diversity conceptualization itself (the "fox" model, compounded) is one alternative to the "hedgehog" model (domination by one central idea or system) for framing analysis.[19]]

A Brief Literature Review: Two Perspectives

There is a fairly sizable literature on guardianship generally,[20] although it does not seem to yet approach that for civil commitment. The literature on public guardianship, especially as it relates to the elderly, and more particularly as it relates to vulnerable, low income and minority elderly, is sparse to nonexistent.

---

18. J. Regan & G. Springer, *supra* note 4, at 41–42.
19. I. Berlin, Russian Thinkers (1978).
20. *See, e.g.,* G. Alexander & T. Lewin, The Aged and the Need for Surrogate Management (1972); Alexander, *On Being Imposed Upon by Artful or Designing Persons— The California Experience with the Involuntary Placement of the Aged*, 14 San Diego L. Rev. 1083 (1977); Frachter, *Toward Uniform Guardianship Legislation*, 64 Mich. L. Rev. 983 (1966); Horstman, *supra* note 6; Levy, *Protecting the Mentally Retarded: Am Empirical Survey and Evaluation of the Establishment of State Guardianship in Minnesota*, 49 Minn. L. Rev. 821 (1976); Morris, *Conservatorship for the Gravely Disabled: California's Nondeclaration of Nonindependence*, 15 San Diego L. Rev. 201 (1978); Pickering, *Limitations on Individual Rights in California Incompetency Proceedings*, 7 U. Cal. Davis L. Rev. 457 (1974); Regan, *Intervention Through Adult Protective Services Programs*, 18 Gerontologist 250 (1978) (hereinafter Intervention); Regan, *Protective Services for the Elderly: Commitment, Guardianship, and Alternatives*, 13 Wm. & Mary L. Rev. 569 (1972); Comment, *North Carolina Guardianship Laws—The Need for Change*, 54 N. C. L. Rev. 389 (1976); Note, *The Disguised Oppression of Involuntary Guardianship: Have the Elderly Freedom to Spend?*, 73 Yale L. J. 676 (1974).

In an early article,[21] Virginia Lehmann makes the following points:
1. Guardianship is a concept which is known in a large number of western countries and has a long history in both common law and civil law.
2. Traditionally, the intent of guardianship arrangements has been to provide for those who cannot care for themselves or cannot manage their "business" affairs.
3. At a minimum, any guardianship arrangement must provide a codified set of procedures for determining who is in need of a guardian, for selecting and appointing a guardian, for specifying the nature of the guardian-ward relationship and determining how this affects the ward's relationship with others, and for terminating the guardianship.
4. A primary concern and difficulty in applying guardianship to adults, including the aged, is the assessment of need and continuing need. That is, when is incapacitation due to "mental illness", "mental deficiency", or some other factor so serious that a guardian is needed, and how does one determine when an established guardian-ward relationship is no longer required?

Each of these points is rather obvious. However, in connection with the fourth point, Lehmann raises three less obvious and very important issues.

First, termination of a guardian-ward relationship may occur before the ward's demise. That is, the ward may recover sufficiently that the services of a guardian are no longer needed and continuation of the guardianship may constitute an intolerable infringement on the ward's civil liberties. However, if one assumes that the adverse effects of the aging process are, by their very nature, inexorably cumulative and irreversible, provision for short-term termination of a guardian-ward relationship may be overlooked. On the other hand, if we recognize that the debilitation which sometimes accompanies, though is not necessarily caused by aging is subject to alleviation, even "cure," through treatment, training, or other forms of intervention, then the need to place time limits on guardianship becomes evident.

Second, Lehmann raises the possibility that guardianship may be limited not only with respect to time, but to function as well. Thus the concept of guardianship need be construed as having sufficient flexibility so that not all guardian-ward relationships are automatically viewed as total or absolute. For example, a prospective ward may be physically incapacitated and thus lack sufficient mobility to provide for his basic physical

---

21. Lehmann, *supra* note 13.

needs. This same person, however, may be possessed of strong and undiminished intellect; the person may be quite capable of making all decisions concerning their business affairs.

Finally, though partly incapacitated and perhaps somewhat less able to make all decisions regarding personal affairs than the person once was, the prospective ward may still be able to make some decisions without assistance, and to offer sound advice regarding others. A guardianship arrangement which does not allow for this kind of participation by the ward in cooperation with the guardian errs in the direction of absoluteness and totality.

For at least these three reasons, flexibility must be built into any statutes regulating guardianship. The concept of "limited guardianship", with limits applied in a variety of ways and over varying ranges of activity, must be explicitly recognized and dealt with.

Lehmann concludes with the following points:

5. The concept of limited guardianship (Pflegschaft) is codified in the civil code of West Germany. The provisions of the German Civil Code which regulate limited guardianship are separate from and in addition to provisions for total or absolute guardianship.

6. In most instances, the German Civil Code allows the appointment of a limited guardian only at the request of or with the consent of the prospective ward. It is the ward who specifies the nature of the relationship between himself and the guardian, and the ward determines if and when the relationship should be terminated.

While the German case is interesting because of its flexibility and the initiative which it gives to the ward, Lehmann lists a number of difficulties which have been encountered repeatedly in using this arrangement, and which are probably characteristic of any guardianship procedure.

First, persons who might benefit from some sort of guardian-ward relationship may be unable to initiate guardianship proceedings. This may occur either because they do not know that such arrangements are possible, or because they are already incapacitated and have no one to assist them in the interim.

Second, no one may be available who is willing to serve as guardian or limited guardian. This, of course, might be taken as a statement of need for public guardianship arrangements, and Lehmann cites the existence of such institutions in England and California. However, she offers no details or comments on the actual working and consequences of public guardianship, and has nothing to say of evaluative interest.

A final suggestion, only obliquely made and not developed in Lehmann's article, is that the primary function of any institutionalized arrangement for public guardianship may be the coordination of already available but often inaccessible social services. In effect, the public guardian might function as an ombudsman, mediating between a needful ward and sometimes inefficient public service agencies. This, of course, raised the possibility that in many instances an "agent-client" relationship might be much more appropriate and useful than a "guardian-ward" relationship. On the other hand, the difference between this alternative and usual social casework is not readily apparent.

A later article[22] by John Regan makes the following points:

1. The number of adult protective services programs is growing rather rapidly throughout the nation. In part, this is a consequence of passage of Title XX of the Social Security Act of 1974. In many instances, however, new protective services programs exist alongside antiquated, inefficient, inflexible, potentially oppressive legal means for intervening in the absence of request or consent by a client. This criticism extends to laws regulating guardianship.

2. A clear distinction must be maintained between protective services, on the one hand, and means of unsolicited, unwanted intervention, on the other. The aim of protective services is to coordinate the activities of social services agencies and other public institutions to promote independent and healthful living for elderly persons. Legal intervention may be needed only when ostensibly needy elderly persons refuse assistance and the court intervenes to assure that the unwanted services are provided. In such instances, a legal guardian may be appointed to act as "substitute decision-maker," one who acts on behalf of a person judged to be incompetent.

3. In practice, use of a guardian-ward relationship to assist putatively incompetent and incapacitated adults readily lends itself to abuse, and may result in oppression and exploitation of aged persons. Particularly dangerous in this connection is over-reliance on the "medical model" of aging-as-disease, especially when applied by a psychiatrist or other physician who "examines" an elderly adult but who has no direct knowledge of the adequacy of the adult's day-to-day behavior. This problem is further exacerbated by the tendency of many, including physicians, to regard old age as sufficient evidence for a diagnosis of "senility" or "senile psychosis," both of which necessarily entail incompetence or incapacity.

---

22. Intervention, *supra* note 20.

4. Court proceedings concerning guardianship cases tend to be "informal" to the point of jeopardizing clients' rights. The alleged incompetent is often absent from the hearing; the respondent is often unrepresented or inadequately represented by counsel; and judges often routinely follow physicians' recommendations and grant petitioners' requests for guardianship.
5. Guardianship are typically total and absolute. Thus, whatever the ward's physical and mental condition,he becomes legally incompetent and incapacitated.

Using these observations as a point of departure, Regan offers a list of suggested changes in guardianship laws:

1. In making decisions as to whether a guardian-ward relationship is necessary in a particular instance, emphasis should be placed on behaviorally manifested disability—that is, demonstrated incapacity or incompetence—rather than on medical diagnoses.
2. In guardianship hearings, all the constraints of due process should apply, and the proceeding should be genuinely adversarial. The existence of "court teams" in which public defenders routinely comply with effectively predetermined decisions of "incompetence" or "incapacity" should be discouraged.
3. Comprehensive evaluations of prospective wards should be accomplished by a multidisciplinary team. The detailed information which they provide should be used by the court not simply to determine whether or not a client is incompetent or incapacitated, but to assess the degree of his impairment.
4. Guardian-ward relationships should be limited in terms of the capabilities of the prospective ward. That is, emphasis should be placed on what he can do rather than what he cannot do.
5. Guardianships should terminate automatically unless renewed by the court.
6. Private social agencies should be available to serve as guardians.
7. An office of public guardian should be created to act as a guardian of last resort.
8. The consent and active participation of the ward should be obtained whenever possible, and infringements on wards' independence should be sharply minimized. In short, flexibility should be built into statutes regulating guardianship, and the courts should remain constantly aware of the need for flexibility in decisionmaking regarding such arrangements.

As with Lehmann, Regan does not deny the need for guardian-ward relationships under certain, apparently rather extreme, circumstances. He, too, emphasizes the need for new, flexible legislation and for flexibility in judicial decisionmaking to minimize the total and absolute character of conventional guardian-ward relationships. As a means of making legal guardianship of adults a more useful procedure for assisting those in need, both Lehmann and Regan offer public guardianship as an alternative to guardian-ward relationships involving two private citizens.

It seems clear that the concept of "limited guardianship" is of overriding concern to both authors. The reasons for this have already been mentioned and seem persuasive. Nevertheless, neither Lehmann nor Regan has given us much that is new in addressing the admittedly very difficult question of when—if ever—it is appropriate to intervene without consent of the client. And neither seems to appreciate the legal and administrative complexity involved in dealing with a concept as flexible as limited guardianship.

In the absence of empirical research on guardian-ward relationships of limited scope, one can only speculate that the primary virtue of the concept—its flexibility when compared to absolute or total guardianships—might also be the primary stumbling block standing in the way of its effective legal codification, judicial interpretation, and day-to-day implementation.

In instances in which a limited guardian-ward relationship is requested by and freely consented to by the ward, problems created by the amorphous nature of the concept may be effectively minimized. This seems especially likely if the prospective ward is the dominant participant in specifying the nature of the guardian-ward relationship.

In cases of forced intervention by the courts, however, the potential utility of limited guardianship becomes problematic. Experience with probation and parole and related types of limited intervention, such as forced restitution and compulsory participation in mental health and drug-abuse outpatient programs, suggests that partial control of limited aspects of persons' behavior is difficult to enforce and not very useful. All too often, "official" participants in such limited, noninvoluntary endeavors either give up or resort to much more drastic means of achieving total compliance and control.

Issues for Consideration

There is a perhaps obvious point which needs to be made explicit in any discussion of public guardianship. That is, public guardianship is not an issue which can be usefully treated in isolation from knowledge of American society and the subordinate position of a growing but still unorganized and therefore powerless elderly population.

Thus, the emphasis in discussions of public guardianship for the elderly should be placed on the intrinsically social character and meaning of age and aging. Otherwise, stereotyped, sometimes convenient misconceptions concerning the capabilities of the elderly and the consequences of aging may mislead us into placing near-exclusive focus on the gross and inevitably incapacitating deterioration which ostensibly occurs in any aging individual. Such misunderstanding and misplaced emphasis can only hopelessly distort discussion of various proposals for rendering services to the aged, for they make any efforts to promote independent and healthful living seem doomed from the start.

On the other hand, if we recognize that relatively little is known about the aging process as it manifests itself physically and psychologically, and that erroneous notions, such as invariant decline in measured intelligence with increasing age, have framed our orientation to the aged for too many years, we will be in less danger of blaming the victim. We will also be less likely to provide only the harshest, most drastically restrictive measures when these are inappropriate. In short, measures aimed at containing aged individuals pending their imminent demise are in no sense legitimate solutions to the problems of, or the social problems posed by, an expanding elderly population.

Instead of placing undue emphasis on the real or imagined degeneration of the aging individual, we may begin to investigate institutional arrangements and their outcomes. We may ask questions as to the adequacy of the most basic social services, including not only conventional "welfare" programs but taken-for-granted services such as transportation, protection from harassment and violence, and the creation and maintenance of places to live which are not prohibitively expensive and which promote the development of social support systems that constitute the rudiments of community. Perhaps the most basic and important issue we can raise concerns the availability of the bare means of subsistence and the social institutional factors which facilitate or hamper aged persons in obtaining the minimum resources necessary to keeping body and mind intact.

At first glance, the growing interest in public guardianship might be taken to be evidence of "official" recognition of the injustice inherent in the social ascription of devalued status to the elderly. Public guardianship might be viewed as a progressive measure, perhaps an alternative to institutionalization, aimed at minimizing the constraints and discomfort which are widely accepted as inevitably accompanying old age.

Alternatively, however, one might view the spreading interest in public guardianship arrangements as a manifestation of a mind-set which cannot assimilate the notion of a healthy maturity. From this perspective, the only useful strategy may seem to be the progressive wrestling from the elderly of more and more of the day-to-day responsibility for their lives. In effect, public guardianship becomes just another institutionalized means for regulating the poor. Hard data to support the notion that there is a large number of incapacitated, incompetent, uncared-for elderly seems to be missing in 1982. Why, then, widespread interest in a legal solution to a problem which may not exist, at least not on a scale to match the manifest concern?

Obviously, we are raising questions which cannot now be answered. Just as obviously, there undoubtedly are extreme and unusual cases in which the services of a public guardian might be indispensible. Nevertheless, one comes away from the gerontological literature with the distinct impression that the widespread perception of a need for public guardianship arrangements has little to do with the characteristics of the aged themselves. Instead, it seems to stem directly from erroneous assumptions about the elderly and the failure of existing public agencies to provide even the modest prevailing level of services and opportunities in a way that the elderly can make best use of them.

Research Findings

The literature had indicated that about fifteen states had some provision for public guardianship. One of our first discoveries was that there are not only explicit public guardian statutes, but also what we are calling "implicit" public guardian statutes. Implicit public guardian statutes are statutes that seem to provide for a mechanism equivalent to public guardianship, without actually denominating the mechanism as "public guardian."

We found fourteen states which provide explicitly for public guardianship: Arizona, California, Delaware, Illinois, Maine, Minnesota, Missouri, Nevada, New Hampshire, New Jersey (for veterans), Oregon, Pennsylvania (by court order), South Carolina, and Tennessee. In addition, we found twenty-five states with some provision for an implicit public guardian: Alabama, Arizona, Colorado, Connecticut, Georgia, Hawaii, Idaho, Indiana, Kentucky, Maryland, Michigan, Minnesota, Mississippi,

New Hampshire (statute), New Jersey (for mentally retarded), North Carolina, North Dakota, Ohio, Pennsylvania, South Dakota, Texas, Utah, Virginia, Wisconsin, and Wyoming. With New Hampshire, New Jersey, Pennsylvania, and South Carolina counted twice, there are only sixteen states with no provision, either explicitly or implicitly, for a public guardian. Thus, public guardianship seems to be a more widespread legal possibility than expected.

A second discovery, however, was that there are not as many active programs. Only nine of the fourteen explicit states have active programs, and sixteen of the twenty-five implicit states have active programs. Furthermore only seven of the fourteen explicit states and about nine of the twenty-five implicit states provide public guardian services to significant numbers of elderly individuals. Public guardianship is more widespread in theory than anticipated, but less widespread in practice.

We first visited public guardian offices in Maryland and Chicago, and we then visited private guardian offices in Jacksonville and Tampa-St. Petersburg. We also visited public guardian offices in Delaware, Arizona, and California, and private guardians in three south Florida cities. Given the clear need, it is reasonable to suggest that public guardianship should be adopted or implemented more widely.

Nevertheless, there are problems with public guardianship. The Maryland program is located in the state office on aging, but there are plans to move the public guardian services to county offices on aging. The small staff in the state office seems to be able to handle its caseload of thirty quite well at the moment. However, when that caseload expands without staff expansion, or when the guardian services are transferred to county offices which are also providing other social services, it is possible that guardian service will deteriorate and that its independence will be contaminated by the conflict of interest within a social service delivery agency. A strong feature of Maryland's program is its statutory provision prohibiting a guardian from hospitalizing a ward without a civil commitment adjudication, in addition to its current independence from direct social service agencies.

The Cook County public guardian in Chicago was in the national news charging a hospital with unauthorized experimental surgery on mental patients. Such advocacy is a distinct departure from his predecessor's alleged systematic looting of ward's estates and engagement in such practices as the notation of visits to some wards who turned out to have been dead for as long as two years.

Nor is such scandal an isolated example of Cook County tomfoolery. The public guardian in Los Angeles has been sued for the inappropriate institutionalization of large numbers of wards. In Arizona, the institutionalization of a high percentage of wards is defended as an appropriate response to the difficult case that a guardian receives. The Arizona guardian offices are mini-bureaucracies apparently funded by fees from wards' estates.

Florida does not yet have any provision for a public guardian. A recent amendment allowing a private, nonprofit corporation to serve as guardian or a recruitment service has been implemented in Jacksonville and Tampa-St. Petersburg. The efforts of the Cathedral Foundation in Jacksonville are particularly commendable, but they suggest a need for expansion of their one staff, three wards, and thirty-five protective services clients by three or four times in Duval County, the same in Volusia County, and by a similar factor for the remaining rural counties in the one state Health and Rehabilitative Services district. Despite some private sector activity in Florida, there are still such phenomena as 600 mental patients at Florida State Hospital who are classified as "voluntary," but who are legally incompetent and without a guardian. At the same hospital, the director of the forensic unit was the guardian of the person for eighty other patients within the hospital which he helped administer.

Conclusion

One can tentatively conclude perhaps that there should be more meaningful review of public guardian activity, that public guardians should not be responsible for estates, that public guardians should be prohibited from committing their wards, that caseloads per guardian should be limited to thirty, that public guardians should be independent of social service agencies, and the like. But perhaps the real problem is conceptual rather than administrative.

The Benjamin Rose Institute study seemed to indicate that, compared to a control group, even the best protective services and staff for the group receiving services could not avoid a higher death rate and a higher institutionalization rate than for the group for whom nothing was done.[23] A study of mental patients released from Alabama's mental institutions by court order concluded that "family members adjusted expectations and accepted the patient home" when the state did not provide the alternative of a mental hospital.[24]

Admittedly, the evidence is limited and perhaps premature, but why should government necessarily become involved in another activity that

---

23. Blenkner, Bloom & Nielson, *A Research and Demonstration Project of Protective Services*, 52 Soc. Casework 483 (1971).

24. Leaf, *Patients Released After "Wyatt": Where Did They Go?*, 28 Hosp. & Community Psychiatry 366 (1977).

it is not only intrinsically incapable of performing, but that also unfairly and perhaps less humanely competes with such fundamental social units as the family? If public guardianship is only as good as guardianship statutes, which are even worse than state civil commitment statutes, or if public guardianship is utilized more where protective or social services are worse, why should another paternalistic public entity proliferate?

Chapter 5

Summary and Discussion of Major Findings from a National Study of Public Guardianship and the Elderly

Winsor C. Schmidt, Jr.
Kent S. Miller
William G. Bell
B. Elaine New

The major conclusions presented in this chapter follow the order in which the study was conducted. Initial concerns were with a telephone survey of public guardianship states, an analysis of state statutes and proposed legislation, and a review of court decisions. This was followed by intensive case studies and field research of five public guardianship states (Arizona, California, Delaware, Maryland, Illinois), as well as the in-depth examination of Florida as a state without provision for public guardianship. It will be apparent that some conclusions are less empirically based than others and thus should be taken primarily as tentative findings or recommendations, subject to future investigation of different data.

One of the first tasks was to identify those states with public guardian statutes and programs of any kind. Earlier sources had suggested that there were from twelve to fifteen such states, but our analysis uncovered thirty-four states with some statutory provision for public guardian services, whether or not they were specifically designated "public guardian." There are fourteen states with explicit provision for a public guardian and twenty-five states with implicit provisions for the functional equivalent of public guardianship. (Five states, Minnesota, New Hampshire, New Jersey, Pennsylvania [explicit by court order], and South Carolina, have both explicit and implicit provisions.) The explicit-implicit distinction is not particularly significant, since some of the states with implicit statutes had the most active and progressive programs.

This study began with the expectation that guardianship services would vary considerably across the states, and this expectation was confirmed on almost every dimension examined. The organizational models[1] were found to exist in modified form with many qualifications and exceptions, with some states having aspects of more than one model. The state programs were finally classified and compiled as follows[2]: court model, six states; independent state office model, three states (including Illinois); social service agency model, nineteen states; and county model, ten states.

Beyond this crude classification, generalizations and groupings that cut across programs were difficult to make. There were problems because some of the programs reviewed were at the state level, with others in local communities. Some were highly organized and staffed, with others run on a part-time basis. Quantitative data—such as the number of wards under the public guardian—were not available in many instances, and some of the figures given in the survey represent only knowledgeable estimates, The general theme of heterogeneity in public guardianship services is reflected in the following observations from the survey and the analysis of the state statutes.

Individuals Served

Of the thirty-four states under analysis, sixteen provide public guardianship services specifically for the elderly, twenty provide public guardianship services for "incompetent" persons, seventeen provide services for the mentally retarded, eighteen offer services to the mentally or physically disabled, and ten provide a form of public guardianship for minors. Some of the programs serve defined populations—for example, residents of institutions or veterans.

Responses to our survey revealed that more than half of the public guardian wards are female. Minorities constituted more than half of the total number of wards in some programs and were rarely present in others. Nearly all of the public guardian wards were described as having low

---

1. J. Regan & G. Springer, Protective Services for the Elderly, p. 111 (July 1977) (a working paper prepared for the U.S. Senate Special Committee on Aging, 95th Cong., 1st Sess.) (court model, independent state office, division of social service agency, county agency).

2. Some states have more than one model. See W. Schmidt, K. Miller, W. Bell & E. New, Public Guardianship and the Elderly, pp. 63–70, 205–228 (1981) (hereinafter Public Guardianship) (table summarizing public guardian operations by state, and descriptions of state public guardianship statutes).

See also Bell, Schmidt & Miller, *Public Guardianship and the Elderly: Findings from a National Study*, 21 Gerontologist 194 (1981).

incomes. Most wards are institutionalized. Whether the death rate of public guardian wards is disproportionate to that for private wards or for some other control group is difficult to say at this time.

Program Characteristics

Staff size varied across programs from a single part-time person to a staff of over one hundred. Caseloads ranged from a low of thirty per staff person in Colorado and Maryland to a high of 341 in New Jersey, with the average for all states being over 100 cases per worker. Several programs held guardianship for over 6000 wards. The time spent with individual wards was reported to range from one or two hours per year to over twenty hours per week.

With respect to staff training and background, public guardians tend to be either social workers or attorneys; the larger offices are likely to be headed by an attorney, with social workers responsible for direct services for the wards. But it should be noted that public guardianship offices are staffed by people from a number of disciplines and with highly variable qualifications.

Guardianship of Person and Property

All but two of the thirty-four states provide for guardianship of the person. Five states prohibit the public guardian from assuming guardianship of property, with other states placing a limit on the size of the estate eligible for public guardianship. Many of the state statutes that contain provisions for guardianship of the person do so without elaboration, and programs have not been developed. The historical interest in the management of money seems to continue to outweigh the response to the social needs of the individual.

Funding of Programs

State statutes are usually silent on funding for public guardianship services, and many states do not have a specific budget allocation for this purpose. In those states that do have allocations, these are based on various combinations of federal, state, and local funds. Twelve of the states do not charge fees for services, and fees are not a prerequisite in the remainder. However, a number of offices are heavily dependent upon the generation of fees, and as a result there is the potential for abuse. Programs may be induced to accept only cases able to pay and to terminate them where they are unable to do so, regardless of the need for services.

Due Process Protections

Although the states vary considerably in the amount of protection provided a potential ward, given the significance of a declaration of incompetency, there are a number of significant deficiencies. These deficiencies relate primarily to hearings, standard of proof, vagueness of criteria, and review functions. When the survey respondents were queried regarding the need for changes in public guardianship laws, an improvement in due process protections was one of the most commonly mentioned needs.

There are some built-in conflicts of interest in a number of states— particularly in those nineteen states where a state or county agency is specified to act as public guardian and is simultaneously responsible for the delivery of social services. Advocacy needs of the ward may not be compatible with general practice in the delivery of social service.

Proposed Legislation

The fifty states were surveyed regarding pending legislation on public guardianship, and twelve states (in addition to Florida) were found to be considering changes. Eight of these involved significant updates, frequently focusing on review procedures, provisions for program funding, and concern for the development of protective services.

The activity reported for twelve states does not accurately reflect the overall degree of interest in legislative change, in that it relates only to currently pending legislation. An unknown number of states have guardianship acts in preparation for appearance in other legislative sessions, and a number of the survey respondents seemed to be unfamiliar with or unclear about the concept of public guardianship. It is our overall impression that there is considerable sentiment in favor of legislation on guardianship, without much consensus over the exact form that it should take.

Court Cases Involving Public Guardianship

Litigation in the public guardianship area is a recent phenomenon and encompassed a total of less than fifty or so lower court cases. A majority of the cases involve wards who have due process complaints against their public guardians and are represented by nonprofit legal aid organizations. But there have also been cases of the public guardian suing on behalf of wards. The impact of this litigation on legislation and programs is not clear, with the exception perhaps of cases in New Hampshire and Pennsylvania. It should be noted that the litigation has dealt primarily with establishing and protecting the rights of the incompetent. The majority of the cases have occurred in three states, but it is a reasonable prediction that litigation in this area could be expected to expand rapidly.

Findings From the Case Studies

Our field research took us into only six states, but in most of these there was contact with more than one program, and in every instance a number of people were interviewed who had widely differing perspectives and roles in guardianship. Whenever possible, records and reports were consulted, wards were visited in the company of guardians, and existing quantitative data relating to guardianship were considered. The summary comments that follow are based primarily on these data, but to some extent draw also upon the work alluded to above.[3]

1. There seems to be no question that there is a population of unspecified size in need of guardianship services. This was affirmed by a very large majority of the people interviewed, by the fact that state institutions contain many patients who have been declared incompetent but have no guardian, and by a sizable number of citizen groups organizing to provide such services.
2. When there is an estate of some size ($50,000–75,000 or more), there is little difficulty in obtaining a guardian.
3. Public guardian offices seem to be understaffed and underfunded, and many of them are approaching the saturation point in number of wards.
4. As a consequence of point three above, most of the wards of public guardians receive very little personal attention, with many being seen for a total of only a few hours per year.
5. When an application for guardianship is filed, it is almost invariably granted. Critics say that this reflects the failure to have critical evaluations and confirms the rubber-stamping tendencies of the court. Supporters argue that guardianship is shunned whenever possible, and the failure to find any discrimination at the decisionmaking level confirms the argument that the wards have been thoroughly screened and are at "the end of the line."
6. Restoration to competency is so rare as to be functionally nonexistent.

---

3. Most of these observations are dealt with in greater detail in Public Guardianship, *supra* note 2.

7. Partial or limited guardianships are rarely established, and voluntary guardianships are next to nonexistent.
8. Incompetency proceedings tend to be nonadversarial, exceedingly brief, and subject to a large number of apparent due process deficiencies.
9. The review of guardianships by the court or other official bodies is perfunctory (if it is done at all), and there are limited protections for those wards who have estates.
10. Most of the wards of public guardians are extremely poor, but a good number have some limited assets, and the public guardian office needs to be prepared to manage these. A number of interviewees suggested that the uncovering of assets for the benefit of the ward should be a major function of the public guardian.
11. No particular patterns were observed regarding minorities and guardianships. Minorities are clearly represented in the programs, but it is not possible to conclude whether the representation is disproportionate.
12. Guardianship is frequently sought for purposes of medical consent, and this trend seems to be upward. When guardianship has been invoked for this purpose, it was our impression that it was primarily for management purposes and paper compliance with the law rather than due to concern over the ward.
13. There are a surprising number of nonprofit private agencies involved in providing guardianship services. Many of these are favorably regarded by professionals in the community, but they tend to deal with an extremely small number of wards.
14. A significant number of private individuals were discovered who hold guardianships for many wards—for example, a private attorney who has fifty wards at any one time and a minister with ninety-five wards. It is not clear how common this is, but in almost every community visited, the existence of such people seemed to be common knowledge.
15. Public guardianship programs seem to be particularly subject to the interests and personality of the program's director.
16. Instances of flagrant abuse of the office of public guardian were discovered, as well as instances of genuine concern and advocacy for the wards.
17. A number of respondents believed that there is an inverse relationship between guardianship and the use of civil commitment for mental illness.

Conflicting Perspectives

The majority of the people with whom we had contact had no doubt about the need for guardianship services and in general supported the concept of the public guardian.

The critics of public guardianship said essentially what we expected on the basis of a review of the available literature.[4] Some claimed that there was no unmet need. Others objected to the development of another bureaucracy that would necessarily become impersonal and incapable of responding to the emerging needs associated with guardianship. A frequently expressed concern was that the establishment of public guardianship services would lead to overutilization—that workers would be tempted to "find" wards who did not need guardianship or to utilize guardianship when less restrictive alternatives would be more appropriate. Related to this concern was a fear that families would be "let off the hook" and that public guardianship would be another instance of the state inappropriately assuming a responsibility better left to the family. There was also some concern about competition with and stifling of the private market.

The supporters of public guardianship held differing perspectives on each of the above points and also cited the advantages of a public program. They argued that there is a large unmet need and that the program is for individuals who do not have a willing or responsible family member or friend to serve as guardian. The expertise that would come from serving a number of wards was seen as providing a more effective service than could be given by private individuals. In addition, a public guardian would serve as a central contact on all matters of guardianship and would be more subject to audit, scrutiny, and review. In contrast with private guardians, such an office would presumably become more effective in such activities as uncovering resources of wards, exploring alternatives to institutionalization, coordinating services for other agencies, and the like. The supporters of a public program also pointed to the perceived deficiencies of the private system—an inability to meet the need, a greater concern with property than person, the absence of review, and the lack of expertise regarding other services.

There were some concerns voiced by those who support public guardianship. A frequent complaint related to the frequency with which the office discouraged guardianship and pushed alternatives that the referring workers felt had already been exhausted. Related to this was the fact that many of the programs were close to capacity. Some of the interviewees object-

---

4. *See* Public Guardianship, *supra* note 2, at 7–23.

ed to the "legal trappings" associated with guardianship, feeling that the process should be informal, based on the expertise of the participating professional. Others held an opposite position and called for additional due process protections.

Recommendations

Our specific recommendations are contained in the introductory comments to the model statute, and in the statute itself.[5] But we would like to underscore several of the conclusions and recommendations. Public guardianship is being endorsed, but only if it is done properly. By "properly" we mean with adequate funding and staffing, including specified staff-to-ward ratios, and with the various due process safeguards that we have detailed. Guardianship should continue to be a very rare event, and less restrictive alternatives must be considered in each instance. The determination of incompetency and the appointment of a guardian should occur within an adversary context. There should be provision for partial, voluntary, and time-limited guardianships. The office should be prepared to manage guardianship of person and property, but it should not be dependent upon the collection of fees for service.

The functions of the office should include the coordination of services, working as an advocate for the ward, and educating professionals and the public regarding the functions of guardianship. The office should also be concerned with private guardianship, in the sense of developing private sources and to some extent carrying out an oversight role.

Information Gaps

As a result of this study, we feel there is a good understanding of the context within which guardianship is established and of the problems and benefits of guardianship as they are seen by the people involved (except for significant numbers of wards). That is, the perceived reality is now known, and further understanding will have to come from direct systematic observation of the wards and their experiences. Some of the important questions and issues raised in the literature[6] remain unanswered and should be posed again at this point.

1. Frequent references were heard to the need for guardianship in order to prevent the victimization of the frail elderly (with the estimates that such situations compose at least one-third of the caseloads of

---

5. See *infra* chapter 15.
6. See Public Guardianship, *supra* note 2, at 7–23.

some public guardians). It would be worthwhile to know the incidence and type of victimization, with the idea that alternatives short of guardianship might be found appropriate.

2. It was noted that voluntary guardianship is an extremely rare event. Should it be encouraged? Is there a proportion of wards who would elect voluntary guardianship if they had the opportunity? How often are the wards resistant to compulsory guardianship?

3. Wards were systematically described to us as people with severe problems who were at "the end of the line." Yet many wards were observed who appeared to be intact and competent to make life decisions. What proportion of the wards are severely confused and disturbed?

4. Mental health and medical professionals are frequently involved in guardianship proceedings. Yet it is not at all clear whether they play a meaningful discriminatory role; widely differing opinions were received on this point. Are their evaluations mainly ceremonial? Are their findings and recommendations related to individual needs and conditions?

5. Whose interest is being served by guardianship? Earlier studies on the guardianship of property have suggested that the ward is not the beneficiary. Does this apply to guardianship of the person also?

6. The provision of counsel is seen as one of the major due process safeguards. To what extent do the attorneys assume an advocacy and adversarial role in guardianship?

7. A number of wards are served by private guardians who are not family members. To what extent are the rights of these wards protected?

8. Very little is know about the economics of guardianship. It is our impression that some individuals in the private market find that guardianship of limited estates, combined with third party or governmental payments, is profitable. Are the rights of the wards suitably represented under these arrangements, and what implications would this have for the funding of public guardians?

9. The argument has been made that the availability of strong protective services negates the need for guardianship. Critics have argued that such services are themselves inappropriately paternalistic, subject to considerable abuse, and would be likely to result

in an increase in the discovery of clients who need guardianship. There is no empirical basis for deciding between these conflicting opinions.[7]

10. What proportion of guardianships are established solely because of the inability of the person to care for one's medical needs? The answer to this question could have implications for partial guardianship as well as alternative mechanisms.

11. In spite of our findings that thirty-four states have provisions for public guardianship, the number of active programs is much smaller, and some large states (e.g., New York) had no such provision. Assuming that the need must exist, how is it being met? Is civil commitment being used to meet the need? Are there other mechanisms?

All of the questions noted above can be answered only by more direct evaluation of potential wards and of the process by which guardianship is granted.

---

7. [*But cf.* Wilber, *Alternatives to Conservatorship: The Role of Daily Money Management Services*, 31 Gerontologist 150 (1991) ("no significant difference in rates of conservatorship between those who were offered daily money management service and those who were not"; conservatorship appointment associated with severity of psychiatric symptoms and cognitive impairment regardless of daily money management).]

Chapter 6

Alternatives to Public Guardianship

Winsor C. Schmidt, Jr.
Kent S. Miller
William G. Bell
B. Elaine New

> *Abstract.* Public guardians are officials appointed by state or local government agencies and courts to serve "wards" who do not have family or friends to serve as guardians. This chapter reports on the need for guardians among the elderly and certain handicapped populations, the extent of current guardianship, and public guardianship alternatives in a state (Florida) that may represent America's demographic future. There seems to be a dilemma created by inadequate guardianship services for indigents on the one hand, and, on the other, the new phenomenon of public guardianship that does more harm than good if not inadequately stuffed and funded.

Public guardianship is the process and responsibility of surrogate, encompassing the individual or entity known as the "public guardian." The public guardian is commonly described as the official appointed by a state or local government agency or court to serve a legal incompetent, called a ward, who does not have willing and responsible family members or friends to serve as guardian. Public guardianship is the process by which a public official becomes "lawfully invested with the power and charged with the duty, of taking care of the person and managing the property and rights of [a] person, who, for some peculiarity of status or defect of age, understanding or self-control, is considered incapable of administering his own affairs."[1]

Historically, the office of public guardian was created with the presumption that a public official would act with a higher degree of care in managing the affairs of an incompetent than would a private guardian. This presumption has been challenged. A public guardian in Los Angeles has been sued for inappropriately institutionalizing elderly wards in two

---

1. Black's Law Dictionary 834 (1968).

cases.[2] A former public guardian in Chicago was accused of systematically looting estates, allowing experimental medical procedures on mental patients, and noting visits to wards who in fact had been dead at the time of those visits.[3]

Partly because of an "old age" criterion, older persons are principal subjects of public guardianship. This chapter will report on alternatives to public guardianship for the elderly in Florida. With its high proportion (17.6 percent in 1977) of residents older than sixty-five, Florida may represent the demographic future for other states as the population ages and may be archetype for the Sun Belt.

Florida did not provide for public guardianship in 1982, although members of the 1980-81 legislative sessions considered several different proposals. Whether Florida should have public guardianship is problematic. One national study concludes that there seems now to be a need for public guardianship, but only if it is done properly.[4] Public guardianship must be adequately staffed and funded, and the guardianship statute must be amended to include functional rather than categorical (e.g., senility, old age) eligibility criteria and enhanced due process.[5] If public guardianship is not carried out properly, it can do more harm than good to older persons and to the other constituencies of pubic guardianship: juveniles, developmentally disabled, mentally ill, alcoholics, addicts, and the physically incapacitated.

The Need for Guardians

Any assessment of the need for guardians is necessarily an elusive and arbitrary endeavor. One study of six states (Delaware, Minnesota, North Carolina, Ohio, Washington, and Wisconsin) indicates that petitions for guardianship are initiated annually for less than one-tenth of one percent of the population.[6] However, petitions for guardianship are a poor index of need. In Florida, for example, petitions for guardianship are sometimes not initiated for an alleged incompetent when someone is not specif-

---

2. McNairy v. Altmann, No. 77-3112 (C. D. Cal., filed Aug. 19, 1977); Snyder v. Altmann, No. 77-4520 (C. D. Cal., filed Dec. 2, 1977).

3. P. Murphy, First Interim Report of the Acting Public Guardian of Cook County, Chicago: Public Guardian of Cook County, pp. 1, 5 (1979). See W. Schmidt, K. Miller, W. Bell & E. New, Public Guardianship and the Elderly, pp. 86-88 (1981) (hereinafter Public Guardianship).

4. Public Guardianship, *supra* note 3.

5. *Id.* at 179-203.

6. M. Axilbund, Exercising Judgment for the Disabled: Report of an Inquiry into Limited Guardianship, Public Guardianship, and Adult Protective Services in Six States (Executive Summary), p. 21 (1979).

ically identified as a prospective guardian. The need for guardianship may increase with the availability of guardian services and decrease with the availability of protective and social services. Otherwise, it may vary with willingness to intrude, the desire to maintain community placement, and faith in everyone's ability to manage their own affairs.

One clear need for guardians in Florida is found in public mental institutions. Florida State Hospital in Chattahoochee has at least 600 patients who have been adjudicated legally incompetent but who have no guardian. Florida's three other mental institutions have had thirty percent of their populations in the same predicament. Patients without guardians have been discharged without restoration of legal competency. Florida's institutions for the mentally retarded may exhibit a similar need. An April 1977 statewide survey of social workers in the Aging and Adult Service Program Office identified 987 legally incompetent clients who did not have a guardian. Most of these people had been involuntarily committed. The extent of overlap with the incompetents in the state hospitals is unknown.

The need for guardians in these situations is clear because of the legal and practical effects of an adjudication of incompetence. Incompetence can restrict or remove the right to make contracts; sell, purchase, mortgage, or lease property; make gifts; travel, or decide where to live; vote, or hold elected office; initiate or defend against suits; make a will, or revoke one; engage in certain professions; lend or borrow money; appoint agents; divorce, or marry; refuse medical treatment; keep and care for children; serve on a jury; be a witness to any legal document; drive a car; pay or collect debts; or manage or run a business.[7]

The absence of a guardian for a legal incompetent means that not even a surrogate exercises or watches over an incompetent's rights. One glaring example is the legally incompetent patients without guardians in Florida mental institutions. These people are administratively classified as "voluntary" in an arbitrary manner and they cannot exercise the rights of voluntary patients in consenting to treatment, planning for discharge, and the like. A legally incompetent person without a guardian is a non-person.

The statewide Aging and Adult Services survey also identified 1,781 clients who, in the opinion of the social workers, needed to be adjudicated incompetent and appointed a guardian. More than 1,700 of these clients were age sixty or older. This needs assessment, of course, is a subjective one.

Further support for the subjective, elusive, and arbitrary nature of the need for guardians comes from local sources. The Broward County Social

---

7. R. Brown, The Rights of Older Persons, p. 286 (1979).

Services Division in 1978 sent questionnaires to thirty individuals from legal, mental health, and social service agencies.[8] Twenty of twenty-one respondents felt there was a significant need for a guardianship program. The extent of the need was identified as ranging from two to three persons per month to thousands.

In Tampa, a 1977 survey of medical opinions identified 700 mental people as needing to be adjudicated incompetent and a guardian appointed.[9] Carol Stahl, a representative of the Hillsborough County (Tampa) Mental Health Association, estimated that 600 people needed guardianships. Other respondents expressed the extent of need in terms of a percentage of their caseload. For example, "ten to fifteen percent of protective services cases require guardianship" and "one percent of the 13,000 elderly people below the poverty level in Duval County need guardianship," said David Atkins of the Duval County Area Agency on Aging. These estimates should be considered cautiously, but there is no doubt that those close to the situation feel there is an unmet need for guardians.

The Extent of Current Guardianship

The only available uniform statewide guardianship data are from the Florida State Courts Administrator.[10] The data are limited, beginning in 1977, to the number of guardianships opened and the number closed in Florida's sixty-seven counties. In 1977, for example, a total of 4,724 guardianships were opened and 3,340 closed. Assuming these data represent other years, the annual net gain is approximately 1,400 to 1,500 guardianships.

An unknown number of existing guardianships include wards who could in other states be clients of the public guardian. These wards do not have sufficient incomes or estates to compensate a guardian or willing and responsible family members or friends to serve as guardian.

A common practice in Florida is for probate judges to appoint attorneys as guardians under such circumstances. One Palm Beach County law firm has thirty-seven wards, ten of whom are on Medicaid. One attorney is guardian of person and property for sixty-seven wards himself. Appointing attorneys as guardians is also a practice in Lake, Pinellas, and Hillsborough counties.

---

8. A. Mahan, Broward County Guardianship Project, Fort Lauderdale: Broward County Social Services Division, p. 24 (1978).

9. Ad Hoc Committee on Guardianship, Position Paper on Guardianship, Tampa: Mental Health Association of Hillsborough County, Inc. p. 2 (1978).

10. Public Guardianship, *supra* note 3, at 148.

Few attorneys seem to assume this responsibility by choice. The more likely procedure is the one described in Broward County where a judge "picked the next one to walk through the door." Many practicing attorneys would find declining such a request difficult.

An attorney appointed under these circumstances is likely to feel put upon, to have limited knowledge about service possibilities, and to be poorly motivated in the face of a time-consuming and unremunerative situation. One Aging and Adult Services worker expressed concern about the motivation of private attorneys serving without compensation and indicated reluctance to use them.

Other Alternatives

In addition to appointing private attorneys as guardians for indigent and friendless wards, a range of other alternatives to public guardianship exists.

Benign Neglect

An unwritten policy of benign neglect results in certain individuals being victimized, failing to receive needed medical and related care, being institutionalized, and dying. Other characterizations of benign neglect are possible, but the predominant perspective is negative.

Informal Guardianship

There are frequent instances in which a neighbor, friend, relative, or nursing home assumes a surrogate function without legal guardianship. Such individuals or entities might become the representative payee of a Social Security check or might hold the power of attorney. Others operate even less formally in obtaining a check signature, cashing a check, and maintaining control of money. Rural areas particularly can have well-developed, informal surrogate mechanisms through neighbors and friends.

Mental Hospitalization

When a guardian is not available, commitment to a public mental hospital may occur. The absence of a guardian also inhibits discharge from a hospital.

Civil commitment to a mental hospital is considered to be the poor man's guardianship. Misuse of civil commitment occurs when prospective wards resist medical evaluation of their competence; emergency involuntary commitment provisions are used to secure guardianship evaluations.

Banks and Trust Companies

Banks and trust companies will assume guardianships of property when a sizable estate is involved. Apparently, though, troublesome reporting requirements and other regulations make these agencies reluctant to assume guardianships when enough money is not involved. The definition of enough varies from one community to another: some Pinellas County banks will handle mid-size estates, but some Hillsborough County banks will not.

A related alternative in other states involves the pooling of estates to make their management more attractive.

Nonprofit Corporations

Florida law allows nonprofit corporations to be appointed as guardian. Several nonprofit organizations act with the specific avowed intent to serve as alternatives to public guardianship. The strengths of nonprofit corporations serving as guardian are continuity (eliminates the problems of guardian relocation, unavailability, or death), probable knowledge of and access to more services, no profit motive, and altruism with respect to the ward. The principal weakness is the potential for impersonality, compared to the love of selfless family or friends in a one-to-one personal guardianship.

Cathedral Foundation, Jacksonville. Affiliated with the Episcopal Church, the Cathedral Foundation provides residential housing and medical care to elderly clients. A program of protective services[11] includes a small guardianship project partially supported through a Title III grant under the Older Americans Act.

This seems to be one of Florida's best guardianship projects. Restricted to a select few, guardianship is a last resort. The range of services and individual, personal attention is considerable, and the wishes of the ward, notwithstanding legal incompetence, seem to be honored to a very high

---

11. See generally Horstman, *Protective Services for the Elderly: The Limits of Parens Patriae*, 40 Mo. L. Rev. 215 (1975).

degree. The Cathedral Foundation maintains that it can respond to such immediate needs as groceries or a light bill that a government agency would take at least thirty days to process. Another cited advantage is the willingness to work themselves out of a job, an inclination less likely in the public sector.

Two aspects of the Cathedral Foundation guardianship project could be improved. Instead of being a passive receptor of appointment as guardian by the court, the Foundation becomes active in the initiation of guardianship. Were the Foundation not so resistant to inappropriate guardianship, this conflict of interest could lead to self-aggrandizement. Also, it seems incongruous for an enterprise as sophisticated as this one to include a contractual provision with serviced clients limiting the opportunity to sue. Notwithstanding these deficiencies, Cathedral Foundation is a highly commendable effort.

Jewish Children and Family Services, Miami Beach. This agency was primarily responsible for changing the Florida law in 1971 to permit nonprofit corporations to serve as guardian. Protective services are provided with the intent of searching for alternatives to guardianship. Limited resources dictate that all of their wards are maintained in nursing or residential homes. Most clients, all of whom are Jewish, have some resources, estimated at approximately $10,000 each. A curious dynamic provides for those who resist services to be adjudicated incompetent and appointed a guardian, while volunteers for services are declared to have no need for guardianship.

The very small number of clients (seven caseload wards, eighteen since 1973) may reflect a highly desirable situation where the agency is succeeding in finding alternatives to guardianship. The agency is also less concerned with victimization as a justification for guardianship than with the basis of care for self. On the other hand, there are continuing references to a large number of individuals in Miami Beach needing guardianship services.

Broward County Gerontology Program. This program was developed and administered by the county social service division and was specifically intended as an alternative to public guardianship. It provides crisis intervention services, makes arrangements for evaluation and treatment services, and petitions for guardianship. One unique feature is its "volunteer guardian bank", composed of retired professionals. Each volunteer guardian has from one to three wards, almost all of whom are in retirement, boarding, or nursing homes. Using these volunteers is said to provide the personal contact that is likely to be missing in public agencies. Using volunteers has the secondary benefit of employing the talents of retired persons. The program staff retains power of attorney to act on behalf of a volunteer guardian if necessary.

In 1979 there were fifty wards, with seventy to ninety cases at some stage in the process during any one month. This is one of Florida's largest guardianship programs.

Other nonprofit corporations with guardianship programs include the Catholic Service Bureau in West Palm Beach, the Guardian Association in Pinellas County, Leon-Wakulla Guardianship Services in Tallahassee, and a developing organization in Chattahoochee. The first is small and similar to the Jacksonville and Miami Beach efforts. The Pinellas Guardian Association features educational programs, a guardian handbook, and monthly meetings. The Tallahassee organization seemed to exist primarily on paper, had no liability insurance, and was virtually indistinguishable from the local government social service agency. The Chattahoochee group was the product of Florida State Hospital's Model Legal Services Program, was seeking liability insurance, intends to rely upon community volunteers, and has developed a good guardian manual. However, the group's ability to serve adequately the hospital's 600 or more legally incompetent voluntary patients, or those requiring a guardian advocate, was doubtful. Under Florida law, a guardian advocate must be appointed for any involuntary mental patient who has been determined as incompetent to consent to treatment.

Summary Observations and Conclusions

Public guardianship did not exist in Florida in 1982. It seemed that the existing alternatives to public guardianship sufficed to meet the need for guardianship services for the indigent. Some of the alternative programs appeared to be doing a competent job, although the majority dealt with a very limited number of wards and were not likely to expand their caseload significantly.

Available information about the effectiveness of the various alternatives to public guardianship has been presented. There is clearly a need for more than a descriptive level study of both alternative programs to public guardianship and public guardian programs. The two approaches have received only preliminary assessment.[12] It is clear, however, that

---

12. Public Guardianship, *supra* note 3; M. Axilbund, *supra* note 6. [*See also* L. Lisi, A. Burns, P. Hommel, K. Baird, C. Lindgren, E. Roe & S. Brewster, National Study of Guardianship System and Feasibility of Implementing Expert Systems, Ann Arbor, MI: Center for Social Gerontology (1992) (study of limited guardianship in 10 states: percentages of limited guardianships in California, Indiana, Kansas and Michigan is 3% or less; 54% of guardianships in Minnesota are limited; five states granted limited conserva-

public guardianship seems qualitatively deficient and that alternatives to public guardianship seem quantitatively deficient.

There is reason for concern about protecting the rights of the elderly in the guardianship process in Florida. Some of these concerns are clearcut: the infringement on the autonomy of individuals, the significance and implications of establishing a guardianship, and the need for due process. It is less clear that such principles are implemented on a day-to day basis. The following tendencies are noted:

1. Proceedings seemed uniformly non-adversarial and when disagreement occurs it relates primarily to which family member will be appointed as guardian.
2. Examining committees almost always recommended guardianship rather than find competence.
3. Once a petition for guardianship was filed, it was almost always granted.
4. Hearings were frequently waived by attorneys, and potential wards were seldom present during the proceeding.
5. Partial or limited guardianships were not employed.
6. Guardianships were rarely, if ever, removed and legal competence restored.
7. The court review process was extremely weak, and if it occurred at all, it usually consisted of checking for computational errors in financial accounts.
8. The principle of utilizing the least restrictive alternative placement was frequently violated.

Some would argue that these concerns are inappropriate because guardianship is a last resort, with the screening process causing any nondifferentiation. However, this argument is not compatible with some experience of guardianship petition rejection in other jurisdictions. In the analogous area of civil commitment, representation of defendants by vigorous and sophisticated attorneys substantially reduces the commitment of individuals about whom there otherwise exists a consensus.[13] At the same

---

torship 7% or less; none of the 10 had conservatorship limitations in more than 15% of conservatorships, except Minnesota which placed limitations in 33% of conservatorships); Keith & Wacker, Guardianship Reform: Does Revised Legislation Make a Difference in Outcomes for Proposed Wards?, 4 J. Aging & Soc. Pol'y 139 (No. 3/4, 1992) (least restrictive alternatives seldom employed in Iowa and Missouri).]

13. *See* A. Brooks, Law, Psychiatry and the Mental Health Systems: 1980 Supplement, pp. 115-118 (1980); Wenger & Fletcher, *The Effect of Legal Counsel on Admissions to a State Mental Hospital: A Confrontation of Professions*, 10 J. Health & Soc. Behav. 66 (1969).

time, some caseworkers in Florida's guardianship process, ready to intervene inappropriately in the lives of their client, seem to feel that anything they do will be in the best interest of their clients and that guardianship is a very desirable outcome.

The public sector does not necessarily provide a panacea in the area of public guardianship. In addition to the difficulties with public guardianship in Chicago and Los Angeles mentioned earlier, one project reports that an experimental group receiving state of the art protective services had higher death and institutionalization rates than did a control group receiving referral agency services or no services.[14] A study of mental patients released from Alabama mental institutions by court order concluded that "family members adjusted expectations and accepted the patient home" when the state did not provide the alternative of a mental hospital.[15] But the alternative guardianship services for the elderly in Florida seem not to be meeting the need satisfactorily.

---

14. Blenkner, Bloom & Nielsen, *A Research and Demonstration Project of Protective Services*, 52 Soc. Casework 483 (1971).

15. Leaf, *Patients Released After "Wyatt": Where Did They Go?*, 28 Hosp. & Community Psychiatry 366 (1977).

Part IV

The Functioning of Guardianship Court: What Happens to People in the Court of Last Resort?

Chapter 7

Guardianship of the Elderly in Tallahassee, Florida

Roger Peters
Winsor C. Schmidt, Jr.
Kent S. Miller

> *Abstract.* Incompetency and guardianship proceedings in Leon County, Florida were examined by observing court hearings and evaluating probate court records for 1977–1982. All incompetency petitions were affirmed by the court, often without evidence describing alleged disabilities. Evidence from Leon County indicates a clear mandate for administrative changes providing 1) more comprehensive assessment of client disabilities and 2) more rigorous financial accounting and management of guardianships. The evidence also supports recommendations in the available literature for statutory change, judicial remedy, and education and training.

Changes in mental disability law have significantly affected methods of processing forensic and civilly committed patients but have largely bypassed a smaller and less vocal group of mentally disabled individuals who are subject to guardianship procedures. One study of six states (Delaware, Minnesota, North Carolina, Ohio, Washington, and Wisconsin) found only 17,000 guardianship petitions filed in one year for a total population of 29,000,000 people.[1] A similar filing rate of 4,729 new guardianships for a population of 8,432,927 was reported for Florida in 1977.[2]

Guardianship is a legal phenomenon consisting of the authority of a guardian and the relation between guardian and ward. A guardian manages the person and/or property of another, the "ward," who is adjudicated incompetent and considered incapable of self-administration. Most

---

1. M. Axilbund, Exercising Judgment for the Disabled: Report of an Inquiry into Limited Guardianship, Public Guardianship, and Adult Protective Services in Six States (Executive Summary) (1979).
2. Schmidt, *Guardianship of the Elderly in Florida: Social Bankruptcy and the Need for Reform*, 55 Fla. B. J. 189 (1981).

states employ a bifurcated process in establishing guardianships. The initial stage involves an incompetency hearing to examine and discuss threshold criteria of "inability to do business, manage property, or conduct personal affairs" by reason of conditions "affecting mental capacity, such as mental illness, alcoholism, addiction, or old age."[3] Incompetency hearings serve as a forum for the court to consider the extent of physical and mental incapacities of the ward and to assess the available human resources in the community to oversee these incapacities.

The second stage of the process involves a guardianship hearing to assign decision-maker responsibilities to either a private or public guardian. The guardian is usually a family member or friend, but in the absence of willing and responsible family members or friends to serve as private guardians or of resources to acquire professional guardian services from private attorneys or banks, a public official can be appointed as public guardian.[4] Public guardians are affiliated with the court in some states and with social service agencies in others. In several states, such as Arizona, public guardians are independent of other judicial or service agencies.[5]

Procedural and Substantive Issues

Guardianship leads to a deprivation of civil rights and has been referred to as a "highly restrictive method of providing supervision and assistance" to the mentally disabled by the President's Commission on Mental Health.[6] Because of the similarities and necessary overlap between guardianship and involuntary commitment proceedings, the Commission recommended that research in the area of guardianship be given a "high priority." Concern is growing among those involved in law and social gerontology about the expanded use of guardianship.[7] Proponents of guardianship

---

3. J. Regan & G. Springer, Protective Services for the Elderly, p. 36 (1977) (a working paper prepared for the U.S. Senate Special Committee on Aging).

4. W. Schmidt, K. Miller, W. Bell & E. New, Public Guardianship and the Elderly (1981) (hereinafter Public Guardianship).

5. J. Regan & G. Springer, *supra* note 3.

6. Report of the Task Panel on Legal and Ethical Issues in President's Commission on Mental Health (vol. 4), p. 43 (1978).

7. *See, e.g.,* Mitchell, *The Objects of Our Wisdom and Our Coercion: Involuntary Guardianship for Incompetents,* 52 S. Cal. L. Rev. 1405 (1974); Regan, *Adult Protective Services: An Appraisal and a Prospectus* in National Law and Social Work Seminar: Proceedings and Prospects, Portland: Univ. of Southern Maine, pp. 12–19 (1982) (hereinafter Appraisal); Regan, *Protecting the Elderly: The New Paternalism,* 32 Hastings L. J. 1111 (1981) (hereinafter Protecting); Sherman, *Guardianship: Time for Reassessment,* 49 Fordham L. Rev. 350 (1980).

reform contend that several procedural and substantive issues demand attention and militate against further use of guardianship statutes.[8]

Incompetency and guardianship hearings do not always reflect the need to preserve maximum liberties of the potential ward. Notifications of incompetency and guardianship hearings often do not describe their legal implications,[9] and legal counsel for the alleged incompetent is frequently absent in guardianship proceedings.[10] Many states do not provide counsel to indigents compelled to appear at incompetency or guardianship hearings or instead provide guardians ad litem, whose responsibilities are statutorily vague.[11] It is unclear, for example, what the guardian ad litem's role might be in initiating appeals of incompetency or guardianship hearings, if this is desired by the ward, or refusing unwanted treatment on behalf of the ward.

Once established, guardianships are rarely monitored by the court. Only ten states sanction regular court reviews of legal guardianships.[12] Even when required by law, reviews often provide little more than a financial accounting of the ward's estate and offer little evidence about changes in the ward's intellectual or physical status that might be of interest to the court in reevaluating the need for guardianship. Further, no statutory incentives are provided for the guardian to initiate restoration of competency on behalf of the ward.

Guardianship represents both a transfer of decisionmaking power from one individual to another and a significant sacrifice to the party yielding this power. Yet, in many cases, a ward may retain some degree of intellectual competence, especially in the care of immediate property or decisions about personal needs. Most states, however, do not recognize a state of partial incompetence.[13] As a result, guardianship proceedings divest the ward of all major decisionmaking power, which can facilitate physical and psychological deterioration.[14] The intrusiveness and rigidity of plenary guardianship provisions, employed by about two-thirds of the states, have been heavily criticized. It has been demonstrated that the loss of decision

---

8. *See, e.g.*, Appraisal, *supra* note 7; Protecting, *supra* note 7; Schmidt, *supra* note 2.

9. B. Sales, Guardianship and Conservatorship: Statutory Survey and Model Statute (1979).

10. G. Alexander & T. Lewin, The Aged and the Need for Surrogate Management (1972); Horstman, *Protective Services for the Elderly: The Limits of Parens Patriae*, 40 Mo. L. Rev. 215 (1975).

11. Sherman, *supra* note 7; Solender, *The Guardian ad Litem: A Valuable Representative or an Illusory Safeguard?*, 7 Texas Tech. L. Rev. 619 (1976).

12. Sales, *supra* note 9.

13. M. Axilbund, *supra* note 1.

14. Schmidt, *supra* note 2.

making power actually leads to individual dysfunction in both social and domestic settings.[15] Thus, plenary guardianship can become a self fulfilling prophecy of sorts—the finding and judicial ratification of incompetence discourage individual creativity and intellectual pursuits, leading to a progressive dependence on appointed guardians, loss of self-esteem, and loss of motivation to maintain self-help and management skills. Further, the serious consequences of guardianship actually deter caretakers from seeking protective services for individuals who require only moderate supervision and who are at least partially competent to care for themselves.[16] In order to remedy such shortcomings, some states have begun to adopt limited guardianship statutes.[17]

Guardianship Research

Although studies have identified the need for substantive and procedural reform of guardianship statutes, few have systematically examined the impact of statutory deficiencies on the guardianship process. Alexander and Lewin[18] conducted an archival search of incompetency and guardianship records in New York in order to investigate procedures for determining incompetency and administration of guardianships established by the court. They discovered that findings of incompetency were based on inadequate information, often in the form of conclusory psychiatric or medical conjecture. None of the incompetency records attempted to specify the functional nature of the person's incapacity. The incompetency hearing was found to be a "rubber stamp approval" of the incompetency petition, previously agreed to by both the petitioner and the guardian. Rarely did the guardian ad litem or counsel raise any objections to the incompetency finding.

Alexander and Lewin also found that guardianships were poorly monitored. In 82% of the cases sampled, financial records or annual accountings were incomplete. Although authorized by law, the court failed to impose sanctions on delinquent guardians. Finally, the study concluded that guardians were not encouraged to develop the management skills of their wards. As a result, except for those supervised within veteran's hospitals, few wards were restored to competency.

---

15. Horstman, *Protective Services for the Elderly: The Limits of Parens Patriae*, 40 Mo. L. Rev. 215 (1975).
16. Sherman, *supra* note 7.
17. M. Axilbund, *supra* note 1.
18. G. Alexander & T. Lewin, *supra* note 10.

Field research by Schmidt and colleagues[19] examined a sample of incompetency and guardianship hearings in six states, substantiating claims made by Alexander and Lewin that these hearings were procedurally inadequate. Applications for guardianship were rarely denied, and hearings were brief, nonadversarial, and subject to several due process deficiencies. Restorations to competency were rare, as were voluntary guardianships and meaningful reviews of guardianships by the court. Schmidt and colleagues found that guardianship proceedings were also substantively deficient. Among the states surveyed, the authors found that partial or limited guardianships were rarely established, although this option was available to the courts.

Thus, recent studies of guardianship law and proceedings help to elaborate potential violations of due process rights and abuses of the supervisory privileges in such caretaking relationships. Few studies, however, attempt to analyze incompetency and guardianship proceedings at the microcosmic, or client, level. Review of research in the area of guardianship suggests that several areas in particular warrant further investigation.

(1) Identification of client population served. Does guardianship serve primarily an elderly population? What is the financial status of wards adjudicated incompetent and of appointed guardians? Are guardianships established only for wealthy clients? To what degree are wards mentally and physically incapacitated? How often do relatives assume responsibility for guardianships?

(2) Legal bases for incompetency determinations. Is psychiatric testimony contested in determining incompetency? Does an independent examination by medical personnel assist the court in determining the need for guardianship and the type of guardianship to be established? Is the original petition to determine incompetency screened by the court for statutory deficiencies? On what basis does the court make its final decision regarding competency?

(3) Substantive issues. Does the court consider use of limited guardianships when a ward is only partially incapacitated? How often are reviews of guardianships submitted or solicited by the court? Are penalties assessed against guardians who are negligent in submitting annual accountings to the court? Are affirmative treatment goals established?

---

19. Public Guardianship, *supra* note 4.

(4) Procedural issues. Is the potential ward and his or her family notified in advance of an impending hearing to determine incompetency or to select a guardian? What is the length of time between the petition to determine competency, the incompetency hearing, and the guardianship hearing? Does the court allow more time to select guardians in cases involving large estates? Do a variety of doctors participate in examining committees? Are the bonds required of newly appointed guardians reasonable? Are bonds assessed in a uniform and consistent manner? Is counsel provided for indigent alleged incompetents?

The present study attempts to address these issues by analyzing both the content and process of incompetency and guardianship hearings. The content of eight hearings was sampled both through direct observation by the authors of all the hearings for several months and by an archival search of court records. The study was undertaken by examining all records of incompetency and guardianship hearings referred to the District 2B Circuit Court, Probate Division, in Tallahassee, Florida, from January 1977 to May 1982. Records contained all correspondence initiated or processed by the court, including petitions, notification, orders, and reports, as well as all documents adjudicating incompetency and appointing guardians. The District 2B Probate Court is responsible for reviewing all petitions for incompetency and guardianship in Leon County, Florida.

Guardianship Law in Florida

The Florida guardianship statute requires that a ward be adjudicated incompetent before a guardian may be appointed. A finding of incompetency must be predicated on "minority, mental illness, mental retardation, senility, excessive use of drugs or alcohol, or other physical or mental incapacity."[20] The incapacity should be such that the person "is incapable of caring for himself or managing his property or is likely to dissipate or lose his property or inflict harm on himself or others."[21] The petition to determine incompetency may be filed by either the immediate family of the ward, any three citizens of the state, or the medical director of a stale correctional institution on behalf of an inmate. After a petition has been filed, the court is obligated to establish a hearing date and to send written notice of the hearing to the alleged incompetent and one or more members of his or her family. No provision is made concerning maximum elapsed time allowed between written notice and incompetency hearings.

---

20. Fla. Stat. section 744.102(5) (1983).
21. Fla. Stat. section 744.331(1) (1983).

Incompetency hearings in Florida are to be conducted in an "informal" manner. If the alleged incompetent cannot afford legal counsel, an attorney is appointed for him or her. No provision is made for juries to hear either incompetency or guardianship cases. An examining committee, consisting of two physicians "who shall not be associated with each other in the practice of medicine" and one other Florida citizen, is used to determine the physical and mental condition of the individual.[22] (Thirty-two other states have some statutory provision for an examination, usually by at least one physician.)[23] A committee finding of competency invalidates the original petition; an incompetency finding must be subsequently verified by the probate court in a hearing.

Upon a finding of incompetency, an individual must be assigned a guardian of the person. In Florida, individual or nonprofit corporations may be appointed as guardians and are responsible for providing humane care and treatment for the ward. Each ward must be provided an annual physical examination by a licensed physician. In addition, annual reports must be submitted to the court detailing the guardian's activity, the personal status of the ward, and the financial status of the ward's estate. The court is allowed a wide degree of discretion in appointing guardians, choosing from among residents of Florida, non-residents, trust companies/banks, or nonprofit corporations.

One aspect of Florida law providing some flexibility to the court is the provision for "limited" guardianship.[24] By this mechanism, a limited guardian of the property may be appointed "[w]hen it appears to the satisfaction of the court that an incompetent is over the age of 18 years and wholly or substantially self-supporting by means of compensation from employment." A limited guardian of property is, for example, empowered to handle financial transactions, including property other than wages or other monetary compensation.

Demographic Findings

Forty-two pairs of incompetency/guardianship cases from 1977–1982 were evaluated. Three cases involving guardianships for minors were not included in the study. Table 1 describes several demographic, diagnostic, and financial characteristics of individuals referred for incompetency/guardianship hearings. The average age of individuals referred for incompetency and guardianship hearings was seventy-three years. Almost

---

22. Fla. Stat. section 744.331(5)(a) (1983).
23. B. Sales, *supra* note 9.
24. Fla. Stat. section 744.303 (1983).

Table 1. Characteristics of Incompetency/Guardianship Referrals in Leon County, Florida

Characteristic	n	%
Age		
90 and above	2	5
80–89	15	36
70–79	14	33
60–69	6	14
Less than 60	5	12
(Range: 18–96, m 73)		
Gender		
Female	29	69
Male	13	31
Residence at time of hearing		
Private home	28	67
Nursing home or home for aged	9	21
Hospital	4	10
Unknown	1	2
Size of estate		
Greater than $100,000	9	21
$50–$100,000	11	26
$25–$50,000	5	12
Less than $25,000	13	31
Unknown	4	10

Characteristic Diagnosis	n (At time of petition)	% (At time of petition)	n (Of examining committee)	% (Of examining committee)
Age related[a]	16	38	30	71
Reference to simple "medical" or "physical" incapacity	16	38	0	0
Medical disorders[b]	6	14	10	24
Retardation	0	0	2	5
Unknown	4	10	0	0

a. Organic brain syndrome, senility, Alzheimer's disease.
b. Stroke, brain damage, epilepsy.

75% were seventy years of age or older, and only 12% were younger than sixty. Fully two-thirds of the wards were females. The preponderance of wards lived in private homes, but 31% resided in rest homes or hospitals at the time of the petition. Relatives were available and willing to serve as guardians in 70% of the cases surveyed.

Incompetency Hearings

The court relied on a large group of physicians from the community to serve on examining committees. In forty-two incompetency hearings, forty-five different physicians were employed by the court, including eight psychiatrists. Psychiatrists were appointed in 60% of cases in which doctors were asked to serve on more than one examining committee. No physician appeared on more than seven examining committees (mean = 1.7 appearances per physician and 3.8 appearances per psychiatrist on examining committees in our sample).

This experience in Leon County should be contrasted with the results of a grand jury investigation in Dade County (Miami), Florida.[25] The grand jury's study of 200 randomly selected files chosen from guardianship cases opened between 1979 and 1981 revealed that the same two physicians were appointed to the examining committee in every case, generating fees of $75 apiece for each examination at a rate of forty to fifty examinations per month over several years. The grand jury cited a need to broaden the composition of the examining committee and suggested that the appointment of physicians should not necessarily be limited to psychiatrists.

All petitions requesting an incompetency hearing in Leon County were heard by the court. In 38% of cases, no specific functional or descriptive analysis was provided explaining the rationale for such a petition. The alleged incompetent was simply described in conclusory fashion as having "mental or physical incapacities"—terminology from the Florida statute. Thus, in a large portion of the cases, the court did not require behavioral evidence of incompetency in the petition but deferred to the summary statements of the examining committee in order to establish the threshold question of mental/physical disabilities.

In the vast majority of cases the court issued notification of an impending hearing to the alleged incompetent and family members within one day of the petition. In 29% of cases surveyed, the court scheduled incompetency hearings within a week of petitions. In these cases it appears that alleged incompetents, family members, legal counsel, or other inter-

---

25. Dade County Grand Jury, Final Report of the Grand Jury, Miami: Office of the State Attorney (1982).

ested parties were allowed minimal opportunity to marshal arguments challenging the basis for petitions. There was no indication that the petitions concerned emergency situations such as consent to surgery.

In only 57% of cases did probate court records contain reference to attorneys appointed on behalf of alleged incompetents. In half of the remaining cases (21% overall), petitioner's attorneys were named in court records without reference to attorneys for the alleged incompetent. It is unclear whether these omissions represent clerical oversight or failure of the court to appoint legal counsel for alleged incompetents. Florida Statutes section 744.331 (4) provides that the opportunity to be represented by counsel must be accorded and mandates the appointment of an attorney if the alleged incompetent cannot afford one. The Florida Supreme Court has ruled that "a trial judge must specifically find whether or not the alleged incompetent is represented by counsel in any hearing where incompetency is to be determined, and whether or not counsel should be afforded. Failure to make such a finding constitutes reversible error."[26]

Of forty-two hearings, all resulted in a finding of incompetency. Findings appeared to be heavily influenced by psychiatric diagnoses. Judges did not depart significantly from these diagnoses or from the psychiatric determinations of incompetency rendered by the examining committee. Judges concurred with all forty-two of the incompetency decisions and did not appear to solicit additional behavioral or psychiatric evidence regarding functional incompetence of the potential ward. In most cases, the diagnosis provided by the examining committee was reiterated verbatim by the court in adjudicating incompetency.

The composition of diagnoses provided by the examining committee differed significantly from those provided by the petitioner. Instead of relying on statutory criteria for a determination of incompetency, examining committees defined incompetency using medical and psychiatric terminology. About 71% of these diagnoses were based on findings of age-related disorders (senility, organic brain syndrome, Alzheimer's disease), compared to only 38% of age-related disorders specified in incompetency petitions. Examining committees also tended to designate other medical disorders (stroke, epilepsy, brain damage) more frequently in determining incompetency. Reliance on more formal diagnostic categories may be explained at least in part by the medical/psychiatric background of members of the court-appointed examining committee. Fully 98% of alleged incompetents were characterized by chronic (vs. acute) disorders, according to the examining committee. Eighteen percent were allegedly in need of physical restraints as a result of their incapacitating disorders.

---

26. *In re* Guardianship of Paunack, 355 So.2d 1195 (Fla. 1978).

Despite the use of more technical and seemingly more precise language, diagnoses rendered by the examining committee did not significantly improve upon those set forth in incompetency petitions. In only 15% of incompetency cases did the diagnosis refer to the etiology, onset, or history of the incapacitating disorder (e.g., brain damage secondary to head injury). Perhaps more importantly, examining committee diagnoses failed to describe the nature or extent of physical incapacity in 93% of cases. Mental incapacities were not behaviorally described in 88% of cases. Thus, in about 90% of cases reviewed, examining committee reports did not provide specific behavioral information for the court that is statutorily required[27] pursuant to an adjudication of incompetency.

Guardianship Proceedings

As indicated by Alexander and Lewin,[28] the size of estates identified for guardianship is often substantial. Of the guardianship files examined, nine (21%) involved estates valued greater than $100,000, and twenty (47%) involved estates above $50,000. The mean size of estates was about $75,000. Florida law allows the judiciary discretion to require appointed guardians to place a bond deposit with the court before assuming financial responsibility for an estate. In practice, bond deposits were mandated in almost 85% of cases reviewed. The average bond levied was $10,000 and constituted an average of 13% of the estate value. Although most bond deposits waived by the court were in cases of estates less than $25,000, there were several notable exceptions. One guardian assuming an estate worth $250,000 was charged no deposit. The two judges presiding over guardianship hearings levied bond deposits inconsistently. One judge handled two-thirds of all cases but charged bond deposits averaging only 10% of the estate value. A second judge, presiding over one third of the cases, charged bond deposits averaging 25% of the estate value (difference between the judges was significant at the .005 level, using chi-square analysis).

Almost all guardianships established were provided for both person and property. In only one case was a limited guardianship option utilized to establish guardianship of property. In this case, the ward was living with a close relative (not the guardian of property), who supervised personal needs but was apparently unwilling to oversee financial management of the estate. In many cases, the examining committee's incompetency decision was predicated on a finding of either mental or physical

---

27. Fla. Stat. section 744.331(1) (1983).
28. G. Alexander & T. Lewin, *supra* note 10.

incompetency. In relatively few cases were both physical and mental incompetency cited by the committee. It appears likely, then, that, at least in several cases, the ward would be capable of circumscribed responsibilities, such as looking after his or her self-care needs.

One 82-year-old woman, for example, was adjudicated incompetent because she could "not manage business relationships" and was "forgetful." The examining committee made this decision based on the diagnostic finding of primary senile-onset degenerative dementia, uncomplicated, without delirium, delusions, or depression. This diagnosis suggests an absence of psychotic ideation or other debilitating symptoms that might prevent the ward from caring for herself, given minimal supervision. In another case, an incompetency hearing determined that an 80-year-old ward manifested physical disabilities, based on the examining committee diagnosis of obesity, a recently broken hip, osteoarthritis, and senile dementia. Here, the ward's intellectual functioning or ability to manage her own estate was apparently not addressed by the court, yet a plenary guardianship was established.

As noted earlier, most appointed guardians were relatives of the ward, many of whom were presumably serving as de facto guardians. Relatives were significantly more likely to assume guardianships when the size of the estate was greater than $50,000. Of these cases, 80% of guardians were relatives, whereas only 60% of estates less than $50,000 were supervised by relatives (difference significant at the .005 level, using chi-square analysis). Only one guardianship case in the sample was contested; this action was taken by relatives of a ward who had both assumed partial responsibility for her estate prior to the guardianship hearing.

The correlation between the size of the estate and the assumption of guardian responsibilities by a relative may be consistent with Alexander and Lewin's finding[29] that guardianship serves the interests of third persons rather than those of wards. The correlation provides some empirical support for a theme suggested in a psychiatrist's observation that " 'for every $100,000 in a given estate a lawyer shows up, for every $25,000 a family member shows up.' "[30]

Financial reviews of established guardianships in Leon County were almost nonexistent. Although annual accountings of each estate are required by law, only one financial review was included in our sample. Several activities were noted in this case: 1) two medical doctors serving on the incompetency examining committee saw the patient two or three times each during the year subsequent to establishment of the guardianship; 2) a pri-

---

29. *Id.*
30. Public Guardianship, *supra* note 4, at 109.

vate psychiatrist was also paid to examine the ward every three months for a "stabilized" psychiatric condition; 3) petitioner's attorney fees totalled $1,369 and were charged to the ward's estate; 4) the newly-appointed guardian charged $2,819 for "reimbursement of administrative costs"; 5) a total of $17,000 was charged to the ward's estate in the first fiscal accounting, including $1,200 in interest for a loan.

The Dade County Grand Jury[31] similarly found that personal annual reports were not up to date 87% of the time, 75% of the guardianship cases did not have timely financial reports, and the required physical examination reports were absent in 91% of the cases. Such practices in Miami interfered for two years with the discovery of a 92-year-old woman "living in squalor"[32] in an adult congregate living facility owned by her guardian, in violation of Florida law, despite a $150,000 bank account. In another Miami case undiscovered for two years, a lawyer for a ward was also appointed as guardian and then submitted "identical billings for the same functions in both capacities in the amount of $77,000."[33] One of the billings to the estate was $1,018 for three hours spent purchasing a $200 clock for the ward.

The average duration of time for adjudication of incompetency in Leon County was thirty-five days. Although the examining committee submitted its findings twenty-three days after the incompetency petition was filed, the court spent an average of about twelve days before actually acting on the incompetency issue. In six of the forty-two cases, the order adjudging incompetency was signed subsequent to the petition for appointment of a guardian by an average of fifteen days. Here, despite a legal presumption of competence, the court allowed petitioners to file guardianship papers prior to a ruling on the incompetency issue, but it did not date or serve notice on these petitions for appointment of a guardian until after an incompetency ruling had been promulgated. In 82% of cases examined, the petition for guardianship was filed simultaneously with the incompetency ruling. In 73% of cases, the court order appointing a guardian was issued the same day as the incompetency ruling and guardianship petitions. For the remaining 27% of cases, guardianships were ordered on an average of fifteen days after the petition was filed. Cases involving small estates were litigated more rapidly. Elapsed time between guardianship petitions and appointment of guardians in cases involving estates of $50,000 or more averaged about nine days, and elapsed time for estates of less than $50,000 averaged about three days (difference significant at the .01 level, using chi-square analysis).

---

31. Dade County Grand Jury, *supra* note 25.
32. *Id.* at 29.
33. *Id.* at 30.

Summary and Recommendations

Guardianship in north Florida served an elderly population suffering from age-related disorders such as organic brain syndrome and senility. Typically, guardianship serves female wards residing in private homes, who were provided court-appointed supervision by relatives living in the vicinity. Wards tended to be moderately wealthy, although the value of estates varied considerably.

Incompetency and guardianship proceedings were not conducted as rigorously as criminal, forensic, or other civil mental health proceedings. Notification of impending hearings mailed to alleged incompetents did not allow adequate time to challenge petitioners' evidence in some cases, and whether legal counsel was regularly appointed by the court is unclear. Hearings were essentially non-adversarial in nature. The court appeared to intervene minimally, allowing medical examiners full discretion to establish the incompetency of the prospective ward.

Neither attorneys nor judges challenged the nominal and inexplicit evidence presented in support of incompetency petitions or the similarly terse medical diagnoses submitted by examining committees in support of incompetency rulings. In both cases, the judiciary appeared to endorse evidentiary standards of incompetency that were insufficient.[34] As a result, the behavioral incapacities of individuals adjudicated incompetent remain sketchy. Compliance with statutory guidelines might be expedited by the use of more careful (written) instructions to the examining committee and a revision of the examining committee report format. At present, this format attempts to solicit diagnostic information by asking examiners to provide evidence of incompetency. The failure to present the minimum statutory criteria for incompetency in the examining committee report encourages the committee's reliance on psychiatric rather than legal definitions of incompetence. The former are most accessible to medical/psychiatric personnel who serve on the examining committees but are less helpful to the court than legal or more functional definitions of behavior.

The appointment of guardians in north Florida appears to be an unexceptional process, often involving close relatives of the ward and formalizing supervisory relationships that have actually been in practice for some time. Consistent with Alexander and Lewin's findings,[35] relatives in our study appeared to be more willing to involve themselves in guardianships when a large inheritance was apparently at stake. In the majority of cases, guardians were available to the court at the initiation of the

---

34. Fla. Stat. section 744.331(1) (1983).
35. G. Alexander & T. Lewin, *supra* note 10.

incompetency petition. For these cases, guardianship hearings were quite streamlined and often were held on the same day as incompetency hearings. In a minority of cases, additional time elapsed. In all cases, the selection of a guardian appeared to be noncontroversial.

The court did not choose to appoint limited guardianships, even when wards appeared capable of caring for themselves or when they were physically incapacitated but able to make financial decisions regarding their estates. The court's reluctance to invoke limited guardianship provisions may be due in part to the fact that examining committees insufficiently appraised and documented functional disabilities of prospective wards. However, little effort was exerted to gather additional information (e.g., by contacting relatives or friends knowledgeable about the ward's physical/mental condition) that might have clarified the need for limited guardianship.

Financial reviews of guardianship were inadequate. Having established guardianships, the court is obliged to see that exploitation and irresponsible management of the ward's person and estate are avoided. This obligation is enumerated by the Florida guardianship statute in two areas. First, it is the duty of the guardian to provide affirmative treatment to the ward, pursuant to rehabilitation or restoration of competence.[36] Second, it is incumbent upon the court to encourage the guardian's financial accountability and judicious use of the estate's assets.[37] The court did not seem to monitor either area. Guardians negligent in presenting yearly fiscal accounting to the court have not been notified or sanctioned, and the court has evidently not audited even the few accountings that have been returned.

An attempt to remedy this situation might include the expansion of the probate court clerk's office activities in order to enable more comprehensive supervision of legal guardianships. One function of the office would involve the development of a uniform estate review format to be used by court-appointed guardians. Presently, each guardian is asked to prepare annual reviews without clear guidelines detailing expected contents, length, style, and the like. Uniform review formats would standardize the documentation and subsequent judicial review processes. In addition, they would serve to delineate statutory parameters of supervision and treatment, including medical and psychiatric care and financial management of the estate. Another function of the expanded clerk's office would be to disseminate annual review forms (well in advance of deadlines) and to train guardians to compile these reviews accurately.

Perhaps most importantly, the clerk's office would serve to evaluate guardianships on an ongoing basis. For this purpose, the office might enlist

---

36. Fla. Stat. section 744.367 (1983).
37. Fla. Stat. section 744.311 (1983).

the services of social workers or paralegal staff who would help to advise guardians in means of complying with treatment and financial guidelines of the Florida guardianship statute. For those guardians refusing to comply with judicial standards, the clerk's office would recommend appropriate sanctions to be levied by the court. A public guardianship office might carry out the same functions. Such an office might also assist the court in locating relatives, friends, or interested individuals or agencies in the community who would consent to supervise limited guardianships. The probate court is currently ill-equipped to survey eligible members of the community for this purpose due to its lack of contact with social resources and conclusory information provided the court by the examining committee concerning the ward's mental and physical incapacities.

This study of guardianship is limited by the small number of cases, in an essentially archival review, over a relatively brief period of time in one county of north Florida, although it did cover all of the guardianship cases in the county of Florida's capital, Tallahassee, during a five-year period. The significant findings are similar to contemporaneous results found by a grand jury in more cosmopolitan south Florida, and the Florida findings do not differ significantly from Alexander and Lewin's New York study.[38] The Florida findings are consistent with the opportunities for disservice in guardianship, about which considerable consensus appears in the available literature.

The literature and empirical research on guardianship to date suggest that contemporary problems may go beyond administrative bromides to the design and structure of guardianship itself. Existing commentary is replete with statutory suggestions aimed at making eligibility criteria more behavioral and less categorical and at enhancing procedural protections. The literature also identifies opportunities for judicial remedies and pleads for education and training. The suggestions for reform remain appropriate.

---

38. G. Alexander & T. Lewin, *supra* note 10.

Chapter 8

Accountability of Lawyers in Serving Vulnerable, Elderly Clients

Winsor C. Schmidt, Jr.

> *Abstract.* This chapter assesses the need for greater accountability of lawyers charged with protecting the financial interests and personal welfare of elderly and disabled clients and wards, and with representing guardians of elderly and disabled wards. The chapter synthesizes the relevant behavioral research and ethical and professional standards. Greater accountability can be accomplished through standards and training for guardians, better court monitoring of guardians, stronger ethical rules for lawyers representing vulnerable clients, and stronger enforcement of such rules.

Vulnerable elderly and disabled clients of attorneys are potentially defenseless against unscrupulous lawyers who might prey upon or neglect them. If the disabled client's lawyer does not speak for the client, no other advocacy may occur. The viability of such legal processes involving the elderly and disabled as guardianship and civil commitment is contingent on presentation of evidence and advocacy to a judge or jury and representation of the vulnerable person's interests against the interests of a petitioner for guardianship or civil commitment.

Guardians of vulnerable elderly and disabled persons are in a similar situation. Guardians who are not lawyers are dependent upon legal counsel for navigating such increasingly formalistic processes as guardianship and civil commitment. Poor quality legal representation of guardians leaves the guardian, and the guardian's vulnerable ward, adrift in unfamiliar legal waters.

The thesis of this chapter is that there is a need for greater accountability of attorneys who represent vulnerable elderly and disabled clients and their guardians. In a review of existing behavioral research and ethical and professional standards, the extent of poor quality legal representation provided to disabled clients and their guardians and the need for greater accountability will be demonstrated.

Quality of Legal Representation

The *Model Rules of Professional Conduct* assert that "disabled clients are often provided substandard representation."[1] The deficiency is attributed to "communication difficulties, the lawyer's ambiguous relationship with the disabled client, and especially in quasi-adversarial proceedings, uncertainty and confusion concerning the proper role of the lawyer."[2]

Reisner observes that various legal studies suggest appointed counsel "all too often carried out their defense functions very perfunctorily."[3] He suggests that such findings are accounted for by attorneys' erroneous perception that their role is limited to assuring non-violation of rights during the legal commitment process; by the reluctance to challenge supposedly authoritative medical opinions because of limited clinical training or civil commitment experience;[4] by inadequate compensation discouraging significant time and effort; and by some attorneys' perception of their role in the "non-traditional legal terms" of explicitly accepting their clients' need for compelled treatment when disordered and at

---

1. Annotated Model Rules of Professional Conduct 160 (1984) (hereinafter cited as Model Rules) *citing*: Litwack, *The Role of Counsel in Civil Commitment Proceedings: Emerging Problems*, 62 Calif. L. Rev. 816, 817 (1974) ("With few exceptions, patients receive considerably less than adequate legal assistance"); Mickenberg, *The Silent Clients: Legal and Ethical Considerations in Representing Severely and Profoundly Retarded Individuals*, 31 Stan. L. Rev. 625, 632 (1979) ("Reports on the quality of legal representation provided to retarded clients...tell of inadequate effort, unjustified compromise of clients' rights and distorted perceptions of legal ethics."); *accord* Andalman & Chambers, *Effective Counsel for Persons Facing Civil Commitment: A Survey, a Polemic, and a Proposal*, 45 Miss. L. J. 43, 43–44 (1974); Cohen, *The Function of the Attorney and the Commitment of the Mentally Ill*, 44 Tex. L. Rev. 424, 424–25, 446–47 (1966).

2. *Id. citing*, *e.g.*, Miller v. Quatsce, 332 F.Supp. 1269 (E.D.Wis. 1971); Mickenberg, *supra* note 1, at 626–27.

3. R. Reisner, Law and the Mental Health System: Civil and Criminal Aspects 406 (1985); *citing*: Andalman & Chambers, *supra* note 1; Cohen, *supra* note 1; Wexler & Scoville, *Special Project-The Administration of Psychiatric Justice: Theory and Practice in Arizona*, 13 Ariz. L. Rev. 1, 51–60 (1971); Note, *Involuntary Hospitalization of the Mentally Ill Under Florida's Baker Act: Procedural Due Process and the Role of the Attorney*, 26 Fla. L. Rev. 508 (1974).

See also R. Reisner & C. Slobogin, Law and the Mental Health System: Civil and Criminal Aspects 728 (2d ed. 1990) *citing, e.g.*, Poythress, *Psychiatric Expertise in Civil Commitment: Training Attorneys to Cope with Expert Testimony*, 2 L. & Hum. Behav. 1 (1978) (lawyers avoid careful cross-examination because of belief that it is not in clients' best interests).

4. R. Reisner, *supra* note 3, at 406 *citing* Elkins, *Legal Representation of the Mentally Ill*, 82 W. Va. L. Rev. 157, 181, 185 (1979).

risk.[5] Patterns of ineffective representation of clients in civil commitment proceedings have been documented in Arizona, Illinois, Michigan, Missouri, Tennessee, Texas, Virginia, and Wisconsin.[6]

Nor is substandard, perfunctory, and ineffective representation of vulnerable clients limited to civil commitment proceedings for the mentally ill and retarded. The American Bar Association Commission on Legal Problems of the Elderly and the National Judicial College convened a National Conference of the Judiciary on Guardianship Proceedings for the Elderly in June 1986. The judicial leaders from states with the highest population and percentage of elderly persons identified significant national deficiencies in guardianship proceedings that could be traced directly or indirectly to inadequate legal representation.[7]

Notice to the alleged incompetent is sometimes insufficient.[8] Time for hearing preparation is as little as one week or less.[9] Notice frequently fails to appropriately convey the nature and potential consequences of the proceedings.[10] The respondent is absent from the hearing as much as eighty-

---

5. *Id. Cf.* 2 M. Perlin, Mental Disability Law: Civil and Criminal 817–20 (1989) (beneficial hospitalization presumption, power imbalance with hospital, client credibility doubt, witness difficulties, self-perceived rolelessness, ignorance about psychiatry, third party pressures, inexperience with differentness).

6. Nelson, Schmidt & Miller, *The Legal Needs of the Mentally and Developmentally Disabled-A Florida Study*, 6 Mental Disability L. Rep. 418, 423–24 (1982) (citations omitted).

For an excellent overview of the "Right to Advocacy Services and Effective Counsel," *see* M. Perlin, *supra* note 5, at 739–873 (1989).

7. *See* Statement of Recommended Judicial Practices Adopted by the National Conference of the Judiciary on Guardianship Proceedings for the Elderly (June 1986) (Erica F. Wood compiled this report) (hereinafter cited as Statement). For a summary of this report concentrating on judicial guardianship practices in Florida and other states, *see* Schmidt, *Recommended Judicial Practices in Guardianship Proceedings for the Elderly*, 61 Fla. B. J. 35 (May 1987). *See also* American Bar Association, Guardianship of the Elderly: A Primer for Attorneys (1990) (representation, ethical dilemmas, evaluating capacity, communication, alternatives, guardian advising); Center for Social Gerontology, National Study of Guardianship System and Feasibility of Implementing Expert Systems Project (1992) (majority of respondents not represented by legal counsel); L. Frolik & M. Brown, Advising the Elderly or Disabled Client: Legal, Health Care, Financial and Estate Planning (1992) (ethical considerations); National Senior Citizens Law Center, Representing Older Persons: An Advocates Manual 15, 22–23 (right to counsel and role of attorney in guardianship and alternatives).

8. *See, e.g.*, Legal Services for the Elderly, Inc., Guardianship and Conservatorship in Maine's Counties 7 (1985) (service of the papers not made in hand).

9. *See* Peters, Schmidt & Miler, *Guardianship of the Elderly in Tallahassee, Florida*, 26 Gerontologist 532, 535 (1985) (29% of the cases).

10. *See, e.g.*, Schmidt, *supra* note 7, at 35 (Florida).

four percent of the time.[11] Court accessibility and the respondent's participation in the hearing are sometimes not facilitated as much as they could be.[12] The respondent is represented by counsel as little as three percent of the time.[13] Counsel's investigation and preparation are such that he or she too frequently functions "'as no more than a clerk ratifying the events that transpire, rather than influencing them.'"[14] Counsel who decide client needs rather than advocating client wishes subvert the effective functioning of adversarial guardianship procedures.[15] Attorneys frequently allow medical determination of incompetency rather than legal evidentiary determination.[16] Counsel could more frequently seek an independent second medical (or mental health or social service) evaluation of the respondent.[17] Attorneys could more vigorously seek less restrictive alternatives to guardianship or implementation of limited guardianship.[18]

---

11. See Horstman, *Protective Services for the Elderly: The Limits of Parens Patriae*, 40 Mo. L. Rev. 215, 235–36 n.81 (1975) (1973–74 study in Los Angeles).

12. Statement, *supra* note 7, at 18.

13. Legal Services for the Elderly, *supra* note 8, at 9.

14. Schmidt, *supra* note 7, at 36 *quoting* Perlin, *Representing Individuals in the Commitment and Guardianship Process*, in Legal Rights of Mentally Disabled Persons 501 (1979). *Accord* Pecora, *The Constitutional Right to Court Appointed Adversary Counsel for Defendants in Guardianship Proceedings*, 43 Ark. L. Rev. 345 (1990).

15. See, e.g., Frolick, *Plenary Guardianship: An Analysis, a Critique and a Proposal for Reform*, 23 Ariz. L. Rev. 599, 634–35 (1981).

16. See *In re* Von Bulow, 22 Misc.2d 129, 470 N.Y.S.2d 72 (Sup. Ct. 1983); Horstman, *supra* note 11, at 227; New, *A Proposal for Guardianship Oversight Commission in Florida*, 58 Fla. B. J. 45, 48 (1985); Peters, Schmidt & Miller, *supra* note 9, at 535; Final Report of the Grand Jury, Dade County, Fla., p. 31 (Nov. 9, 1982); Legal Services for the Elderly, *supra* note 8, at 13–16 Table 10C.

17. See, e.g., Schmidt, *supra* note 7, at 37; Saunders & Simon, *Individual Functional Assessment: An Instruction Manual*, 11 Mental and Physical Disability L. Rep. 60 (1987).

18. See W. Schmidt, K. Miller, W. Bell & E. New, Public Guardianship and the Elderly 91, 172 (Ballinger 1981); Peters, Schmidt & Miller, *supra* note 9, at 536 (limited guardianship used only once in five years in Leon County, Florida, despite appearance of capacities in at least several other cases); M. Axilbund, Substituted Judgment for the Disabled: Report of an Inquiry into Limited Guardianship, Public Guardianship and Adult Protective Services in Six States (1979); M. Kapp & J. Detzel, Alternatives to Guardianship for the Elderly: Legal Liability Disincentives and Impediments, Wright State University School of Medicine (1992); Statement, *supra* note 7, at 41; R. Steinberg, Alternative Approaches to Conservatorship and Protection of Older Adults Referred to Public Guardian, Institute for Policy and Program Development, Ethel Percy Andrus Gerontology Center (1985) (money management and transitional decisions are the most frequent reasons for guardianship referral); L. Stiegel, Alternatives to Guardianship: Substantive Training Materials and Module for Professionals Working with the Elderly and Persons with Disabilities, Ameri-

Concerning the submission and review of guardian reports in Miami, Florida, the Dade County Grand Jury concluded: "Most attorneys for guardians either do not know about the report responsibilities of their guardian clients or they are not effectively communicating those responsibilities to their clients."[19] Attorneys could do much more to meet the unmet need for guardianship services by the thousands of elderly and disabled persons who are legally or functionally incompetent but do not have willing and responsible family members or friends to serve as guardian or resources to compensate a professional private guardian.[20] It seems likely that legal representation of vulnerable clients in (involuntary) adult protective services proceedings is similarly problematic, but access to the proceedings and focused inquiry have been limited.[21]

---

can Bar Association (1992); Legal Services for the Elderly, *supra* note 8, at 4–5.

But see S. Brakel, J. Perry & B. Weiner, The Mentally Disabled and the Law 385 (1985) (abuses like "representation by unprepared attorneys" may occur more easily with limited guardianship).

For a compilation of quantitative guardianship research, *see* Center for Social Gerontology , *supra* note 7; Schmidt, *Quantitative Information About the Quality of the Guardianship System: Toward the Next Generation of Guardianship Research*, 10 Probate L. J. 61 (1990).

19. Final Report of the Grand Jury, *supra* note 16, at 32.

See generally S. Hurme, Steps to Enhance Guardianship Monitoring 63–66 (1991) (monitoring role of attorney for petitioner, attorney for guardian, attorney for ward); G. Zimny, B. Gilchrist & J. Diamond, A National Model for Judicial Review of Guardians' Performance (1991) (six courts in California, Connecticut, Kentucky, Michigan, Minnesota, Missouri); Perry & Hurme, *Guardianship Monitoring and Enforcement Nationwide*, 15 Mental & Physical Disability L. Rep. 304 (1991) (monitoring statutes and practices in the states); Zimny, Gilchrist, Grossberg & Chung, *Annual Reports by Guardians and Conservators to Probate Courts*, 3 J. Elder Abuse & Neglect 61 (1991) (return and review of financial reports achievable).

20. *See* S. Brakel, J. Parry & B. Weiner, *supra* note 18, at 390; W. Schmidt, K. Miller, W. Bell & E. New, *supra* note 18, at 183, 193; Hightower, Heckert & Schmidt, *Elderly Nursing Home Residents' Need for Public Guardianship Services in Tennessee*, 2 J. Elder Abuse & Neglect 105 (1990), Schmidt & Peters, *Legal Incompetents' Need for Guardians in Florida*, 15 Bull. Am. Acad. of Psychiatry and L. 69 (1987) (at least 11,147 persons reportedly needed a guardian in Florida in 1983).

21. *See* Kapp, *Adult Protective Services: Convincing the Patient to Consent*, 11 L. Med. and Health Care 163 (1983); Regan, *Adult Protective Services: An Appriasal and a Prospectus*, in National Law and Social Work Seminar: Proceedings and Prospects (1982); Regan, *Protecting the Elderly: The New Paternalism*, 32 Hastings L. J. 1111 (1981); Schmidt, *Adult Protective Services and the Therapeutic State*, 10 L. & Psychology Rev. 101 (1986); Schmidt & Miller, *Improving the Social Treatment Model in Protective Services for the Elderly: False Needs in the Therapeutic State*, 1 J. Int'l & Comp. Soc. Welfare 90 (1984); M. Axilbund, *supra* note 18.

Ethical and Professional Standards for Legal Representation

The general ethical and professional obligations and responsibilities of attorneys in serving vulnerable clients in such situations as civil commitment, guardianship, and adult protective services are prescribed. Rule 1.1 of the *Model Rules of Professional Conduct* states: "A lawyer shall provide competent representation to a client. Competent representation requires the legal knowledge, skill, thoroughness and preparation reasonably necessary for the representation."[22] Compared to the *Model Code of Professional Responsibility*, "Rule 1.1 more fully particularizes the elements of competence."[23] The "legal background" to the rule observes that suggested remedies for dealing with criticism of the legal profession include "mandatory continuing legal education, changes in law school curricula, testing and performance review."[24] It singles out peer review as a "promising approach."[25] The background emphasizes the stakes as ultimately being the "ability of the legal profession to resist government intervention and be self-regulating."[26] Problems of defining competence in the disciplinary context are similar to those in the malpractice and sixth amendment right to effective assistance of counsel, contexts.[27]

Rule 1.3 of the *Model Rules* provides: "A lawyer shall act with reasonable diligence and promptness in representing a client."[28] The comment elaborates that an attorney's work load should be controlled enough for adequate handling of each case.[29] Procrastination "can cause a client needless anxiety";[30] disabled clients may be particularly vulnerable to exacerbation of already existing anxiety. Lawyers should clarify any doubt about the existence of a client-lawyer relationship in writing. Before relinquishing responsibility for an adverse administrative or judicial proceeding, the attorney "should advise the client of the possibility of appeal."[31] In sum, "'Lawyers...everywhere are, themselves, on public trial... The pro-

---

22. Model Rules, *supra* note 1, at 13.
23. *Id.* at 14.
24. *Id.*
25. *Id.*
26. *Id.* at 16.
27. *Id.*
28. *Id.* at 30.
29. *Id.*
30. *Id.* at 31.
31. *Id.*

crastination of one of us results in the condemnation of all and, in this context, we must stand responsible for each other as we discharge our obligation to our clients, the courts, and the public at large.'"[32]

Rule 1.14 of the *Model Rules* more specifically states:

(a) When a client's ability to make adequately considered decisions in connection with the representation is impaired, whether because of minority,[33] mental disability or for some other reason, the lawyer shall, as far as reasonably possible, maintain a normal client-lawyer relationship with the client.

(b) A lawyer may seek the appointment of a guardian or take other protective action with respect to a client, only when the lawyer reasonably believes that the client cannot adequately act in the client's own interest.[34]

Clients are presumed to retain degrees of capacity for making decisions, even when lacking legal competence or being of "advanced age."[35] However, "If the person has no guardian of legal representative, the lawyer often must act as de facto guardian."[36] The legal background clearly states: "Ordinarily as in any client lawyer relationship, the lawyer has the duty to advocate the wishes of the client and the client is entitled to competence, preparation, and communication..."[37] The attorney "should see to the appointment of a guardian or legal representative"[38] if in the client's interest. The attorney "must represent the representative's decisions and determination as to which interests are in the best interests of the client, absent evidence of fraud or collusion on the part of the representative."[39] But conflicts between the client's interests and the representative may be "resolved judicially."[40] And finally, "If the lawyer represents the guardian as distinct from the ward, and is aware that the guardian is acting adverse-

---

32. *Id. quoting* Mendicino v. Magagna, 572 P.2d 21, 23–24 (Wyo. 1977).

33. A "redraft" of the Model Rules specifies "abnormality" instead of "minority". M. Perlin, *supra* note 5, at 822–23 *citing* ABA/BNA Lawyer's Manual on Professional Conduct, Model Rules of Professional Conduct Rule 1.14, at 01:134 (1988).

34. Model Rules, *supra* note 1, at 156.

35. *Id.* at 157. *See* Tremblay, *On Persuasion and Paternalism: Lawyer Decision-making and the Questionably Competent Client*, 1987 Utah L. Rev. 515 (1987). "Advanced age" is a potentially pejorative, ageist, and discriminatory phrase. *See, e.g.*, Schmidt, *supra* note 7, at 37.

36. Model rules, *supra* note 1, at 157.

37. *Id.* at 159 (citations omitted),

38. *Id.* at 161. *Cf.* Saunders & Simon, *supra* note 17.

39. *Id.*

40. *Id.*

ly to the ward's interest, the lawyer may have an obligation to prevent or rectify the guardian's misconduct."[41]

There is some debate among attorneys regarding the relevance of the *Model Rules,* especially Rule 1.14(b), in representing vulnerable clients. Devine concludes that Rule 1.14(b) breaches the spirit and letter of ethical provisions regarding confidences and conflicts of interest.[42] He suggests a new Rule 1.14(b) [43] under which "the lawyer would be permitted to advise others that the authority to act for the client is absent, thereby preventing the lawyer from being personally liable and preventing a material misrepresentation of fact to the third party with whom the lawyer has dealt on behalf of the client."[44] This suggested new rule constitutes a further attempt "to resolve the best interests/advocacy dichotomy by adopting a philosophy which sees the lawyer as an advocate for the disabled client."[45]

State legislatures are taking more direct steps at assuring accountability of lawyers in representing proposed wards in guardianship proceedings. The attorney for the proposed ward is required to take a zealous, advocate role representing the client's expressed wishes.[46] Some statutes prescribe minimum duties, including: personal interviews with the pro-

---

41. *Id.* at 157 *citing* Rule 1.2 (d).

Cf. M. Perlin, *supra* note 5, at 822–32 (five major problems with the Model Rules: internal inconsistency of "'normal' lawyer-client relations" with "'quasi-adversarial'" commitment proceedings; unresolved issues of extent of deference to guardian decisions, and of conflict between client views and "'best interests'" perception of lawyer; ignore issues of disabled client refusal of psychotropic medication, and wish to control own funds; implies client decision rather than counsel mandate to raise incompetency defense; characterize commitment as "'quasi-adversar[ial]'" and "'quasi-judicial'").

42. Devine, *The Ethics of Representing the Disabled Client: Does Model Rule 1.14 Adequately Resolve the Best Interests/Advocacy Dilemma?,* 49 Mo. L. Rev. 493 (1984). *Accord* Alles, *Representing Older Persons: Ethical Dilemmas,* 8 Bifocal 3 (1987). *See generally* Pennell, *Ethics in Estate Planning and Fiduciary Administration: The Inadequacy of the Model Rules and the Model Code,* 45 Rec. 715 (1990).

43. *Id.* at 514:
When, after undertaking representation of a client it becomes reasonably clear to the lawyer that the client is suffering from a disability and is thereby no longer capable of aiding the lawyer in furthering the attorney-client relationship, the lawyer may make such disclosure of this fact to third parties as is reasonably necessary to comply with the provisions of Rule 4.1 [prohibiting false statement of material fact and failure to make necessary disclosure of material fact], except that no such disclosure is authorized where the lawyer is employed for the limited purpose of representing the client in any matter wherein the disability of the client is the subject matter of the representation.

44. *Id.*

45. *Id.* at 515.

46. *See* D.C. Code section 21-2-33 (b) (1987); Fla. Stat. Ann. section 744.102 (1) (1990);

posed ward; explanation of proceedings, possible consequences, alternatives, and rights in understandable language, communication mode, and terms; securing and presentation of evidence and testimony; and, offering arguments to protect the rights and further the interests of the proposed ward.[47]

The judiciary has addressed the liability of attorneys and guardians who provide poor service for wards. One court recognized a duty by an attorney to the guardian and ward to discover that the guardian had engaged in misappropriation, conversion, and improper investment.[48] Another court found a breach of fiduciary duty by the guardian to the ward where the guardian failed to investigate the effect of liquidating real estate on the ward's eligibility for public assistance, and to seek public assistance.[49]

Recommendations

This recital of the ethical and professional responsibilities of attorneys in serving vulnerable clients is not congruent with the deficient representation described at the outset. Accountability for such attorneys could be improved.

Legal malpractice is an increasing, but not crisis, concern.[50] When legal malpractice reaches the crisis level of medical malpractice, and of the tort crises stimulating no-fault automobile insurance and workmen's compensation, it will probably be appropriate to institute Bar or government client compensation funds for victims of lawyer malpractice.

Bar discipline and peer review may be no more effective than medical licensing at assuring quality professional service.[51] Just as medical licensing should more closely scrutinize the small number of physicians responsible for a disproportionate amount of medical malpractice, so should Bar discipline and peer review focus more closely on lawyer malpractice experience.

N.M. Stat. Ann. sections 45-5-303.1, 45-5-404.1 (1989) (conservatorship); Wash. Rev. Code Ann. section 11.88.045 (1992).

47. *See* D.C. Code section 21-2003 (6); N.M. Stat. Ann. sections 45-5-303.1, 45-5-404.1 (conservatorship); N.D. Cent. Code section 30.1-26-01 (1989 Supp.).

48. Fickett v. Superior Court of Pima County, 27 Ariz. App. 793, 558 P.2d 988 (1976).

49. Guardianship of O'Connor, 170 Ill. App. 3d 759, 121 Ill. Dec. 408, 525 N.E. 2d 214 (1988).

50. *See, e.g.,* Tabac, *Crossfire at the Bar: Legal Malpractice Suits are Altering the Way Attorneys Deal with Clients — and with Each Other*, N. Y. Times Magazine, May 3, 1987, 30.

51. *See, e.g.,* R. Fellmeth, Report on the Performance of the Disciplinary System of the California State Bar (1987).

A Bar survey "revealed the absence of comprehensive [Bar] programs on technical [mental disability] legal issues aimed specifically at lawyers and legal advocates."[52] If patterns of deficient representation continue, Bar certification of elder and disability law specialists should be provided, including mandatory continuing education to keep pace with the rapid developments occurring in these complex fields.

Recommendations for improvement of legal services in civil commitment proceedings abound.[53] The most important recommendation is a right to effective assistance of adversary counsel in adversary civil commitment (and guardianship) proceedings, including the privilege of government funding and appointment of counsel for indigents. Without such assistance, few other rights are meaningfully exercised. Reformers have elaborated the desirable role of attorneys in guardianship cases.[54] There seems to be an emerging consensus that the desirable role is that of advocate for the disabled client. If the client's lawyer does not act as advocate, who will?

The National Conference of the Judiciary on Guardianship Proceedings for the Elderly made numerous recommendations for guardianship change, including the establishment and implementation of standards and training for guardians and better court monitoring of guardians.[55] States adopting such recommendations as mandatory training of guardians and annual audits of the ward's person and property are beginning to report favorable experiences that can serve as guides for the other states.

The closer scrutiny of adult protective services has begun.[56] The well-intentioned veil of confidentiality shielding such services should not block enhanced evaluation and accountability efforts. Legal services in the protective services process can increase confidence that results match good intentions.

The *Model Rules of Professional Conduct,* especially related to clients under disability, seem to be at least incrementally stronger than the *Model Code of Professional Responsibility.* Devine's suggested new Rule 1.14(b) is endorsable.[57]

---

52. ABA Commission on the Mentally Disabled, Survey of Continuing Legal Education Programs on Mental Disability Law (1986).

53. *See, e.g.,* sources cited *supra* notes 1, 3, 4. *See also, e.g.,* Stefan, *Right to Counsel in Civil Commitment Proceedings,* 9 Mental & Physical Disability L. Rep. 230 (1985) (role of counsel).

54. *See, e.g.,* Wang, Burns & Hommel, *Trends in Guardianship Reform: Roles and Responsibilities of Legal Advocates,* 24 Clearinghouse Rev. 561, 563–69 (1990).

55. Statement, *supra* note 7. *See* sources cited in *supra* notes 7, 19. *See also* Saunders & Simon, *supra* note 17.

56. *See* sources cited in *supra* note 21.

57. Devine, *supra* notes 42–45.

The judiciary, and their officers of the court, have been at the forefront of positive change on behalf of the elderly and mentally disabled. Breakdowns in the legislative-political and executive-managerial response to vulnerable people have been balanced by judicial-legal action. To avoid increasing government intervention in the delivery of legal services to vulnerable clients, attorneys must each perform their advocacy role. They must represent their clients and their clients' wishes rather than judge them. They are obliged to prevent or rectify guardian misconduct. There should be stronger self-enforcement of ethical rules. The state of legal services for vulnerable clients is not good, but it is better, and there is capacity for improvement.

Chapter 9

Recommended Judicial Practices In Guardianship Proceedings for the Elderly

Winsor C. Schmidt, Jr.

In June 1986, the American Bar Association Commission on Legal Problems of the Elderly and the National Judicial College convened a National Conference of the Judiciary on Guardianship Proceedings for the Elderly in Reno, Nevada.[1] This chapter reports the recommended judicial practices in guardianship proceedings produced by that conference and summarizes practices in Florida and other states in 1987. The conference and its recommendations are intended to encourage similar state efforts, changes in statutes and court rules, coordination between the judiciary and the aging network, and testing in individual courtrooms.[2]

Procedure: Notice to the Alleged Incompetent

1. Personal service upon respondent should be by a court officer in plain clothes trained in dealing with the aging. In addition to the respondent, notice should be given by mail to the spouse, all the next of kin, the custodian of the respondent, the proposed guardian, and the providers of service.

In Florida in 1987, notice to the alleged incompetent is provided by service of the petition for determination of incompetency in the manner required for service of a summons.[3] A copy of the petition and notice of

---

1. The 28 participants included 24 probate and general jurisdiction trial judges selected as judicial leaders from states with the highest population and percentage of elderly.
2. *See* Statement of Recommended Judicial Practices Adopted by the National Conference of the Judiciary on Guardianship Proceedings for the Elderly (June 1988) (Erica F. Wood compiled this noteworthy report) (hereinafter cited as Statement).
3. Fla. R. P. & G. P. 5.570(a) *citing* Fla. R. Civ. P. 1.070.

hearing must be served on one or more members of the alleged incompetent's family if any are known residents of the county.[4] Notice of the petition for appointment of the guardian involves similar procedures.[5] Considerable judicial discretion is allowed and local practices vary.[6] A study of guardianship practices in Maine showed that service of the papers giving notice to the alleged incompetent is not made in hand.[7]

2. *There should be at least fourteen days notice before the hearing unless the court otherwise orders.*

There is no statutory provision in Florida regarding how much time must elapse between provision of notice and the date of the hearing.[8] Many courts reportedly try to provide two weeks notice to allow the alleged incompetent and the examining committee adequate time for preparation, examination and report filing, but some counties only require five to ten days.[9] A study of guardianship cases in Leon County between 1972 and 1982 found that the court scheduled incompetency hearings within one week of petitions in 29% of the cases.[10] The Uniform Probate Code 1-401(a) requires fourteen days notice.

3. *Notice should be in plain language and in large type. It should indicate the time and place of hearing, the possible adverse results to the respondent (such as loss of rights to drive, vote, marry, etc.), and a list of rights (such as the right for court-appointed counsel or guardian ad litem.) A copy of the petition should be attached.*

Florida forms for notice and petition for adjudication of incompetency and appointment of guardian use legal language and small type;[11] they specify neither possible adverse results[12] nor list of rights. The U.S.

---

4. Fla. R. P. & G. P. 5.570(a).

5. Fla. R. P. & G. P. 5.570(b). *See also* Fla. Stat.§ 744.377(1) (1987).

6. Brennan, *Procedure to Establish Guardianship* in Florida Guardianship Practice, pp. 28, 47 (1978).

7. Legal Services for the Elderly, Inc. Guardianship and Conservatorship in Maine's Counties, p. 7 (1985).

8. There are 22 other states that are statutorily silent on timeliness of notice. Parry, *Incompetency, Guardianship, and Restoration* in S. Brakel, J. Parry & B. Weiner, The Mentally Disabled and the Law (1985).

9. Brennan, *supra* note 6, at 47.

10. Peters, Schmidt & Miller, *Guardianship of the Elderly in Tallahassee, Florida*, 25 Gerontologist 532, 535 (1985).

11. Brennan, *supra* note 6, at 25–27, 29, 45–46.

12. A person adjudicated incompetent in Florida is statutorily "presumed to be incapable of managing his own affairs or of making any gift, contract, or instrument in writing that is binding on his or his estate." Fla. Stat. § 744.331(8) (1987).

In most states a finding of legal incompetence restricts or takes away "the right to: make contracts, sell, purchase, mortgage, or lease property; make gifts; travel, or decide where to live; vote; or hold elected office; initiate or defend against suits; make a will, or revoke

Supreme Court in *Mullane v. Central Hanover Bank & Trust Co.*, 339 U.S. 306 (1950), held that due process requires notice appropriate to the nature of the case by means that one desirous of actually informing might reasonably adopt, and in *Covey v. Town of Somers*, 351 U.S. 141 (1956), that notice by mail to a known incompetent regarding foreclosure of tax liens is inadequate because the individual is unable to understand the proceedings.

Procedure: Presence of the Alleged Incompetent at the Hearing

1. Respondent has a right to be present and should be present if at all possible.

Florida in 1987 has no statutory provision assuring the right of the respondent to be present at the hearing. A study of 1,010 filings in Los Angeles in 1973–74 found the judge, the petitioner and the petitioner's attorney to be the only persons present at the incompetency hearing in 84.2 percent of the cases.[13] Excusing the respondent's attendance is in some jurisdictions a routine practice leading to proceedings that lack any substance.[14] Forty-four percent of the judges responding to a recent national survey indicated that under 20% of respondents are present during the hearing.[15]

2. The court should do everything possible to encourage access to the courts by the elderly, including making the court facilities accessible and training court staff as to available services and resources. However, this shall not diminish the court's ability to convene at any other location if in the best interest of the respondent.

The court provides a forum for determining the incompetency and need for surrogate decisionmaking of elderly persons. Since the forum is a service for elderly citizens, it is appropriate that the court is physically accessible and comfortable. Some area agencies on aging have special transportation systems for the elderly. The court should be accessible to the physically handicapped. The court could convene in appropriate nursing

---

one; engage in certain professions; lend or borrow money; appoint agents; divorce, or marry; refuse medical treatment; keep and care for children; serve on a jury; be a witness to any legal document; drive a car; pay or collect debts; manage or run a business." R. Brown: The Rights of Older Persons, p. 286 (1979).

13. *See* Horstman, *Protective Services for the Elderly: The Limits of Parens Patriae*, 40 Mo. L. Rev. 15, 235–36 n. 81 (1975) (National Senior Citizens Law Center Study).

14. Mitchell, *Involuntary Guardianship for Incompetents: A Strategy for Legal Services Advocates*, 12 Clearinghouse Rev. 451, 454 (1978).

15. Statement, *supra* note 2, at 63.

homes, board and care homes or senior housing facilities. Videotaping or telephone interviewing might enhance accessibility by elderly persons. Guardianship proceedings should serve alleged incompetents first, and then petitioners and third parties.[16]

3. *To make participation of the respondent and others as meaningful as possible, courts should make all possible resources available for impaired persons, including interpreters for the deaf and non-English speaking persons and visual aids.*

Meaningful participation and opportunity to be heard are facilitated by accommodation to possible sensory losses of elderly persons. Judges should encourage supportive company, establish eye contact, provide extra time and patience, paraphrase, talk slowly and distinctly without background noise, keep the movements visible, assure bright but diffuse lighting, avoid glare, use large type or double and triple-spaced written materials, and assure that signs are large with well-spaced lettering.[17]

Procedure: Representation of the Alleged Incompetent

1. *Counsel as advocate for the respondent should be appointed in every case, to be supplemented by respondent's private counsel if the respondent prefers. If private funds are not available to pay counsel, then public funds should be used, not to exceed the rates ordinarily paid to court appointed counsel.*[18]

The study of guardianship in Leon County from 1977 to 1982 found that probate court records contained reference to attorneys appointed on behalf of the alleged incompetent in only 57% of the cases.[19] The Maine study found that only 3% of alleged incompetents were represented by

---

16. G. Alexander & T. Lewin, The Aged and the Need for Surrogate Management (1972) (guardianship seems beneficial only to persons other than the ward).

17. Statement, *supra* note 2, at 18.

18. An alternative view, adopted by a minority of the conference, was that the following paragraph should be added: "A guardian ad litem, who is an attorney, should be appointed initially in all incompetency proceedings. The guardian ad litem's duty is to explain to the respondent the rights of the respondent and the meaning of the proposed hearing. The guardian ad litem must report back to the court, in writing, the results of the interview with the respondent with respect to the respondent's physical, mental and financial condition. The report should also state whether a guardian should or should not be appointed." *But see, e.g.,* Solender, The Guardian Ad Litem: A Valuable Representative or an Illusory Safeguard?, 7 Texas Tech. L. Rev. 619 (1976).

19. Peters, Schmidt & Miller, *supra* note 10, at 535. *See* Brennan, *supra* note 6, at 49.

counsel statewide.[20] Thirty-three percent of the surveyed judges reported that the alleged incompetent was "sometimes" or "seldom" represented by counsel.[21]

The Florida Supreme Court in *In re Paunack*, 355 So.2d 1195 (Fla. 1978), has ruled that "a trial judge must specifically find whether the alleged incompetent is represented by counsel in any hearing where incompetency is to be determined, and whether counsel should be afforded. Failure to make such a ruling constitutes reversible error." Legal scholars argue that alleged incompetents are constitutionally entitled to counsel, including court-appointed counsel for indigents.[22]

2. *Counsel for the respondent should make a thorough and informed investigation of the situation. After accomplishing the investigation, counsel should proceed to represent the respondent in accordance with the rules of professional conduct governing attorneys of that state.*

Legal protections for alleged incompetents are neither meaningful nor implemented if effective assistance of counsel is not rendered. Commentators have too long observed that counsel in such mental disability cases as guardianship function "as no more than a clerk, ratifying the events that transpire, rather than influencing them."[23] Such practice in mental disability cases is arguably unconstitutional.[24]

The dilemma in representing an alleged incompetent is whether to act in the client's best interest, or to advocate the client's interests to the maximum extent possible as the client determines them. Problems with counsel determining the client's best interest include: the counsel is less likely to challenge expert testimony; determination of effective assistance and quality of representation is more difficult; counsel may provide only procedural formality legitimizing routine approval of petitions; and counsel lacks expertise to decide the mental capacity and psychological needs of the client.[25]

---

20. Legal Services for the Elderly, *supra* note 7, at 9.
21. Statement, *supra* note 2, at 63.
22. *See* Dudovitz, *Protective Services and Guardianships: Legal Services and the Role of the Advocate*, in National Senior Citizens Law Center, Representing Older Persons: An Advocate's Manual 77–88 (1985); Horstman, *supra* note 13, at 236, 245.
23. *E.g.*, Perlin, *Representing Individuals in the Commitment and Guardianship Process*, in Legal Rights of Mentally Disabled Persons 501 (1979).
24. State *ex rel.* Memmel v. Mundy, No. 441–417 (Wis. Cir. Ct., Milwaukee Cty., Aug. 18, 1976) (1 Mental Disability L. Rep. 183, (1976), *aff'd* 75 Wis. 2d 276, 249 N.W. 2d 573 (1977).
25. Frolick, *Plenary Guardianship: An Analysis, A Critique and A Proposal for Reform*, 23 Ariz. L. Rev. 599, 634–35 (1981).

One commentator acknowledges:

> The judge may not want this adversary model, rather preferring a cooperative informal atmosphere in which all the participants explore together what would be in the elder's best interest. However, history shows that a nonadversarial system may result in significant loss of rights by the individual being subjected to the proceedings.[26]

An attorney who decides the client's needs usurps the function of the judge and undermines the purpose of the adversary process.

Evidence: Assessment of Medical Diagnosis of the Alleged Incompetent

1. The court has ultimate responsibility to assess medical evidence and to determine incompetence. A doctor's input should be required but a doctor's medical diagnosis should not be the sole criterion for a court's adjudication of incompetency.

Appropriate functioning of guardianship proceedings is jeopardized not only by paternalistic counsel, but also by medicalization of the process. The study of guardianship in Leon County between 1977 and 1982 determined:

> Findings appeared to be heavily influenced by psychiatric diagnosis. Judges did not depart significantly from these diagnoses or from the psychiatric determination of incompetence rendered by the examining committee. Judges concurred with all 42 of the [psychiatric] incompetency decisions and did not appear to solicit additional behavioral or psychiatric evidence regarding functional incompetence of the potential ward. In most cases, the diagnosis provided by the examining committee was reiterated verbatim by the court in adjudicating incompetency.[27]

In fact, "in about 90% of the cases reviewed, examining committee reports did not provide specific behavioral information for the court that is statutorily required (Florida Guardianship Law, Fla. Stat. § 744.331(1), 1983)."[28] The 1985 Maine study found that only 31% of the physicians' statements contained specific behavioral information.[29] Such practice renders the issue of incompetency "a medical rather than a legal question."[30]

---

26. Dudovitz, *supra* note 22, at 74.
27. Peters, Schmidt & Miller, *supra* note 10, at 535.
28. *Id.* at 536.
29. Legal Services for the Elderly, *supra* note 7, at 13–16, Table 10c.
30. Horstman, *supra* note 13, at 227.

In reasserting the primacy of incompetency as a legal determination by legal standards and procedures with legal consequences, the Dade County Grand Jury recommended that the criteria by which each committee member reaches a diagnosis should be more precise, and "that a standardized test be selected for this purpose."[31] A New York court in *In re Von Bulow*, 22 Misc. 2d 129, 470 N.Y.S. 2d 72 (Sup. Ct. 1983), has ruled that incompetency cannot be based on a physician's affidavit to which all parties concur, but rather that competency is a triable issue of fact based on evidence submitted to the court.

2. *Respondent has a right to cross-examine the physician, but a physician's letter or affidavit may be admitted if stipulated to by the respondent. The respondent, or the court on its own motion, has the right to ask for an independent evaluation by a physician or other mental health or social service professional.*

The Dade County Grand Jury concluded that the composition of the examining committee should be broadened to include lay advocates for the elderly and developmentally disabled, and nonpsychiatrist physicians.[32] The grand jury had found that the same two physicians were appointed to the examining committee in all Dade guardianship cases for several years, and that three individuals rotated the lay assignment on the committee every four months.[33]

The makeup of the examining committee has varied among Florida counties[34] with some courts appointing committee members from a panel, and some courts involving the family or other petitioners in seeking willing members.[35] The occupational makeup of the committee may also vary widely from two psychiatrists and a nurse to a family doctor, an independent psychiatrist, and a lay person, often a deputy sheriff.

---

31. Final Report of the Grand Jury, Dade County, Fla., p. 31 (Nov. 9, 1982). *See* New, *A Proposal for a Guardianship Oversight Commission in Florida*, 58 Fla. B. J. 45, 48 (1985).

A model statute allows expert witnesses in guardianship to describe present mental functioning, prognosis, and whether a severe mental disorder exists, but prohibits opinion testimony about any applicable diagnosis category unless raised by the respondent. American Bar Association Commission on the Mentally Disabled, *Legal Issues in State Mental Health Care: Proposal for Change—Suggested Statute on Guardianship*, 2 Mental Disability L. Rep. 449, 453 (1978) (hereinafter cited as Mentally Disabled Guardianship).

32. Schmidt, *The Evolution of a Public Guardianship Program*, 12 J. Psychiatry & L. 349, 356 (1984).

33. Final Report of the Grand Jury, *supra* note 31, at 30.

34. Compare Final Report of the Grand Jury, *supra* note 31 (same appointees in Dade County) *with* Peters, Schmidt & Miller, *supra* note 10 (45 different physicians in 42 incompetency hearings in Leon County).

35. Brennan, *supra* note 6, at 48.

Evidence: Use of Investigative Resources to Assist the Court

1. *The court should have guardians ad litem, visitors or court investigative agencies available to it to investigate the respondent's situation and condition.*

2. *The investigator's report should cover the issues of incompetence, who should be guardian, placement of respondent, services available, and an assessment of less restrictive alternatives to the creation of a guardianship. The report should be made available to the court and all counsel.*

3. *Investigators should be professionally trained and familiar with the problems of the elderly.*

These recommended judicial practices relating to investigative resources essentially enhance the capacity of the court to receive more and better information about the alleged incompetent. Since remedies for the criticisms of guardianship are aimed at developing and implementing criterial and procedural protections against inappropriate guardianships, improving investigation risks increasing the burden faced by respondents. Better investigation alone makes alleged incompetents dependent upon the objectivity and quality of the unilateral investigation. In this sense, enhanced investigation may be inconsistent with an adversarial truth-finding model, especially when the investigation is court-associated, rather than petitioner-associated. A model statute provides, "The evaluation shall be conducted to minimize interference with respondent's activities and intrusion with the respondent's privacy."[36]

Evidence: Advanced Age of the Alleged Incompetent

1. *"Advanced age," in itself, should not be a factor in determining incompetence.*

2. *Judges handling guardianship cases should be educated at local, state and national programs about the aging process, and the societal myths and stereotypes of aging.*

---

36. American Bar Association Commission on the Mentally Disabled, Guardianship and Conservatorship: Statutory Survey, Model Statute 93 (1979) (hereinafter cited as Developmental Disabilities Guardianship). *See* Mentally Disabled Guardianship, *supra* note 31, at 451–52 (evaluation conducted with minimum interference, right to remain silent and accompaniment by attorney, right to independent examiner to testify on respondent's behalf).

The use of the term "advanced age" as a factor in determining incompetence "is a blatant instance of age discrimination."[37] "Advanced age," and arguably such pejorative terms as "senility," perpetuate the following examples of social myths and stereotypes about older persons: chronological aging determines mental, emotional and physical status; older persons are unproductive; older persons prefer disengagement from life; older persons are inflexible; older persons are forgetful and have limited attention spans; older age involves serenity.[38] Age discrimination is "ageism."

> Ageism can be seen as a process of systematic stereotyping of and discrimination against people because they are old, just as racism and sexism accomplish this with skin color and gender. Older people are categorized as senile, rigid in thought and manner, old-fashioned in morality and skills.... Ageism allows the younger generations to see older people as different from themselves, thus they subtly cease to identify with their elders as human beings.[39]

Ironically, judges involved with guardianship and other protective services may themselves appear to be rigid, "whereas actually they are unacquainted with the subject of impairment in older persons...; a valid, sound training program should be inaugurated."[40]

Court Order: Maximizing Autonomy of the Ward

1. The court should find that no less restrictive alternative exists before the appointment of a guardian.

The constitutional doctrine of the less restrictive alternative provides that an otherwise legitimate and substantial governmental purpose cannot be implemented through means that broadly stifle personal civil liberties "when the end can be more narrowly achieved. The breadth of legislative abridgment must be viewed in the light of less drastic means for achieving the same purpose."[41] Several model guardianship statutes imple-

---

37. Statement, *supra* note 2, at 33 quoting Recommendation to the ABA House of Delegates by the Young Lawyers Division through its Committee on the Delivery of Legal Services to the Elderly, Aug. 1983 (Commission on Legal Problems of the Elderly concurred).
38. *See* R. Butler, Why Survive? Being Old in America, pp. 6–11 (1975).
39. *Id.* at 12. *E.g.,* Harvey v. Meador, 459 So.2d 288, 292 (Miss. 1985) ("Advanced age will naturally bring about a decrease in physical prowess and mental efficiency.").
40. Hall & Mathiasen, *Overcoming Barriers to Protective Services for the Aged*, Report of a National Institute on Protective Services, p. 28 (1968).
41. Shelton v. Tucker, 364 U.S. 479, 488 (1960).

ment the doctrine.⁴² Inappropriate loss of autonomy can contribute to physical and mental illness and deterioration, and essentially become a self-fulfilling prophecy.⁴³

Less restrictive alternatives to guardianship include: "power of attorney; durable family power of attorney ('living wills'); appointment of an agent; single transaction court ratification of a particular action; joint tenancy; inter vivos transfers of property; deeds of guardianship; trusts; substitute or representative payee; protective services, and civil commitment [citations omitted]."⁴⁴ A recent study found that money management and transitional decisions are among the most frequent reasons for guardianship referral.⁴⁵

2. *A scheme for limited guardianship and limited conservatorship should be provided, preferably by statute. Courts should always consider and utilize limited guardianships, as an adjunct of the application of the least restrictive alternative principle, either under existing statutory authority or under the court's inherent powers.*

Guardianship in practice is usually an all-or-nothing legal mechanism; either a person is incompetent meriting a plenary guardianship, or the person is competent.⁴⁶ This all-or-nothing approach does not correlate to the functional capacities of individual human beings. Limited guardianship is a product of applying the lease restrictive alternative principle, but also it reflects appropriate tailoring of the legal mechanism to individual human needs.

A risk to limited guardianship is that judges may become less reluctant to impose a limited guardianship than a plenary guardianship, thus poten-

---

42. *See* Uniform Probate Code section 5-306; Developmental Disabilities Guardianship, *supra* note 36, at 98; Mentally Disabled Guardianship, *supra* note 31, at 454; J. Regan & C. Springer, Protective Services for the Elderly, p. 83, working paper prepared for the Special Committee on Aging, U.S. Senate (1977).

43. Statement, *supra* note 2, at 41.

44. Schmidt, *supra* note 32, at 353–54.

45. R. Steinberg, Alternative Approaches to Conservatorship and Protection of Older Adults Referred to Public Guardian, Institute for Policy and Program Development, Ethel Percy Andrus Gerontology Center (1985).

46. *See* M. Axilbund, Substituted Judgment for the Disabled: Report of an Inquiry into Limited Guardianship, Public Guardianship and Adult Protective Services in Six States (1979); Legal Services for the Elderly, *supra* note 7, at 4–5, 18; W. Schmidt, K. Miller, W. Bell & E. New, Public Guardianship and the Elderly 91, 172 (Ballinger 1981); Peters, Schmidt & Miller, *supra* note 10, at 536 (limited guardianship used only once in five years in Leon County, Florida, despite appearances of capacities in at least several other cases).

Cf. Fla. Stat. 744.303 (1983).

tially increasing the number of inappropriate guardianships in the continued absence of adequate procedural protection.[47]

Supervising the Effectiveness of Guardianship Services: Submission and Review of Guardian Reports

Guardians should be required to make a periodic report as to the ward's present condition and the continuing need for a guardian, either limited or plenary. Courts should review such reports and take appropriate action with regard thereto. A system of calendaring such reports should be established to ensure prompt filing, with sanctions provided for failure to comply.

Available evaluations concerning submission and review of annual guardian reports suggest that Florida practice has been poor. Of the 200 random cases reviewed for the 1982 Dade County Grand Jury, "87% were not up to date in annual reports concerning the ward's personal status, 75% of the cases were not timely in financial reports, and 91% of the cases were incomplete in physical examination reports."[48] In Leon County for 1977 to 1982, "[f]inancial reviews of established guardianships... were almost nonexistent."[49] A 1985 Connecticut report identified the same problem and contrasted the successful practice of the District of Columbia and a number of other states.[50]

The Dade County Grand Jury concluded:

> The seriousness of the substantial shortfall in annual reports cannot be overemphasized. Most guardians either do not know about their report responsibilities, or they are not fulfilling their report responsibilities. Most attorneys for guardians either do not know about the report responsibilities of their guardian clients, or they are not effectively communicating those responsibilities to their clients. The clerk's office has either been unable to inform or remind guardians of their report responsibilities, or has not effectively recognized the significance of such reports sufficiently to remedy the problem.[51]

---

47. *See* S. Brakel, J. Parry & B. Weiner, *supra* note 8, at 535.
48. Schmidt, *supra* note 32, at 356.
49. Peters, Schmidt & Miller, *supra* note 10, at 536.
50. Connecticut Probate Administration, Report on Guardianship Accounting, p. 12 (1985) (unpublished).
51. Final Report of the Grand Jury, *supra* note 31, at 32.

Supervision of Guardianship Services: Training of Guardians

The court should encourage orientation, training and ongoing technical assistance for guardians, including an outline of a guardian's duties and information concerning the availability of community resources, including the aging network, and information about the aging process.

While some Florida guardianship practice has been poor, guardian training efforts underway in Florida are setting a strong pace for the rest of the country. At the urging of a circuit judge, the Guardian Association in Pinellas County was established to provide educational programs, exchange ideas and programs, assist in the development of needed services, produce a handbook for guardians and publish a regular bulletin.[52] Following the grand jury report, Dade County probate judges and the Dade County Young Lawyers Section produced a fifteen-minute training videotape for guardians that all perspective guardians must view before letters of guardianship are issued.[53] Public guardians receive frequent calls from private guardians who seek information, guidance and advice.[54]

Ensuring the Effectiveness of Guardianship Services: Use of Guardianship Agencies

When there is no suitable person to act as guardian, the court may utilize any public, private or volunteer office or agency to so act. Such guardians should be expected to observe the same standards of performance required of private guardians, and should not be an employee of the court.[55]

---

52. W. Schmidt, K. Miller, W. Bell & E. New, *supra* note 46, at 155.
53. Statement, *supra* note 2, at 54.
54. *Id.* at 53. *See* W. Schmidt, K. Miller, W. Bell & E. New, *supra* note 46.
55. An alternative view, adopted by a minority of the conference, was that this section should read as follows: "When there is not a suitable person to act as guardian, the court may utilize any public, private or volunteer office or agency to so act. Such guardians should be expected to observe the same standards of performance required of private guardians, and should operate independently of the court and other social service agencies."

This view is consistent with the findings and recommendations of the principal national study of public guardianship funded by the U.S. Administration on Aging. W. Schmidt, K. Miller, W. Bell & E. New, *supra* note 46, at 183, 193. *See* S. Brakel, J. Parry & B. Weiner, *supra* note 8, at 390.

As of 1983, there were at least 11,147 specifically identifiable persons reportedly in need of a guardian in Florida.[56] This did not include persons in need who were private clients of nursing homes and adult congregate living facilities or chronic mental patients not receiving health or social services at the time of the survey.

The 1986 Florida Legislature in F.S. section 744.305 established a public guardian program, but only appropriated enough money for pilot projects. Florida authorizes the eligibility of nonprofit corporations to serve as guardians, and some do, albeit with mixed results.

The empirical need for a supply of guardians for legal and functional incompetents who do not have willing and responsible family members or friends to serve as guardian, or resourees to compensate a professional private guardian, is clear. Yet public guardianship nationally has been associated with inappropriate institutionalization of wards, failure to obtain public benefits for public wards, inappropriate and overutilization of public guardianship as a social service, and provision of conflicting ease management and guardianship services.[57]

To be successful:

> The public guardian must be independent of any service providing agency (no conflict of interest), and the public guardian must not be responsible for both serving as guardian, and petitioning for adjudication of incompetence (no self-aggrandizement). The public guardian must be adequately staffed and funded to the extent that no office is responsible for no more than 500 wards, and each professional in the office is responsible for no more than 30 wards. A public guardian is also only as good as the guardianship statute governing adjudication or incompetence and appointment. Failure in any or these considerations will tip the benefit/burden ratio against the individual ward, and the ward would be better off with no guardian at all. [citations omitted][58]

Conclusion

The purpose of this chapter was to report the recommended judicial practices in guardianship proceedings adopted by the National Conference of the Judiciary on Guardianship Proceedings for the Elderly and to summarize judicial practices in Florida and other states. The intention of

---

56. Schmidt, *supra* note 32, at 358; Schmidt & Peters, *Legal Incompetents' Need for Guardians in Florida*, 15 Bull. Am. Acad. of Psychiatry & L. 69 (1987).

57. Statement, *supra* note 2, at 56–59 citing cases and secondary sources.

58. Schmidt, *Guardianship of the Elderly in Florida: Social Bankruptcy and the Need for Reform*, 55 Fla. B. J. 189, 193 (1981).

the chapter is to stimulate similar state efforts, changes in statute and court rules, coordination between the judiciary and the aging network, and testing of the recommended practices in individual courtrooms.

Part V

The Functioning of Guardian Programs and Services: What Happens to People After the Court of Last Resort

Chapter 10

The Evolution of a Public Guardianship Program

Winsor C. Schmidt, Jr.

Abstract. The available literature on guardianship suggests that this legal device has a poor benefit/burden ratio for individual wards, yet there are 11,147 persons allegedly in need of a guardian in Florida. Florida has begun to test a public guardianship response to this need. Florida's comparison of volunteer and professional models of public guardianship suggests that volunteers are no panacea to guardianship problems. Public guardianship programs risk the self-aggrandizing position of both petitioning for adjudication of incompetency and serving as guardian, the conflict-of-interest position of being part of a social service agency, inadequate staffing and funding, and vague guardianship criteria and lax procedures.

A significant jurisprudential theme is personhood and the extent to which law recognizes personal autonomy.[1] A contemporary arena for determining whether an individual is legally autonomous is guardianship. Guardianship is arguably the key to a series of issues ranging from the right to die[2] to civil commitment[3] and the right to refuse psychiatric treatment.[4] This chapter will trace the development of a programmatic response to the need for guardianship in the public sector.

---

1. *See generally*, J. Craven, *Personhood: The Right to be Let Alone*, 1976 Duke L. J. 699.

2. *See, e.g.*, Superintendent of Belchertown State School v. Saikewicz, 370 N.E.2d 417 (Mass. 1977); N. Cantor, *A Patient's Decision to Decline Life-Saving Medical Treatment: Bodily Integrity Versus the Preservation of Life*, 26 Rutgers L. Rev. 228 (1973).

3. *See, e.g.*, Mental Health Law Project, *Legal Issues in State Mental Health Care: Proposals for Change—Civil Commitment*, 2 Mental Disability L. Rep. 73, 90 (1977) ("incompetency may be a constitutionally required threshold criterion for [parens patriae] commitments").

4. *See, e.g.*, Rogers v. Comm't of Dep't of Mental Health, 390 Mass. 489 (1983); Guardianship of Roe, 421 N.E.2d 40 (Mass. 1981).

Grand Jury Investigation

Additional empirical information concerning deficiencies in guardianship is available as a result of a grand jury investigation in Miami, Florida.[5] The Dade County Grand Jury for the 1982 spring term supervised a review of 200 random guardianship cases opened between 1979 and 1981, and the interviewing of key personnel in the guardianship process.

The grand jury found that the alleged incompetent was present at the competency hearing in only one of four cases.[6]

> Eighty-five percent of the wards in our study were over the age of sixty and fifty-eight percent were over seventy-five years of age. Six of every ten were women. In seven of every ten cases the guardian appointed was a relative of the ward and in two of the cases a non-relative. In the remaining ten percent of cases the guardian was a bank or a lawyer. In 46% of the cases the assets of the ward (control of which, of course, is vested in the guardian) were in excess of $50,000. In 39% of the cases the assets were below $50,000 and 15% of the wards [were] insolvent.
>
> These statistics clearly suggest the basis for concern: elderly persons being divested of control of their assets by a process in which they cannot, or do not, participate, with control of their assets being given to another individual who will, hopefully, act in the ward's interest and not in their own.
>
> The concerns are not without merit....[7]

The grand jury cited one case of a 92-year-old woman "living in squalor" in an adult congregate living facility owned by her legal guardian.[8] Not only did this violate Florida law, but she had a bank account of $150,000 at the time. This situation was unnoticed for two years until uncovered by a Nursing Home Ombudsman Committee member.

In another case, the ward's lawyer was also appointed as guardian, and then submitted "identical billings for the same functions in the amount of $77,000."[9] One billing item was $1,018 for three hours spent purchasing a $200 clock. These irregularities went undiscovered for two years.

The grand jury found that for several years the same two physicians were appointed to the examining committee in all guardianship cases, and that the lay person on the committee was always one of three individu-

---

5. Final Report of the Grand Jury, Dade county, Fla. 26–36 (Nov. 9, 1982). Florida allows civil grand jury investigations and reports on public matters and public officials. *Id.* at 4. [*See, e.g.*, chapter 1, *supra*, for background information.]
6. *Id.* at 28–29.
7. *Id.* at 29.
8. *Id.*
9. *Id.* at 30.

als who rotated their assignment every four months.[10] Florida law provided: "The judge shall appoint an examining committee consisting of one responsible citizen and two practicing physicians who shall not be associated with each other in the practice of medicine. The citizen appointed shall not be associated with, or employed by, either physician."[11] The grand jury noted that "each examination generates a fee of $185 ($75 for each of the two physicians and $35 for the lay member) and approximately forty to fifty examinations occur each month."[12] The grand jury concluded that the need existed to broaden the composition of the committee, including lay advocates for the elderly and developmentally disabled, and non-psychiatrist physicians. The jury also suggested that the criteria by which each committee member reached a diagnosis should be more precise and "that a standardized test be selected for this purpose."[13]

Another grand jury finding related to the filing of annual reports, "the only automatic mechanisms and source of information for review and monitoring of [personal and financial status in] ongoing guardianships."[14] The grand jury found that the "great majority of guardianship files for at least the past four years" were incomplete in annual reports.[15] The total number of open guardianships was unknown. Of the 200 random cases, 87% were not up to date in annual reports concerning the ward's personal status, 75% of the cases were not timely in financial reports, and 91% of the cases were incomplete in physical examination reports. Competency was restored in only four of the 200 cases.[16] The grand jury concluded:

> The seriousness of the substantial shortfall in annual reports cannot be overemphasized. Most guardians either do not know about their report responsibilities, or they are not fulfilling their report responsibilities. Most attorneys for guardians either do not know about the report responsibilities of their guardian clients, or they are not effectively communicating those responsibilities to their clients. The clerk's office has either been unable to inform or remind guardians of their report responsibilities, or has not effectively recognized the significance of such reports sufficiently to remedy the problem.[17]

---

10. *Id.*
11. Fla. Stat. section 744.331(5)(a) (1981).
12. Final Report of the Grand Jury, *supra* note 5, at 30–31.
13. *Id.* at 31.
14. *Id.*
15. *Id.*
16. *Id.* at 30.
17. *Id.* at 32.

In response to the grand jury, the timetable for computerization of the probate division was "dramatically changed" from several years in the future to the following year.[18] The grand jury observed:

> Computerization will also permit a cross-indexing of guardians and wards which will enable one to determine how many wards a given guardian has. In the past allegations that unfit or unscrupulous guardians were assigned to numerous wards have not been susceptible to investigation due to the total absence of any system of cross-indexing.[19]

The last principal finding of the grand jury related to "the dearth of guardians for incompetents who have no willing and responsible family members or friends to serve as guardian, or insufficient resources to compensate a guardian."[20] The grand jury recommended increased staffing of the corporate nonprofit Dade County Guardianship Program, the funding of a pilot public guardianship project for Miami from the state-funded pilot public guardianship program in the Office of the State Courts Administrator, and state authorization and funding of public guardianship.

The Supply of Guardians

Public guardianship is an aspect of the area of guardianship most in need of reform—the supply of guardians.[21] An incompetent with a sizable estate, or with willing and responsible family members or friends, has little difficulty in having someone serve as guardian. A proposed ward without such resources, however, has a very different situation.

In April 1983, an assessment of the need for guardians was completed in Florida. A telephone survey of the seventy-four public receiving facilities, community mental health centers and clinics, thirty private receiving facilities, eleven Aging and Adult Services district offices, and six state mental institutions was performed. Informants reported 2,842 persons

---

18. *Id.*
19. *Id.* at 33.
20. *Id.* at 28. The grand jury also made lesser recommendations that an accountant do a sample audit of property management in guardianship cases, and recommend whether a general audit should occur; that a gerontologist, habilitation specialist, "or other appropriate specialist" do an analogous person management audit; that the legal community address the issue of appropriate legal representation of alleged incompetents; that the "vague" and unreliable statutory definition for incompetence be addressed; that partial or limited guardianship be instituted; and that attorneys for potential incompetents advise their clients about alternatives to guardianship. *Id.* at 34–35.
21. *See generally* W. Schmidt, K. Miller, W. Bell & E. New, Public Guardianship and the Elderly (1982) (hereinafter Public Guardianship).

who are legally incompetent from past civil commitment, but without a guardian, and 6,054 persons whom social workers claim are functionally incompetent and need a guardian, but are not adjudicated because there is no one to serve as guardian. There are also 2,251 Developmental Services clients who reportedly would be eligible for guardianship services, if they were available.

The total of 11,147 persons in need of a guardian in Florida does not include the number of private clients in nursing homes and adult congregate living facilities who may need guardians, or the extent of need among some chronic mental patients who are not currently receiving services. The total does include 421 people in state mental hospitals who could reportedly be discharged to community facilities if provided a guardian.

In response to the need, it was suggested that the Department of Health and Rehabilitative Services make greater efforts to restore inappropriate incompetencies, that greater use be made of alternative legal devices to guardianship, and that research concerning overprediction and overassessment of incompetence take place.

The consequences of guardianship may be serious, but the effect of legal incompetence without a guardian, or of functional incapacity without guardianship assistance, is total lack of protection. In thirty-four other states, there is some statutory provision for public guardianship to address the need for guardians.

Florida's Approaches

Florida has had several approaches to the need for guardians that is met in other states by public guardianship. These approaches include: benign neglect; informal guardianship by neighbors, nursing homes, and the like without legal process or authority; civil commitment to a mental institution ("poor man's guardianship"); private attorneys on a pro bono or nominal fee basis (sometimes with dozens of wards each); banks of trust companies (for modest estates);[22] nonprofit corporations,[23] usually with a religious affiliation; county social service programs utilizing volunteers; citizen groups serving as guardian banks;[24] and a newly appropriated (1982) Public Guardianship Pilot Project in the Office of the State Courts Administrator.

---

22. In other parts of the country, some banks will profitably service small estates that are grouped together. Another idea is such service as a required public contribution.
23. *See* Fla. Stat. section 744.305 (1979).
24. *See* Public Guardianship, *supra* note 9, at 149–56.

Florida's Public Guardianship Pilot Program began with a 1982 appropriation of $160,000 by the legislature to the Office of the State Courts Administrator. Public guardianship programs in other states can be classified into four models: a conflict-of-interest state social service agency model; an independent county agency model; an independent state office model; and a court model.[25] Florida rejected the conflict-of-interest social service agency model for obvious reasons. The independent state office model was rejected because Florida is geographically too large for guardianship services to be delivered from Tallahassee to, for example, Miami. The independent county agency model was rejected because the counties did not want another state-mandated program that they would have to fund.

The court model is working unexpectedly well so far.[26] There was some hesitation about having a court both adjudicate incompetence and provide guardianship service, but the rather accidental Florida remedy of housing the program in the Supreme Court's Office of the State Courts Administrator has insulated public guardians from local judicial pressure and from individual justices, while providing the hierarchical aegis of the Florida Supreme Court.

The original plan for the Florida Pilot Program called for experimentation with contracted professional and volunteer models, respectively, as well as an in-house demonstration professional model in Tallahassee. The in-house demonstration fell to interim budget cutbacks.

Following a request for proposal process, the Office of the State Courts Administrator contracted with the Guardianship Program of Dade County in Miami to provide services with paid staff, and with Lutheran Ministries of Florida, Suncoast Area Public Guardianship Project in St. Petersburg, to provide services with volunteers. Data were gathered from each program through administration of periodic individual client assessment forms, guardianship plans, and guardian activity reports. The pilot projects were prohibited from both petitioning for adjudication and serving as guardian; they could not do any recruitment on specific outreach. They were also limited to a specific client/staff ratio (20/1).

Start-up problems with the projects included a lack of accurate reporting, a lack of conformity of guardianship plans to the deficits identified in the individual assessments, and that guardian activities focused less on medical treatment than on paper work (including program evaluation requirements), financial matters, improving the ward's living condition, and obtaining services/social support.

---

25. *Id.*
26. *See* Office of the State Courts Administrator, Final Report of the Public Guardianship Pilot Program (1984).

The initial overall client functioning was assessed as severely impaired. Most clients were elderly, white females. Initial recommendations included establishing comparison groups to determine the benefits of guardianship, obtaining psychological assistance in monitoring reports and client activities, and encouraging the pilot projects to review each other's activities.

Comparison of Professional and Volunteer Models

After 9 ½ months of guardianship service delivery and data gathering, differences between the professional model of public guardianship in Dade County and the Suncoast volunteer model in St. Petersburg began to emerge.

Despite intake and processing through a common guardianship statutory scheme, the two groups of wards were not homogeneous. The twenty-one Dade wards were younger, ranging from twenty to eighty-eight, with an average age of fifty-two. The twenty-nine Suncoast wards ranged from forty-four to ninety-seven, with an average age of seventy-seven, and a median of eighty-two. The Dade group was more acutely disturbed, but the Suncoast group was more functionally and chronically disabled.

An effort was undertaken to compare the Dade wards with a control group of sixty-two Jacksonville protective services clients who could have been adjudicated incompetent, but for the provision of protective services. The Suncoast wards were compared to a group of 200 Community Care for the Elderly (CCE) clients who also were at risk of being adjudicated incompetent, but for the provision of state community care services. There was enough similarity between the Dade and Jacksonville groups in intellectual functioning and behavior to recommend further investigation into the diversionary attributes of protective services for alleged incompetents who are capable of making choices. There was also reasonable comparability between the Suncoast and CCE groups. However, the overall effort demonstrated the difficulty and ambiguity in attempting to find comparable controls.[27]

The evaluation next measured the changes in functioning level at the time of adjudication, and at the end of the service period. The data suggested that the status of both groups of wards at the final assessment

---

27. [*But cf.* Wilber, *Alternatives to Conservatorship: The Role of Daily Money Management Services*, 31 Gerontologist 150 (1991) (quasi-experimental design used to show no significant difference in rates of conservatorship between those offered daily money management service and those not; daily money management doesn't seem to divert from conservatorship).]

was equal to, or somewhat better than, the status at the outset of guardianship, but there was little evidence to suggest that guardianship is a panacea, or a mechanism for rehabilitation. There appeared to be no clearly measurable advantage to being a ward of the professional model, or a ward of the volunteer model.

Another data source was individual guardianship plans, adapted from treatment and habilitation plans for mental illness and mental retardation. The plans seemed to have considerable potential for planning, management, and monitoring of ward care, but the volunteer guardians found them a considerable inconvenience, and the professional guardians were unable to exploit their potential. There was some likelihood that guardianship practice had not advanced to a stage of experience and professionalism where such devices could be productive.

The third data source was guardian activity reports, adapted from attorneys' timekeeping logs, or work chronology records. The Dade program devoted 5.6 hours to each ward per month; the Suncoast program devoted ten hours to each ward per month. Both programs devoted relatively more time to their wards' medical status, services and social support, and financial status than to participation in activities, self-care skills, nutritional status, and orientation and behavior problems. Otherwise, the differences between professional and volunteer models in nature of guardianship activities were minimal.

The most interesting information from the Florida comparison of professional and volunteer guardianship models concerns the viability of volunteers as guardians. Thirty-eight of forty-seven volunteers in the Suncoast program reported some activity on behalf of a project ward. The range of total reported work for 9 ½ months was from 184 hours to less than ½ hour. Only about one-third of the volunteers were active to any degree in the last month of the program. Volunteers accounted for only 22% of the total volunteer program work. Two-thirds of the volunteers' time involved ward medical status and social support, which essentially was visiting and taking the ward to the doctor.

The volunteer model did not seem viable without staff to recruit, train, monitor, and support the volunteers. This staff attention to the volunteers was at the opportunity cost of providing direct staff service to wards.

The actual average cost of guardianship service to one ward was $42.52 per hour, $238.09 per month, and $2,857.08 per year for the Dade professional model, and $17.25 per hour, $172.41 per month, and $2,068.92 per year for the Suncoast volunteer model. If the volunteer hours are cost-free, the cost of the Suncoast staff time was $22.81 per hour.

The evaluation could not prove empirically that wards of the professional model in the aggregate did significantly better than wards of the volunteer model. However, the Florida Office of the State Courts Administrator indicated that it would not renew the contract with the Suncoast program (Lutheran Ministries of Florida, Inc.) because of numerous individual questions concerning the quality of Suncoast's guardianship services.

Based on these experiences with public guardianship, the Florida Office of the State Courts Administrator has recommended that the legislature establish a Guardianship Oversight Commission similar to that recommended by the American Bar Association,[28] that funding for highest-priority public guardianship services be provided through the Commission in fiscal year 1984–85, that state funding for protective services and case management be increased to reduce the need for public guardianship, and that social service mechanisms be developed to ensure appropriate restoration of legal incompetents, assumption of guardianship by family or friends, and exhaustion of alternatives to guardianship.[29]

---

28. Developmental Disabilities State Legislative Project, Guardianship and Conservatorship: Statutory Survey, Model Statute 86–90 (1979). [*See* New, *A Proposal for a Guardianship Oversight Commission*, 59 Fla. B. J. 47 (Feb. 1985).]

29. Office of the State Courts Administrator, *supra* note 26.

Chapter 11

A Descriptive Analysis of Professional and Volunteer Programs for the Delivery of Public Guardianship Services[1]

Winsor C. Schmidt, Jr.
Kent S. Miller
Roger Peters
David Loewenstein

An Introduction to the Study[2]

The role of the state in relation to "deviants"—for example, the ill, developmentally disabled, and addicts—is the subject of continuing attention and controversy.[3] The inherent conflict is between a citizen's right to privacy, autonomy, and freedom on the one hand[4] and, on the other hand, the interests of the state in protecting society and providing services for

---

1. The authors gratefully acknowledge the assistance of Jose Gay and James Fishback, the cooperation of the Guardianship Program of Dade County, Inc., Miami and Lutheran Ministries of Florida-Suncoast Area, St. Petersburg, and funding by the Office of the Florida State Courts Administrator, Elaine New, public guardianship program director.

2. This study compares "professional" and "volunteer" models for delivering public guardianship services to older adults in Florida who do not have willing and responsible family members or friends to serve as guardians. Data are presented about the older adults' functional status during guardianship, the development and implementation of guardianship plans, the amount and nature of guardian work, the extent to which volunteers are a panacea for public guardianship, and the costs of professional and volunteer models. Questions are raised about the real purpose of incompetence, and the difference between guardianship and social casework.

3. *See* P. Conrad & J. Schneider, Deviance and Medicalization: From Badness to Sickness (1980); N. Kittrie, The Right to be Different: Deviance and Enforced Therapy (1971).

4. *See, e.g.*, N. Kittrie, *id.*

those in need.[5] Problems are limited when a citizen voluntarily seeks services, but there are major concerns when the power of the state is invoked to provide "care and treatment" against the wishes of the individual.[6] When is involuntary intervention appropriate? How do we limit paternalistic intervention and invasions of privacy without rationalizing the neglect of human needs, and how do we avoid the inappropriate use of human service agencies as a means of exercising control?

These problems are particularly acute with respect to the elderly. There is a widespread belief that a number of frail elderly are neglected, subject to abuse, and in need of protection.[7] One traditional mechanism for providing this protection is through the appointment of a guardian.

---

5. The interests of the state are grounded in the police power and *parens patriae*.

"While broad and extending to concern with the welfare of individuals (or their health, safety and morals—thus paralleling the *parens patriae* power), the essence of the police power is its authority to act in furtherance of the general welfare and public safety." S. Brakel, J. Parry & B. Weiner, The Mentally Disabled and the Law 24 (1985) (hereinafter S. Brakel). Police power action is controversial to the extent that (1) it constitutes preventive detention of indiscreetly defined populations; *see, e.g.*, Dash v. Mitchell, 356 F.Supp. 1292 (D.D.C. 1972); (2) subject populations are no more dangerous than the general population; (3) dangerous behavior cannot be accurately predicted, *see, e.g.*, J. Monahan, The Clinical Prediction of Violent Behavior (1981); (4) subject populations are too vaguely defined, *e.g.*, Papachristou v. City of Jacksonville, 405 U.S. 156 (1972) (vagrant persons); Fleuti v. Rosenberg, 302 F.2d 652 (9th Cir. 1962) (psychopathic personality); and (5) individuals are unconstitutionally punished for a status, condition, or illness, *e.g.*, Robinson v. California, 370 U.S. 660 (1962) (narcotics addiction).

The *parens patriae* authority is the alleged authority of the state to act as "the general guardian of all infants, idiots and lunatics." Hawaii v. Standard Oil Co., 405 U.S. 251, 257 (1972) (quoting 3 W. Blackstone, Commentaries, 47).

6. *See, e.g.*, N. Kittrie, *supra* note 3. Difficulties with the *parens patriae* authority are not only that its legal precedent seems to be a 17th century printer's error in the English common law, *see, e.g.*, Custer, *The Origins of the Doctrine of "Parens Patriae,"* 27 Emory L. J. 195 (1978), but also that it justifies dangerously excessive and abusive discretionary power in the legislatures, agencies, and courts which use it. *See, e.g.*, O'Connor v. Donaldson, 422 U.S. 563, 583–84 (1975) (Burger C.J., concurring, "The existence of some due process limitations on the *parens patriae* power does not justify the further conclusion that it may be exercised to confine a mentally ill person only if the purpose of the confinement is treatment"). See also, In re Gault, 387 U.S. 1, 16 (1966) (*parens patriae* is a rationalization with murky meaning and dubiously relevant historical credentials); W. Gaylin, I. Glasser, S. Marcus & D. Rothman, Doing Good: The Limits of Benevolence (1978); Curtis, *The Checkered Career of "Parens Patriae": The State as a Parent or Tyrant*, 25 DePaul L. Rev. 895, 895–96 (1976); Horstman, *Protective Services for the Elderly: The Limits of Parens Patriae*, 40 Mo. L. Rev. 215 (1975).

7. *See, e.g.*, Dalend, Kane, Satz & Pynoos, *Elder Abuse Reporting: Limitations of Statutes*, 24 Gerontologist 61 (1984); Faulkner, *Mandating the Reporting of Suspected Cases of Elder Abuse: An Inappropriate, Ineffective, and Ageist Response to the Abuse of Older Adults*, 16 Fam. L. Q. 69 (1982); Katz, *Elder Abuse*, 18 J. Fam. L. 695 (1979–80).

Until quite recently the use of guardianship received little attention with the exception of some concern over the proper management of estates and the business affairs of wards. Heightened interest in guardianship came about in part because of the rapid growth in the proportion of the population that is elderly, and possibly from a heightened sensitivity to the rights of a number of groups subject to state control. Within the last few years there have been several national studies of guardianship, establishment of large scale programs of public guardianship, and considerable legislative activity in many states.[8]

Many social service providers seem to have only limited concerns about the potential abuses of guardianship. They tend to see it as only one of a number of alternatives in providing care and protection for the elderly, that it should be relatively rare, non-adversarial, and reserved for individuals "at the end of the line."[9] The problem is perceived as one which should be managed by professionals and monitored by peers. Social service providers are likely to feel that the focus on individual rights has led to delay in treatment and protection. On the other hand, the critics of the use of guardianship see it as having the potential for doing harm,[10] and an "initiation rite for the entry of the poor and inept into the managed society,"[11] and applied for inappropriate reasons according to invalid standards.[12] These views are consistent with the questioning of the assumption that social interventions do more good than harm.[13] Other major concerns relate to the findings that guardianship is most frequently established for the interests of someone other than the ward,[14] and that proceedings involve significant due process deficiencies.[15]

---

8. *See, e.g.*, G. Alexander & T. Lewin, The Aged and the Need for Surrogate Management (1972) (hereinafter G. Alexander & T. Lewin); S. Brakel, *supra* note 5, at 369–433; W. Schmidt, K. Miller, W. Bell & E. New, Public Guardianship and the Elderly (1981) (hereinafter W. Schmidt). *See also*, Abstracts of the Spring Seminar, 8 Prob. L. J. 2 (1988).

9. *See, e.g.*, G. Hall & G. Mathiasen, eds., Overcoming Barriers to Protective Services for the Aged (1968); Hobbs, *Adult Protective Services: A New Program Approach*, Pub. Welfare 28 (Summer 1976).

10. *See, e.g.*, Address by E. Cohen, Protective Services and Public Guardianship: A Dissenting View, 31st Annual Meeting of the Gerontological Society in Dallas, Texas (Nov. 20, 1978) (hereinafter Cohen, Address to Gerontological Society).

11. Mitchell, *Involuntary Guardianship for Incompetents: A Strategy for Legal Services Advocates*, 12 Clearinghouse Rev. 451, 466 (1978).

12. *Id.*

13. *See, e.g.*, W. Gaylin, I. Glasser, S. Marcus & D. Rothman, Doing Good: The Limits of Benevolence (1978); Blenkner, Bloom & Nielsen, *A Research and Demonstration Project of Protective Services*, 52 Soc. Casework 483 (1971).

14. G. Alexander & T. Lewin, *supra* note 8, at 13.

15. *See, e.g.*, W. Schmidt, *supra* note 8.

Unfortunately, little information is available to aid in choosing between these conflicting perspectives, and very little information is available on what it is that guardians do. There is some information about guardianship at the system level—such as analysis of statutes, description of programs, and the like[16]—but there is little systematic information based on the study of wards or the activities of guardians. This study does not provide data directly relating to the broad questions raised above, but it is an attempt to provide some information about the functional status of wards, the provision and cost of guardianship services, and, more importantly, what it is that guardians do for their wards.

Previous Professional Literature

Guardianship is a legal mechanism involving "the authority of a guardian and the relation between guardian and ward."[17] A guardian manages the person and/or property of another—the "ward"—who is adjudicated incompetent and considered incapable of self-administration.[18] The law governing guardianship law emphasizes mental incapacity as an eligibility criterion for adjudication of incompetence, with the consequence that "anyone, especially an older person, who needs a guardian is popularly assumed to be mentally ill. The aged person with a few of the symptoms of chronic brain syndrome, such as forgetfulness, is more likely to be judged mentally ill and therefore to be declared incompetent."[19]

Guardianship results in an almost total deprivation of civil rights[20] and is considered a "highly restrictive method of providing supervision and assistance" by the President's Commission on Mental Health.[21] A ward "may be subject to greater control of his or her life than one convicted of a crime."[22] The Commission recommended that research in the area of guardianship receive a high priority.[23]

---

16. *See* Alexander & T. Lewin, *supra* note 8; S. Brakel, *supra* note 5; W. Schmidt, *supra* note 8.

17. *See, e.g.*, Schmidt, *Guardianship of the Elderly in Florida: Social Bankruptcy and the Need for Reform*, 55 Fla. B. J. 189, (1981).

18. *Id.*

19. Staff on Senate Special Comm. on Aging, 95th Cong., 1st Sess., Protective Services for the Elderly (Comm. Print 1977) (prepared by J. Regan and G. Springer).

20. *See* R. Brown, The Rights of Older Persons 286 (1979).

21. President's Commission on Mental Health, Mental Health in America: 1978, Vol. 1 at 43 (1978).

22. Estate of Roulet, 23 Cal. 3d 219, 228, 152 Cal. Rptr. 425, 430, 590 P. 2d 1, 6 (1979).

23. *See* President's Commission, *supra* note 21.

Professionals in law and social gerontology express growing concern about the expanded use of guardianship.[24] Proponents of guardianship reform suggest that numerous substantive and procedural issues require attention and militate against use of guardianship statutes.[25] In his seminal publication, *Adult Protective Services: An Appraisal and a Prospectus*, Regan observes, *inter alia*, that the standards for determining incompetency are too broad and widely applied, that the criteria should be behavioral rather than categorical (e.g., advanced age, mental illness or defect), that determination of incompetency should be situational rather than total, and that judges commonly disregard guardianship procedures.[26]

While commentators identify needs for substantive and procedural reform of guardianship law, there is relatively little quantitative research on what guardianship accomplishes. In New York, researchers Alexander and Lewin conducted an archival search of guardianship records and concluded that wards ended up worse in every case; guardianship primarily serves the interests of third persons and institutions.[27]

In carrying out a quasi-experimental design through Cleveland's Benjamin Rose Institute, Blenkner and associates found that the provision of enriched protective services, including guardianship, to the experimental group not only failed to prevent or slow deterioration or death, but the experimental group actually had a higher rate of institutionalization and death than did the control group who received referral agency services or no services.[28] A reanalysis confirmed the strong effect of experimental group membership on the tendency to be institutionalized.[29] Field research on public guardianship in six states by Schmidt and associates concluded that a high potential exists for public guardian conflict of interest, self-aggrandizement, understaffing and underfunding, and inadequate legal protection for the ward.[30]

The expectations and duties for guardians are statutorily specified, but the guidance is general and protection of the ward from the guardian is

---

24. *See, e.g.*, Mitchell, *supra* note 11, at 466; J. Regan, *Protecting the Elderly: The New Paternalism*, 32 Hastings L. J. 1111 (1981); J. Regan, *Adult Protective Services: An Appraisal and a Prospectus*, National Law and Social Work Seminar: Proceedings and Prospects 11–19 (1982) (hereinafter Regan, "An Appraisal"); Sherman, *Guardianship: Time for Reassessment*, 49 Fordham L. Rev. 350 (1980).

25. *See, e.g.*, Regan, "An Appraisal." *id.*; W. Schmidt, *supra* note 8, at 191.

26. *See*, Regan, "An Appraisal," *supra* note 24.

27. G. Alexander & T. Lewin, *supra* note 8, at 136.

28. M. Blenkner, M. Bloom, M. Nielsen & R. Weber, Final Report—Protective Services for Older People: Findings from the Benjamin Rose Institute Study, Cleveland (1974).

29. Berger & Pilavin, *The Effect of Casework: A Research Note*, 21 Soc. Work 205 (1976).

30. W. Schmidt, *supra* note 8.

limited.[31] Most jurisdictions require the filing of a surety bond to indemnify against financial mismanagement, and twenty-one states impose fiduciary duties.[32] Twenty-two states have a habilitation requirement encouraging guardians to use services that will maximize the ward's personal functioning.[33] Such services are stated to include mental health treatment, physical therapy, education, vocational training, and job placement assistance.[34] Most states allow the collection of a fee by the guardian from the estate for guardian services.[35]

The historical purpose of guardianship is care of another, but the professional literature suggests an alternative:

> Recognize guardianship for what it really is: the most intrusive, non-interest serving, impersonal legal device known and available to us and as such, one which minimizes personal autonomy and respect for the individual, has a high potential for doing harm and raises at best a questionable benefit/burden ratio. As such, it is a device to be studiously avoided.[36]

In this context, another opportunity arose to gather quantitative information about guardianship and guardians.

Description of the Project

In 1982, the Florida legislature appropriated money to establish and evaluate a public guardianship pilot program. Florida, unlike at least thirty-four other states, did not have a statutory provision for "public guardianship".[37] Public guardianship is the judicial appointment and responsibility of a public official in a state or local government agency or court to serve a legal incompetent—the "ward"—who does not have willing or responsible family members or friends to serve as guardians.[38]

This evaluation concerns two programs: Guardianship Program of Dade County, Inc., Miami (hereinafter Dade) and Lutheran Ministries of Florida—Suncoast Area, St. Petersburg (hereinafter Suncoast). The Dade program followed a "professional" model that employed paid staff

---

31. B. Sales, D. Powell & R. Van Duizend, Disabled Persons and the Law: State Legislative Issues 463 (1982) (a tremendous resource to a review of pertinent statutory enactments).
32. *Id.*
33. *Id.*
34. *Id.*
35. *Id.*
36. Cohen, Address to Gerontological Society, *supra* note 10.
37. W. Schmidt, *supra* note 8, at 143.
38. *See, e.g.*, W. Schmidt, *supra* note 17, at 192.

to provide guardian services. The Suncoast program recruited community volunteers to provide the services. Both programs were in existence prior to their contracts with the Office of the State Courts Administrator,[39] but beginning in February, 1983 and continuing through November, 1983, the programs identified and reported on specific wards who were served under the terms of the contracts. The principal subject of the evaluation is this group of wards.

The major purpose of the public guardianship pilot project was to demonstrate and evaluate alternative public guardian service delivery models. In addition to overall comparison of the two models, answers were sought to a number of more specific questions, such as the following:

1. What are the characteristics of the clients served?
2. What are the unmet needs of the wards?
3. What cost/benefits are involved in public guardianship?
4. To what extent are the needs of the wards addressed in guardian plans and activities?
5. To what extent does the provision of public guardians help or hinder incompetents?
6. What are the major activities carried out by guardians?

The target populations for the pilot project were patients in state mental hospitals who could be deinstitutionalized given the availability of a guardian, and deteriorating, oft-time elderly individuals in the community who were unable to meet their daily needs, unable to consent to services, and who might need institutionalization absent a guardian.

Data Sources and Relevant Information for the Study

Sources of Data

In addition to an intake form[40] for recording basic descriptive information and a series of questions regarding financial matters, there were four major sources of data.

1. The Client Assessment Form (CAF). This assessment form, developed and utilized by the Florida Department of Health and Rehabilita-

---

39. Florida law allows non-profit corporations to act as legal guardians. *See* Fla. Stat. Ann. section 744.305 (West 1986).
40. Intake forms record such descriptive information as name, address, telephone number.

tive Services, was used to assess client functioning in the following areas: (1) living situation: (2) activities; (3) functional status (daily skills); (4) nutrition status; (5) medical status; (6) intellectual functioning and behavior; (7) services and social support. The CAF was administered for each client at the time of appointment of the guardian, whenever a major event occurred in the life of the client,[41] and during the final few weeks of the project.

The CAFs provided information about the number and types of wards served, a baseline from which to measure change in the status of the client, data for comparison of the two programs, and a basis for formulating guardianship plans.

2. *The Guardianship Plan.* A guardianship plan, developed for each client for each of the areas noted in the CAF, including the following:

1. A statement of the specific needs of the ward (in particular functioning areas).
2. A statement of the optimal (least restrictive) conditions to meet those needs, and to achieve at least the standard of living enjoyed by the ward prior to incompetency and guardian appoint-ment.
3. A statement of the available services that will be obtained to meet those needs, both within six months, and longer term.
4. A statement of the rationale for provision of any non-optimal service.
5. A notation of the guardian or staff responsible for obtaining or providing the service.
6. A statement of the minimum conditions, for each need in each functioning area, under which the public guardian might be received.

The plans provided information useful in assuring that each need of the ward was addressed, in comparing the planning for each ward program, and in providing a base for determining the extent to which each program's activities was relevant to the needs of each ward.

3. *The Guardian Activity Report.* The third source of data for this evaluation was the guardian activity report. The guardian activity report is similar to an attorney's timekeeping log, or a work chronology record.[42] On each guardian activity report was recorded the name of the worker, the date, the time the activity began, the activity (accomplishment, out-

---

41. Major events included such changes as transfer from home to nursing home, or nursing home to hospital.
42. *See* H. Mintzberg, The Nature of Managerial Work 21–22 (1973).

come), the code for the activity,[43] the duration of the activity,[44] and the name of the client for whom the activity was performed. Guardian activity reports were completed daily and copies furnished to the Office of the State Courts Administrator. The guardian activity reports indicated the quantity and relevance of the work performed for the wards.

4. *Additional Reports and Documents*. A fourth source of data consisted of miscellaneous reports filed by the programs, records kept by the Office of the State Courts Administrator, and observations by the researchers from site visits to each of the programs.

The data are subject to an unknown degree of bias.[45] Several steps were taken, however, to maximize the validity and reliability of the reports. Staff from the Office of the State Courts Administrator ("the contractor") provided training to the workers in the use of the forms, and monitored the weekly reports for inconsistencies. Site visits by the contractor and the evaluators involved face-to-face contacts with staff, volunteers and wards. Finally, note that most of the significant information was descriptive in nature and called for relatively little subjective judgment.

Characteristics of Wards

The original plan was to compare the Dade and Suncoast programs on a number of dimensions.[46] Such comparisons would be most useful if the wards of the programs were reasonably similar in terms of basic descriptive characteristics. Selective factors were operating in Dade, however, so that relative to Suncoast their twenty-one wards were younger (average age fifty-two, median age forty-eight), more acutely disturbed (half were diagnosed as psychotic), and more likely to be in a psychiatric hospital (29%) or general medical hospital (24%).

The fifty-two Suncoast wards had an average age of seventy-seven and a median age of eighty-two. Almost four-fifths were female (compared with two-thirds in Dade), and all but two wards were white (contrasted with 74% in Dade). Forty-two percent were living in nursing homes and 22% in hospitals. As would be expected with the older Suncoast wards, there was a high degree of dependence upon others for assistance

---

43. One of the eight functioning areas listed above, plus a "general indirect services" category, a category for general activities in the support of the program, and for the Suncoast, a category to cover activities directly related to supporting the volunteers.

44. In tenths of hours, or six minute intervals.

45. Stating perhaps that this is broadly recognized in social service evaluation.

46. For example, client functioning and changes over time in living situation, activities, daily living skills, nutrition status, medical status, intellectual functioning and behavior, services and social support.

in daily functioning. The principal difference in the characteristics of the guardians for the older, less disturbed Suncoast wards and the guardians for the younger, more psychiatrically disturbed Dade wards was that the former were generally older volunteers, while the latter were generally younger, paid social service workers. No systematic data were collected on the characteristics of the guardians.

The overall differences with respect to basic characteristics would lead to an expectation of differing needs and services. In fact, there were a number of similarities across the programs. At least for these two guardianship programs, there is no question that wards were highly limited in what they could do for themselves, were generally confused, and were in need of supervision. They led passive and isolated lives limited for the most part to eating, sleeping, and watching television. As a group, their financial situation was marginal, with Social Security and other public benefit programs being almost the sole source of income.

Role of the Family

A frequently expressed reservation about establishing public guardianship programs is that such programs may result in giving to the government responsibilities that best remain with the family.[47] Some limited data spoke to the availability of family members and thus familial support.

A significant number of project wards had no family (30% in Dade, 39% in Suncoast). Where a record of some family existed, it indicated that to an unknown degree they were scattered across the country, or their location was unknown, or they were frail, elderly, and/or otherwise incapable of assuming the responsibilities of guardianship.

Family members were present for a minority of the wards. For example, in Dade, the petitioner for incompetence in five of the twenty-one cases was a relative. At the initiation of the guardianship, 10% of the Dade group and 30% of the Suncoast group (nine out of thirty wards for whom the information was available) were living with relatives. The Dade program reported that when intentions were announced to establish public guardianships for fifteen prospective dischargees at South Florida State Hospital, relatives came forward to assume that responsibility in some instances.

Limited data reveal that many wards have no appropriate family available to serve as guardians, but at the same time, affirm the appropriate-

---

47. *See, e.g.,* W. Schmidt, *supra* note 8, at 71–72, 150, 173–174; *cf.,* Leaf, *Patients Released After "Wyatt:" Where Did They Go?*, 28 Hosp. & Community Psychiatry 366 (1977) (families accepted mental patients at home when they did not have the alternative disposition of a state mental hospital).

ness of a policy that guardianship programs aggressively seek family members as guardians before assuming that role.

Changes in Functioning Level Between the First and Last Assessments

Basic questions relate to the changes that occur in the wards and their situations between the time of appointment of the guardian and the final assessment: Does their environment change for better or worse? Does their level of functioning change in identifiable ways?

Any attempts to answer these questions are based on two different, but related, measures. One measure consists of composite scores developed from the precoded items for each of the seven categories of the CAF. The second measure is the summary rating made by the interviewer, based on the objective precoded items, interview observations, and subjective feelings. The latter is probably of lesser significance because only a limited number of interviewers were involved, and regardless of attempts to be objective in the assessments, the raters are directly involved in the programs. Thus, aware of the purposes of assessments, to an unknown extent, the raters operated with an understandable bias.

Table 1 contains the Average Change Scores for the Dade and Suncoast groups. For the most part, there was very little change in the Average

Table 1. Average Change Scores Changes in CAF Ratings Between First and Last Assessments*

	Possible Range of Scores	Dade Amount of Change	% Change	Suncoast Amount of Change	% Change
Living Situation	0–25+	–.3	–2	.5	2.5
Activities	0–45+	5.0	11	–3.6	–10
Functional Status	0–45+	2.8	8.5	–1.8	–5
Nutritional Status	0–42+	9.3	41	8	2.5
Medical Status	0–79+	2.5	4.5	–1.7	3
Intellectual Functioning and Behavior	0–79+	3.6	9	.9	2.5
Social Supports	0–10+	.4	10	0	0

*Scale size varies for each of the areas.

Table 2. Average Change Scores Changes in Summary Ratings Between First and Last Assessments*

	Dade		Suncoast	
	Amount of Change	% Change	Amount of Change	% Change
Living Situation	−.1	− 4	1.3	44
Activities	1.3	29	4	13
Functional Status	.3	8	.3	9
Nutritional Status	7	3	8	27
Medical Status	.4	12	.6	19
Intellectual Functioning and Behavior	.8	23	.2	6
Social Supports	.8	22	.9	27

*Based on a five point scale, with positive numbers reflecting an improvement in functioning and negative numbers reflecting a loss. The percent of change is based on the amount of change between the first and last assessments divided by the original scores.

Change Scores for the Dade and Suncoast groups. The possible range of scores varies with each of the seven areas, but the limits are relatively large and the amount of recorded change is quite small. Only two areas, both in Dade, are worth noting. Activities and nutrition appear to have improved somewhat.[48]

The summary ratings contained in Table 2 reflect a more positive picture. For Dade, the most significant shift is for activities. The Suncoast rater saw dramatic change in living situation, nutritional status, social supports, and medical status.

Minimally, these data suggest that the status of the clients at the time of the final assessment is equal to or better than it was at the outset of guardianship. Note that consistently negative changes in specific areas of client functioning, e.g., deterioration, might be expected regardless of intervention efforts due to the large number of elderly with severe health problems.

---

48. Statistical tests were not used to assess the significance of the change scores because population data were used. Statistical tests are not appropriate for non-probability samples. *See, e.g.*, F. Kohout, Statistics for Social Scientists: A Coordinated Learning System (1974); Bakan, *The Test of*
 Significance in Psychological Research, 66 Psychological Bull. 423 (1966). The actual change determines substantive importance.

Guardianship Plans

Guardianship plans are similar to the habilitation and treatment plans used to establish goals and methods of treatment on behalf of developmentally disabled, psychiatric, and other clients for which state services are provided. The guardianship plan is intended to serve as a bridge between identified client needs or deficits and specific services necessary to remedy these deficits. The plan may function to alert or reacquaint staff to client needs, and to facilitate long-term planning and coordination of staff and other resources to meet these needs. Federal court decisions have required treatment and habilitation plans as minimum constitutional requirements for adequate treatment of the mentally ill and developmentally disabled.[49]

Guardianship plans were completed for all wards in both the Dade and Suncoast groups during the first assessment period. Plans were completed, however, for only eight of twenty-one Dade wards, and eighteen of thirty-six Suncoast wards during the subsequent assessment period. The follow-up guardianship plans were not completed for twelve Dade wards and sixteen Suncoast wards due to their entry in programs after May, 1983. Because guardianship plans were to be submitted every six months, only a single (first) plan was obtained for each of these wards. Follow-up guardianship plans were missing for one Dade ward and for two Suncoast wards.[50] With information only from a single guardianship plan for the majority of wards, it is difficult to gauge the continuity of programming and treatment provided. Although a discussion of ongoing guardianship plan reporting is included in this study, analysis of guardianship plans will hereafter refer only to those plans completed simultaneous to initial ward assessments.

The greatest need identified for both groups[51] was in the area of living situation, as noted in Table 3. Activities and functional status were identified as needs in about 60% of all cases. The fewest needs were established in areas of nutrition (28% overall) and services and social supports (38% overall). The most frequently cited needs within the Dade group were in the area of activities and living situation.

Living situation was an especially conspicuous need for hospitalized wards, most of whom were in the Dade group. For fifteen of nineteen wards residing in medical and psychiatric hospitals, living situation needs were identified on guardianship plans. Functional and financial status

---

49. See, e.g., Wyatt v. Stickney, 325 F.Supp. 781 (M.D. Ala., 1971), 344 F.Supp. 373 (M.D. Ala. 1972), aff'd sub nom., Wyatt v. Aderholt, 503 F.2d 1305 (5th Cir. 1974).
50. See infra.
51. Identified in about 74% of all cases.

Table 3. Identifiable Needs:
Frequency of Guardianship Plan Needs Cited by Pilot Groups

	FIRST ASSESSMENT						
	Dade (N = 21)		Suncoast (N = 36)		Combined (N = 57)		
	Need Cited	No Need Cited	Need Cited	No Need Cited	Need Cited	% Cited	No Need Cited
Living Situation	13	8	29	7	47	(74%)	15
Activities	14	7	19	17	33	(58%)	24
Functional Status	11	10	25	11	36	(63%)	21
Nutritional Status	5	16	11	25	16	(28%)	41
Medical Status	8	13	21	13	29	(54%)	26
Intellectual functioning	12	9	15	18	27	(50%)	27
Services and Social Support	7	14	14	21	21	(38%)	35
Financial Status	10	11	16	16	26	(49%)	27
	80	88	150	128	230		216

were identified as needs in about half of all cases. Nearly ten to twelve wards residing in hospitals were found to be in need of services to remedy functional deficits.

Interestingly, only four of fifteen wards in medical or psychiatric hospitals were identified as needing help in locating additional services or social support. A variety of these services were provided by the hospital; it is likely that hospitalized wards were ineligible for a variety of services available to wards residing in the community. Equally likely, however, is that a number of hospitalized wards from both groups were eligible for release to community facilities within several years, and perhaps were more needy than most of services intended to ease the eventual transition from institution to community living. Despite probable shortages of services available for these marginally functioning wards, it appears unusual that guardians did not perceive the need for ascertaining additional services (e.g., meals on wheels, adult day care, recreation) that might be provided upon client transfer to the community.

Guardians in the Suncoast group were more likely to identify needs on guardianship plans, although about four needs per client, in eight need areas, were established for both groups. In the Suncoast group, most frequent needs appeared to be in the areas of living situation (80%), functional status (70%), and medical status (62%). Needs in areas of activities and financial status were cited for at least half of all Suncoast clients. The Suncoast group was comprised of an older clientele that appeared to have several unique needs. Eighteen of twenty-six clients over age eighty (in both groups) had needs designated on guardianship plans in the area of living situation. Sixteen of twenty-one clients in this age group were in need of specialized assistance in the area of activities, including twelve of nineteen nursing home clients.

As might be expected, fourteen of twenty-three extremely elderly[52] clients had guardianship plan needs designated in the area of medical assistance. Only nine of twenty-four extremely elderly clients, however, were targeted for assistance in the area of services and social support. Medical or physical disabilities may have rendered this group less mobile and ineligible for certain community services obtained outside the home or facility (e.g., psychiatric or psychological services), although one might expect that this group would then be eligible for a greater number of services featuring home visits. It is also unusual that guardians perceived this group in significantly greater need of assistance in the area of activities, but less in need of services and social support than younger wards.

Correlation Between Assessed Needs and Guardianship Plans

Note that scores or ratings on the CAF assessment instrument were not always equaled directly with client needs. For example, a ward's living situation could be free of physical defects (yielding a high score on the CAF), and yet be unsuitable because of expense or restrictive behavioral eligibility requirements that necessitated the ward moving to another facility. Conversely, some wards could be on a low calorie or restricted diet (yielding a low score on the CAF), yet not be in need of dietary or nutritional improvement. In most cases, however, composite scores and subjective ratings from the CAF appeared to be valid indices of client needs.

Correlation Between Guardianship Plans and Activities

The extent to which guardianship plans reflected the perceived needs of each ward, thus influencing guardians' performance of selected activ-

---

52. Extremely elderly is generally over age eighty.

ities on behalf of the ward, is unclear. We are able, however, to determine whether activities performed were consistent with needs designated on guardianship plans.

1. *The Dade Group.* Those clients who had guardianship plan needs designated in the area of living situation received slightly more assistance from guardians in this area, although all wards appeared to receive about ten hours of time. Very little time was spent by guardians in areas of activities and functional status, despite the fact that activity and functional status needs were identified in over 60% of all cases. Possibly the guardians' time in these areas was recorded mistakenly in other areas such as services and social support or living situation. More likely, however, Dade guardians were ill-equipped to meet client needs in these areas, and were more proficient at securing help for wards in areas of finances, living situation, services and social supports, and medical services.

For most wards, guardians did not appear to have assigned or secured other vendors or interested parties to remedy deficits in areas of activities or functional status. For Dade wards, needs in these areas requiring direct client contact appeared largely unmet. Provision of services intended to increase participation in activities and to enhance functional abilities could have required long-term staff intervention. Contact with Health and Rehabilitation Services (HRS), Department of Developmental Services and Aging and Adult Services could have proved beneficial for wards with needs in these particular areas. Similarly, in the area of nutritional status, guardianship plan needs were established for five wards, yet no activities were apparently performed on behalf of these clients to remedy nutritional deficits. Activities here may have been coded under the category of medical status.

Wards designated as having needs in the area of intellectual status were five times more likely to receive assistance from guardians. Only thirty-four activities, however, were performed on behalf of the twelve wards with intellectual status needs. Wards in the Dade group received equivalent activities from guardians in the area of services and social supports, regardless of whether guardianship plan needs were designated. In the areas of financial status, wards with designated needs received three times the number of activities (an average of eighteen activities per ward) compared to other wards.

2. *The Suncoast Group.* Suncoast wards with designated living situation needs on guardianship plans were provided about ten guardian activities in this area, or about twice as many as other wards. Wards with needs regarding activities and intellectual status were slightly more likely to receive assistance from guardians in these areas, although relatively few activities were performed. Overall only about three per ward had such

needs. Designation of functional, medical, or nutritional status, or services and social supports, on guardianship plans did not render wards more likely to receive related guardianship services. Wards with financial needs detailed on plans received an average of fifteen guardianship activities performed for them in this area, compared to only eleven activities for other wards.

Change in Guardianship Plan Needs

Although a six month guardianship plan was completed for only one-third of wards in the Dade group and one-half of wards in the Suncoast group, several observations may be made. Reporting of needs on guardianship plans appeared to be somewhat more consistent with the Dade group. In two-thirds of Dade cases reported, designation or non-designation of a particular need area is followed by similar designation/non-designation in subsequent guardianship plans.

For Suncoast plans, consistency in designation of needs was achieved in about half of the cases reported. It is unclear whether changing needs of the wards or erratic reporting procedures explain these results. In seven cases for the Suncoast group in which living situation was established as a need in the initial plan, living situation was not designated in the subsequent guardianship plan probably because more appropriate living arrangements were made on behalf of the ward, decreasing the need for further guardian activities in this area.

Two other need areas, services/social supports and financial status, established for Suncoast wards on the first plan were largely absent from subsequent plans. In areas of medical and intellectual status, the preponderance of ward needs were designated in the second guardianship plan, suggesting a degree of physical or intellectual deterioration in the generally older Suncoast population.

Conclusion

Although no more than a single guardianship plan was completed for the majority of wards in either group during the second year of the pilot project, consistent reporting over time probably would have enhanced the ability of staff to: 1) plan and coordinate activities on behalf of the ward; 2) alert staff to on-going needs of the wards; and 3) serve as a gauge of staff performance for evaluation purposes.

When completed by a team of social service and professional staff familiar with the ward, guardianship plans serve as a comprehensive assessment instrument, including a detailed listing of client needs in all eight content areas. Disappointingly, this type of comprehensive assessment was not conducted by either pilot group, although reporting techniques could be expected to improve given more training and experience with guardianship plan formats. Feasibly, guardianship plans revised over time would allow more concise and relevant reporting of ward needs, services to be provided, and staff accountability for securing services.

Guardian Activities

Until now, no systematic data existed on how much time guardians devote to their wards, the kinds of activities guardians perform, or the relative amount of time devoted to various activities. With respect to each of these areas, interest remains in the capability of professional guardians as compared to volunteers. For example, one might expect that volunteer guardians spend greater amounts of time in socializing or "just visiting" with their wards. The guardian activity reports provided answers to these questions.

Table 4 contains the frequency or incidence of activity by category or by program. The categories of activities largely follow those of the CAF and the intake form. Category eight relates to financial status. Category nine, general indirect services, is for guardianship activities where one or two wards could not be identified, but the activity benefits a large num-

Table 4. Frequency of Activities by Guardians

Activity	Dade Frequency	%	Suncoast Frequency	%
1. Living Situation	229	(13)	258	(6)
2. Activities	7	(1)	102	(3)
3. Functional Status	7	(1)	258	(6)
4. Nutritional Status	1	(0)	127	(3)
5. Medical Status	311	(18)	517	(13)
6. Intellectual Functioning	44	(3)	207	(5)
7. Services and Social Support	365	(21)	796	(20)
8. Financial Status	241	(14)	466	(12)
9. General Indirect Services	197	(11)	176	(4)
10. Programmatic	303	(18)	794	(20)
11. Volunteer	0	(0)	298	(8)
TOTAL	1,705		3,999	

ber of wards. Category ten is for activities related to the general program. Category eleven, Volunteer, has a surprisingly low figure for the Suncoast program. This is partially explained by the fact that the full-time volunteer at Suncoast reported only 7% of her time, and thus the figure given is considerably lower than the actual and affects the comparative distribution of the other categories.

The Suncoast program reported more than twice as many (3,999 to 1,705) guardian activities—frequency or incidence—as Dade. This is not a surprising figure, because Suncoast had thirty-six pilot wards contrasted with twenty-one in Dade—42% more wards. Although there are some differences by program, the profiles are highly similar. Neither program reported comparatively significant activities related to stimulating the ward's participation in activities, the ward's ability to provide for his or her basic needs, nutritional status, or orientation and behavioral problems. Although services in these areas may in some cases be provided by facilities, such as ACLF's and nursing homes, it is incumbent upon guardians to monitor and document delivery of services.

Activities for the two programs were distributed in roughly the same amounts for medical status, services and social support, and financial status, with each of these categories accounting for somewhere between one-fifth and one-fourth of the total. The Suncoast program devoted comparatively fewer of its activities to the living situation. Although the two programs report a similar number of activities in the programmatic category, duration data that follow reveal that Suncoast spent a much larger proportion of its time with this category. For the most part, the distribution of activities by category illustrates that the differences between a volunteer model and a professional model are minimal.

The above frequency or incidence information is based on the assignment of an activity to a category based on the guardian's understanding of the categories from the CAF, which was possibly minimal. As a result, in order to get a more detailed understanding of what guardians do for their wards, a second analysis was undertaken. The individual reports and coding of comments were divided into four major categories:

(1) direct work with client;

(2) conferences/consultations with others about the client;

(3) administrative functions;

(4) miscellaneous (including guardian transportation).

Analysis was completed for all guardian activity reports submitted for the weeks of March 14–20, July 14–20, and November 7–13, 1983. These periods were carefully chosen to reflect different points in the history of the guardianship in order to quantify any changes in activity associated with the maturity of a guardianship. Such changes were noted, but they are relatively minor or unsystematic.

Table 5 shows the percentage of the various activities for each category as well as the relative percent of time devoted to each category. A major function of the guardian is that of procuring, as opposed to delivering, direct services, and thus one would expect direct contact with the ward to be limited. For both programs, approximately one-fifth of the guardian's time consuming activities were socializing (6%), shopping (5%), and transportation (6%). For the Suncoast program, socializing was the major activity involving direct contact with the ward (16%). Both programs spent approximately one-third of their time on conferences and consultations with others.

Other minor variation between programs can be seen. The Dade program spent twice as much time as Suncoast in legal consultations (9% versus 4%). Legal counsel was provided by attorneys on the Board of Directors, or by an attorney on retainer. Discussion and action regarding placement was relatively time consuming (14% Dade, 9% Suncoast). Family and friends received little attention, presumably because of their absence or nonexistence. A surprisingly small proportion of time was reported as consultation with social service agencies (1% and 5% for the two programs). Much of this activity was likely to be recorded elsewhere.[53]

Duration of Guardian Activity

Table 6 reports the amount, and distribution by nature of activity, of the work accomplished by the Dade and Suncoast (thirty-six wards) programs. Forty-five percent of Suncoast's time was spent on programmatic activity, compared with 19% by Dade. The distribution of work for Dade indicates that services and social support (30%), medical status (14%), financial status (11%), living situation (10%), and general indirect services (11%) occupy most of a guardian program's time. Neither program was able to devote much attention to the intellectual functioning, activities, functional status, or nutritional status of their wards. Suncoast's preoccupation with programmatic activity makes it difficult to assess the distribution of the guardians' time, but seven percent of their time assessed related to volunteer activity.

Table 7 reports the amount and distribution of work by nature of activity, accomplished for thirty-six wards by paid staff and volunteers in the Suncoast program. Volunteers contributed 22% of the time recorded as work for the Suncoast program. Forty-six percent of volunteer work was

---

53. Note that secretarial time was not reported for the Dade program, but was reported by Suncoast.

Table 5. Percent Distribution of Guardian Activities by Frequency and by Duration

	Frequency (percentages)		Duration (percentages)	
	Dade	Sun-coast	Dade	Sun-coast
I. Work Directly with Ward				
A. Socializing	5	17	6	16
B. Activities (e.g., bowling)	0	0	0	1
C. Shopping	4	1	5	1
D. Discussion About Placement	2	2	4	3
E. Daily Living Needs	0	1	0	1
F. Intervention on Unique Occasions	1	2	0	1
G. Transportation	3	1	6	1
H. Discussion of Medical Issues	2	1	1	0
I. Discussion of Finances	3	0	2	0
Total	20	25	24	24
II. Conferences and Consultations with Others About the Ward				
A. Family/Friends of Ward	2	4	1	4
B. Legal Consultants	13	6	9	4
C. Financing				
SSI/Food Stamps	5	3	3	2
Banking	0	0	0	0
Resolution of Property	2	6	1	0
General Finances	2	7	4	4
D. Medical Consultations				
Assessment	5	4	4	3
Treatment	2	3	1	2
E. Placement of Transfer	14	6	10	6
F. Consultation with Social Service Agencies	2	5	1	5
Total	47	38	34	30
III. Administrative Functions				
A. Program Related Activities	14	19	18	26
B. Sending Out Bills or Checks	2	4	2	8
C. Administrative Meetings/Consultations	5	9	1	6
D. Inservice Training	0	5	0	4
Total	21	37	31	44
IV. Miscellaneous (travel time, etc.)	12	0	12	1

Percentages less than 1 are recorded as 0. Due to rounding, all columns may not add up 100%.

Table 6. Duration of Guardian Activities by Program

Activity	Dade Hours	%	Suncoast Hours	%
1. Living Situation	115	10	105	3
2. Activities	17	1	53	2
3. Functional Status	4	0	68	2
4. Nutritional Status	0	0	31	1
5. Medical Status	153	14	206	6
6. Intellectual Functioning	33	3	59	2
7. Services and Social Support	334	30	427	13
8. Financial Status	123	11	233	7
9. General Indirect Services	128	11	358	11
10. Programmatic	210	19	1462	45
11. Volunteer	0	0	227	7
TOTAL	1117		3229	

Table 7. Duration of Guardian Activities by Paid Staff and Volunteers in Suncoast

Activity	Paid Staff Hours	%	Volunteers Hours	%
1. Living Situation	81	3	30	4
2. Activities	11	0	42	6
3. Functional Status	43	2	25	3
4. Nutritional Status	10	0	21	3
5. Medical Status	69	3	137	19
6. Intellectual Functioning	44	2	15	2
7. Services and Social Support	98	4	328	46
8. Financial Status	214	8	20	3
9. General Indirect Services	359	14	0	0
10. Programmatic	1375	54	85	12
11. Volunteer	242	10	14	2
TOTAL	2546		717	

in the area of services and social support, 19% related to ward medical status, and 12% of their work was programmatic. Fifty-four percent of

Table 8. Duration of Total Reported Activity by Suncoast Paid Staff

Worker Number	Hours	%	First/Last Entry
10	1086.0	29	2/7–11/20
11	794.0	21	2/1–11/18
12	18.0	0	2/1–4/20
13	269.0	7	2/1–11/17
14	812.0	22	3/21–11/19
15	.3	0	2/2–2/2
16	517.0	14	2/1–6/15
17	214.0	6	7/11–11/19
18	.3	0	8/15–8/15
Total	3710.6		

paid staff work was programmatic, 10% was volunteer related, and 8% concerned ward financial status.

Table 8 reports the duration of activity reported for each of the paid staff in the Suncoast program. One worker did 29% of all reported paid staff work for Suncoast. (The paid staff did 78% of all work, including volunteer time, reported for this "volunteer" program.) An estimated 69% of this worker's time was allocated to programmatic activity. Three workers were secretaries. The bookkeeper did 21% of the reported staff work; the volunteer coordinator did 7% of the staff work; and a half-time caseworker did 6% of all reported staff work. These results suggest that this volunteer program accomplished most of its work through paid staff rather than volunteers. Instead of directly serving wards, the Suncoast paid staff recruited, trained, and supervised the volunteers, spending more time in these activities than the volunteers did with the wards. Suncoast in some ways administered a program for volunteers rather than a program for wards.

Volunteer Program

In order to develop a detailed understanding of the operation of the volunteer program, the total time reported by the Suncoast program for all of their wards was analyzed by staff and by volunteer. For each volunteer, the dates of entry of the first and last recorded activity were reviewed, as well as the total time recorded.

During the project period, activities were reported by forty-seven volunteers (thirty-eight of whom reported some activity on behalf of a project ward), but their degree of involvement was highly skewed. The range of total hours worked was from a high of 184 to a low of less than thirty minutes. Four of the volunteers had an entry for only a single date, and thus were never really involved in the program. The time between the first and last entry was less than two months for eighteen of the volunteers (38%). The quality of attention to wards as measured by time could vary from hour to hour, but the skewed quantity of time suggests differing dedication, interest, availability, and talent, affecting the grade of service.

As a further index of the degree of active involvement, the last date on which an activity was recorded was examined. Because program requirements called for a contact with the ward every two weeks, and data were collected through November, it was decided that the absence of an entry subsequent to October 28 would probably mean that the volunteer was not actively involved.[54] Thirty-two (70%) of the volunteers did not have an entry for the last month of the project. The average amount of total time worked by this group was approximately ten hours.

Expressed another way, approximately one-third of the total number of volunteers were active, to any degree, in the last month of the program. A number of volunteers left the program for a variety of reasons.[55] Whether the investment of time in recruitment, training and supervision of volunteers was worth the effort is difficult, at best, to determine. The volunteers accounted for only 22% of the total program time. Considerable staff time went into the volunteer program, including a full-time, on-staff recruiter, with much of the staff time falling into the programmatic category. We conclude that had these resources been diverted to providing direct professional guardianship services, the likely result would have been a significant net gain in services to the wards. It seems that, generally, volunteers underestimated what was involved and the commitment which was necessary.

Regardless, the use of volunteers in any program has some benefits other than the direct work contributed, including: 1) the development of a supportive constituency; 2) a change in public attitudes and knowledge; and 3) some tasks may best be performed by volunteers.

One distinctive feature of the Suncoast program is the frequent overlap of coverage of wards by staff and various volunteers. Approximately two-thirds of the wards had activities performed for them by more than

---

54. This does not assume that any given ward had not been visited, only that the volunteer had not been active.

55. The following was noted on one guardian report: "Being on a fixed income I can no longer afford to finance (client) without being reimbursed. Consider this my resignation."

one volunteer.[56] In some ways this can be seen as a programmatic benefit. The ward was known by more than one volunteer, thus, coverage during vacation or sickness, or transition between guardians, could be more easily managed. When traveling to remote sections of a county, a volunteer could check on another ward. With shared knowledge about a ward, the volunteers derive additional education regarding the solution to problems.

On the other hand, the ward could find that being seen by a number of people results in confusion as to who the guardian is, what function is being served, and understandably, what depth there is to the relationship. Model guardianship statutes encourage a one-on-one relationship, and singular attention is probably preferred in our own lives, especially when ill or disabled.

Frequency of Contact with Wards

Each ward was required to be contacted within every two week period. In order to determine that this requirement was followed, activity reports were examined by date of contact for each ward. For both Dade and Suncoast, better than two-thirds of the wards were subject to at least one violation of this requirement (71% and 70% respectively). In some instances, the period of no contact was only a few days over the two-week requirement, and probably not of much significance. Both programs, however, had five to seven instances for a given ward when the stated time period for contact was exceeded, and on occasion there was two months or longer between contact. In these latter cases, the absence of contact could have significant consequences for the ward. For example, the functional status or living situation of the ward could change—a house fire in one case—without proximate knowledge by the guardian.

If consensus exists that guardian and ward contact should occur every two weeks, concerted administrative coverage is mandated for conformity. Slippage is far too easy, as demonstrated by these results.

Cost Analysis

The Dade and Suncoast pilot guardianship programs respectively received $5,000 per month over the nine and a half month period from February 1, 1983 to November 18, 1983. For this money, the Dade program pro-

---

56. One ward had entries from five volunteers, and five wards had entries from four or more volunteers.

vided guardianship services for twenty-one wards; the Suncoast program provided guardianship services for twenty-nine wards.[57]

For the total of $47,500 to each program over nine and a half months, the Dade program recorded a total of 1,117 hours of work for their twenty-one wards, while the Suncoast program recorded a total of 2,754 hours for their twenty-nine wards. Note that Dade did not include bookkeeper effort for their wards in the reported work, while Suncoast did. These total amounts of work average 5.6 hours per ward per month by the Dade program, and ten hours per ward per month by the Suncoast program.

The average monthly cost of providing guardianship service to one ward was $238.09 for the Dade program, and $172.41 for the Suncoast program. The average cost of one hour of guardianship service was $42.52 for Dade, and $24.14 for Suncoast. The average annual cost per ward was $2,857.08 for Dade, and $2,068.92 for Suncoast.

The Suncoast total of 2,754 hours of work for twenty-nine wards can be broken down to 2,082 hours by the paid staff and 670 hours by the volunteers. If volunteers are assumed to donate time that is cost-free, the cost of the staff's time in the Suncoast program averaged $36.59 per hour (compared with $42.52 per hour in the Dade program).

The question of public guardianship program cost is a significant economic, political and policy issue. The professional (Dade) and volunteer (Suncoast) models piloted and demonstrated here represented the best Florida efforts available for evaluation.[58] For example, other Florida guardianship resources, such as the Cathedral Foundation in Jacksonville, did not apply. The Cathedral Foundation operates a guardianship diversion program of voluntary protective services that is extremely aggressive about exhausting guardianship alternatives and acting as guardian only as a last resort in a very limited number of circumstances.[59]

A threshold means of evaluating the comparative costs of the pilot professional and volunteer models is to compare the amount of service delivered for identical amounts of money. By this measure, the Suncoast program served more wards and, as a program, delivered more hours of guardianship work. The free time donated by the volunteers in the Suncoast program did not account for this advantage, and made up only 24%

---

57. The total number of wards cited elsewhere in this report for Suncoast is thirty-six. This is because the Suncoast program generously provided information on additional wards in their program for purposes of improving the amount of information available for evaluation.

58. There may be some excellent programs that chose not to compete in the proposal process for guardianship program money.

59. W. Schmidt, *supra* note 8, at 152–53.

of Suncoast's work. Note also that these pilot programs were components of larger organizations; one of the organizations might have enjoyed an unknown overhead advantage over the other that facilitated better service to wards in the component pilot programs.[60]

The data from the client assessments, guardianship plans, and guardian activity reports did not indicate conclusively that wards of either program generally did significantly better or worse than the other program. The impossibility of proving a null hypothesis, however, also precludes one from definitively concluding that there is no difference in program accomplishment for the two groups of wards.

Indeed, less data-based indices of program quality were exhibited. The Office of the State Courts Administrator indicated that its contract with the Suncoast program through Lutheran Ministries of Florida, Inc. for guardianship services would not have been renewed even if funds were available, because of numerous individual questions concerning the quality of service. Monitoring staff in the Office of the State Courts Administrator had much contact on a personal basis with each program, and had considerable opportunity to formulate a subjective judgment about quality. Adopting the view of a potential consumer of Suncoast services or Dade program services, one could readily conclude a preference for Dade's guardianship services. Over all, Dade's program exhibited higher beneficial ward contact and superior services.

A final question when considering cost is the extent to which, while one program seems qualitatively superior to another, the guardianship service quality in either program is truly adequate. Because the Florida pilot project was the first public guardianship program to generate quantitative information, there is no optimal or minimally acceptable public guardianship program with which to objectively compare these results.

What can be said, based on the study[61] of other non-profit programs in Florida and the public guardianship programs of five other states, is that there was room for improvement in the Florida pilot programs. Further, the improvement would probably occur more readily with infusion of money rather than with the popular panacea of volunteers.

These two programs were pilot, demonstration, experimental programs. They were not yet model programs. Thus, associated costs should be considered preliminary and tentative, rather than definitive.

---

60. Another consideration of program cost is the quality of service delivered for the money. This is a much more subjective measure, and the point at which cost-benefit analysis becomes particularly problematic.

61. *See* W. Schmidt, *supra* note 8, at 152–53.

The Control Group: The Cathedral Foundation in Jacksonville

In addition to the two programs evaluated here, the original design called for a control group of individuals who were at-risk for having a guardian appointed but for whom one was not available. This comparison group would provide some measure of change in client level of functioning in the absence of guardianship services. The Cathedral Foundation in Jacksonville, Florida, provided data on their clients comparable to that collected from the two pilot projects. Because the Cathedral group differed from the Suncoast clients in significant ways—age, race, independent living, the presence of psychiatric conditions—comparisons for these two groups were not possible. Yet enough similarities existed with the Dade group to permit some limited statements.

The Cathedral Foundation believes that some of its clients could be adjudicated incompetent, but that these individuals can be maintained with protective services as well as, if not better than, persons who are stripped of all their legal rights through guardianship. The Cathedral Foundation believes that there is generally little, if any, difference between its protective services clients and its own guardianship wards.

The Dade wards and the Cathedral clients were demographically different. The Dade wards were generally younger and had a much smaller proportion that was black.[62] Generally, Dade wards had more prior mental hospitalizations. The two groups were comparable by quite a few functional and behavioral variables. Although the Cathedral clients were not comparable to the Dade wards to the extent that they constitute a control group, it is interesting to observe that the Cathedral clients were about five times more likely to live independently and about half as likely to be in an institution than the Dade wards. The Dade staff appropriately lamented the extent to which state and federal fiscal policies continued to provide disproportionate incentives for institutional care over home care. Yet one can respond that this says nothing about the relative quality of life experienced by a person in either group.

The data do allow this question: why are two groups, who have relevant functional and behavioral variables in common, legally incompetent on one hand (Dade), and mere protective service clients (Cathedral) on the other? One possibility suggested during interviews was that there are historical incidents that lead to legal incompetence that are not reflected in functional assessments after adjudication of incompetence. This matter of possibly unique case histories requires further study.

---

62. It should be noted that the need for black guardians is almost completely unmet.

Conclusion

The Project

This study is an evaluation of the two pilot projects of the Florida Public Guardianship Pilot Program in the Office of the State Courts Administrator. Each project pursued one method of guardian service delivery: the Dade project attempted to use paid employees in a "professional" model, and the Suncoast project used volunteers in a "volunteer" model. Each project received $47,500 to deliver guardian services over a nine and a half month period. The data instruments included functional assessment forms, guardianship plans, and guardian activity reports completed by personnel in each project. The evaluation budget allowed one site visit to each project. During each visit, project personnel and wards were interviewed.

The wards in each project, the product of one state guardianship law,[63] were demographically different. The principal significance of this finding debates a perception that incompetent persons without resources to employ a private guardian, and without willing and responsible family or friends to serve as guardian, are homogeneous. The data in this study suggest that wards of a public guardian may not be homogeneous.

Such a finding would stimulate several questions. Are public guardian wards unique, or instead are they virtually indistinguishable from other classes of persons, except for the fact that public guardian wards have been identified and adjudicated incompetent. If public guardian wards are indistinguishable from other groups, what is the purpose of the legal label of incompetence?[64]

The functional assessments for each ward did not change much over the nine and a half month evaluation period, nor did one group of pilot wards change to a greater degree than the other. Each pilot group seemed to have a few wards who can appear competent on a given day, and each group had wards who were clearly incompetent by any legal or medical definition.

Restoration of guardianship is a relatively rare event. A Dade staff person said that out of a total of 261 guardianships, only one restoration was completed, with an additional three or four in process.[65] He added the opinion that this rate would be a reasonable expectation for the future.

---

63. Fla. Stat. Ann. section 744.703 (West 1987).

64. *Cf.* Mitchell, *supra* note 11, at 453 ("Benevolent motivations justify the use of amorphous incompetency standards...").

65. Interview with Frank Repensek, Executive Director of the Guardianship Program of Dade County, in Miami (Spring 1983).

The figures from Suncoast are similar: for all of their wards, there was a total of three restorations.[66]

Some Legal Considerations

Guardianship realistically is a legal, surrogate decisionmaking device to facilitate legal, social functioning concerning persons who are incapable—and perhaps unwilling—of making decisions. If legal incompetents are not functionally or behaviorally distinct from many other persons, the legal definition for incompetence is very important. To the extent false positives are intolerable in guardianship, the legal definition now seems to be very broad,[67] as evidenced by the suspect cases in each pilot project. If the legal definition for incompetence is not narrowed significantly, and enforced, then additional procedural protections for prospective wards seem appropriate[68] on the basis of the marginal cases identified in each of the pilot projects. An alternative response that guardianship should increase exponentially, based on alleged need, is no more realistic under current conditions and circumstances than the notion that guardianship is rehabilitative.

The suspect and marginal cases in such high visibility projects as these also lend support to a finding that much greater use be made of such legal alternatives to guardianship as durable family powers of attorney ("living wills"), single transaction court ratification of particular actions (e.g., consent to a medical procedure), substitute or representative payee, and adult protective services.[69] To the extent that some pilot personnel indicated property management incapacity to be the real problem for incompetents, then such alternatives as trusts should be used much more frequently. Consideration could be given to legislatively allowing a non-family power of attorney to survive incompetence.

One standard for surrogate decisionmaking is the substitute judgment doctrine: what the individual would have done if he or she were competent.[70] A "living will", for example, facilitates implementation of a ward's desires with regard to his other property. Widespread use would mitigate

---

66. Interview with Dade Hyland, Suncoast Lutheran Ministries, in St. Petersburg (Spring 1983).
67. See Regan, "An Appraisal," supra note 24, at 1122–26.
68. Id.
69. See, J. Regan, Protective Services for the Elderly: Commitment, Guardianship and Alternatives, 13 Wm. & Mary L. Rev. 569, 609–15 (1972).
70. See, e.g., Superintendent of Belchertown State School v. Saikewicz, 373 Mass. 728, 370 N.E.2d 417 (1977).

the seemingly "faddish craving" for guardianship pervasive in Florida and other parts of the country.

The pilot projects engaged in little consideration of legal alternatives. Compared to public guardianship programs in other states[71] that are directed by attorneys more at ease with such matters, rather than by social service professionals, a lack of legal advice is perhaps understandable. But to the extent guardianship could be ameliorated by better legal planning and services, a focus on social casework for wards is unfortunate and arguably misplaced for a group in a unique and greatly preventable legal predicament, rather than a necessarily unique social situation. Also, the pilot programs' focus on social casework makes one ask: what is the real difference between guardianship and social casework, other than the rather arbitrarily imposed legal status? Utilization of legal alternatives to guardianship should take place prior to judgment of incompetency and the appointment of a guardian: it should not be considered a responsibility of these programs.[72]

Suggestions for Future Programs

The guardianship plans probably could have their format revised. Project personnel apparently did not understand, or did not effectively communicate to workers, the need for and meaning of such categories as "rationale for providing non-optimal services." Pilot project personnel correctly observe that a major problem with public guardian wards is lack of monetary and legal resources and sufficient public services.

The guardianship plans were designed on the basis of treatment and habilitation plans; such plans are widely used and useful tools. Stating needed services in guardianship plans sets goals for the guardianship of the ward, and documents specific service and resource needs. It is one thing to say that all wards need better food, clothing, shelter, and more money, and another thing to say how much and what kind. Our findings indicate that a rationale for not providing optimal services for documented needs actually protects the responsible guardianship project.

Fairly uniform shortages emerged in reporting six of eight guardianship plan need categories, and in service responses plotted for each need noted in the assessment instrument.[73] Guardians seemed adept at describing needs of wards and services to be obtained in areas of financial sta-

---

71. W. Schmidt, *supra* note 8, at 63–66.
72. A judge might intervene to order services prior to final adjudication of incompetency in a situation involving an emergency medical procedure.
73. See Table 3, *supra*.

tus and living situation, but were less cogent and facile in areas of physical and intellectual needs. Whether the problem is erroneous or inappropriate requirements, or a breakdown in communication and instruction, or whether such requirements are programmatically helpful and could be worked out with experience, is difficult to say. Future programs should experiment further with the guardianship plan format and variations. More consultation of appropriate professional staff in development of guardianship plans could be helpful.

Volunteers in the Role of Public Guardians

A most important accomplishment of the pilot program is the empirical identification of the quantity and nature of work done by a public guardian on behalf of a ward,[74] considering the relatively small number of wards, the difficulty in establishing comparison groups, and the problems in arriving at a definition of, and behaviorally measuring, incompetence. The professional model (Dade) in this pilot, while determined to deliver higher quality services overall,[75] reported less total work, on fewer wards, for the same amount of money, than did the volunteer model (Suncoast). The volunteers do not perform more than 24% of the effort accomplished by Suncoast. Any functional outcome for wards from guardianship is difficult to assess but apparently nominal.

While the philosophy that government can get something for nothing by use of volunteers is not totally debunked by this pilot, the volunteer panacea should be sharply questioned. Volunteers must be recruited, trained, professionally supported, monitored, and replaced. All of this activity is at the opportunity cost of the direct client services that recruiters, trainers, professionals, and monitors could be performing instead. In essence, volunteers are not truly cost-free, and, needless to say, a true volunteer model should consist of nothing but volunteers.

On the other hand, the altruism, energy, caring, and humanity exhibited by the most active Suncoast volunteers are some of the most exhilarating and hopeful findings of this study. Suncoast demonstrates that volunteers can be recruited, trained, supported, and replaced in some kind of guardianship role. The untapped potential in volunteers for guardianship responsibilities should be examined. Retirees, a large demographic influence in Florida, may be an especially productive resource.

Suggestions about volunteers from this study must be limited to relying on volunteers for "friendly visitor" sorts of activities, a job that can

---

74. *See* Mintzberg, *supra* note 42.
75. *See* text preceding note 61, *supra*.

mean more to individual wards than the squadron of lawyers, psychiatrists, and social workers who might otherwise be the ward's only source of direct contact. Public guardianship programs should maximize opportunities to utilize volunteer services. At the same time, care should be taken that the benefits of volunteer services remain greater than the costs to secure them. A volunteer is initially highly motivated, but may not be as continually motivated as someone who is paid to do a job that can be as depressing and frustrating as it can be emotionally and spiritually rewarding.

A Few Final Observations

Finally, several problems and limitations should be noted. The actual delivery of guardianship services covered a relatively short period of time, a total of nine and one-half months, with the average ward having a guardian for about six months. Researchers consider this a short time to establish programs, collect data, and evaluate programs, yet it is a legislatively mandated timetable which had to be observed. A review of wards over a longer period might provide a picture different from the one described here.

The time limitations, combined with relatively tight budget limitations, led to some compromises in the evaluation process. There was only one short site visit, and the data collected were primarily descriptive, ultimately leading to aggregate, somewhat cross-sectional pictures only. As previously stated, it was not possible to get much of a sense for the unique histories of the wards, or the critical incidents that may have led to guardianship, and thus a true picture of the wards' real needs.

The program people were dissatisfied with some aspects of the data collection instruments, feeling that they failed to adequately reflect the richness of activities and events, and in some respects were oriented too heavily to non-institutionalized populations. Certainly, future evaluations should be funded so as to provide for cooperatively developed evaluation instruments.

Regardless, it is clear that the programs are fundamentally aiding people in trouble and that the basic needs of wards are being served. As with many of the social services provided in this country, guardianship services must be enhanced and responsive to legal, demographic and sociological changes and research.

Part VI

Summary of What is Known, and Unknown, about Guardianship

Chapter 12

Quantitative Information About the Quality of the Guardianship System: Toward the Next Generation of Guardianship Research

Winsor C. Schmidt, Jr.

The purpose of this chapter is to describe the state of quantitative knowledge about the guardianship system in order to contribute to improving guardianship services, as well as to facilitate the planning and development of alternatives to guardianship, and of guardianship research. The issues of focus include: the number of people under guardianship; the causes for people being brought into the guardianship system; the characteristics and disposition of people brought into the guardianship system; the characteristics of the guardians; and the extent to which such alternatives to guardianship as power of attorney, representative payee, and limited guardianship reduce the level of guardianship service required, delay the need for guardianship service, and make guardianship service unnecessary.[1]

Definitions

"Guardianship" is the legal "office, duty, or authority of a guardian," and the legal relationship between a guardian and a ward.[2] A "guardian" is "a person lawfully invested with the power and charged with the duty, of taking care of the person and managing the property and rights of

---

1. The United States Administration on Aging requested applications for grant proposals to increase knowledge about these basic questions. Program Announcement, 53 Fed. Reg. 50, 167 (1988).
2. Black's Law Dictionary 636 (5th ed. 1979).

another person [the ward], who . . . is considered incapable of administering his [or her] own affairs."[3] (Some states use such words as "conservator" or "committee" rather than "guardian".) Just as citizens enjoy a legal presumption of innocence until legally proven guilty, so do citizens enjoy a legal presumption of competence until legally proven incompetent and a substitute decisionmaker (the guardian) is appointed by the court.[4]

Guardianship is decentralized. Judicial incompetency determinations are made by local (county-level, probate or general) courts pursuant to state law. Although several bills have been introduced in Congress,[5] there is no federal guardianship law or federal definition of incompetence for purposes of guardianship. Guardianship records are kept in local clerks' offices, with some aggregate statistics reported to state court administrators' offices. There is no national guardianship record repository, and local records are frequently paper files rather than computerized.

The legal definition for incompetence or incapacity varies by state. The definition is also evolving from a 1960s linkage between inability to care for property or personal affairs, and a specified disability, to more clinical definitions that examine an individual's ability "to go through the cognitive process of making rational decisions."[6] At least sixteen states have adopted the Uniform Probate Code definition that an "incapacitated person" is one who "lacks sufficient understanding or capacity to make or communicate responsible decisions concerning his person."[7] The National Guardianship Symposium at the Wingspread Conference Facility, sponsored by the American Bar Association Commissions on Legal Problems of the Elderly, and on the Mentally Disabled, recommended in July 1988 that the National Conference of Commissioners on Uniform State Law

---

3. *Id.* at 635.

4. There may be some question whether the guardianship system, in analogous fashion to the criminal justice system, would rather let ten functionally incompetent persons escape the guardianship system than inappropriately adjudicate one functionally competent person legally incompetent. In fact, there are reportedly many functionally incompetent persons who need guardianship services but have not been adjudicated legally incompetent. Schmidt & Peters, *Legal Incompetents' Need for Guardians in Florida*, 15 Bull. Am. Acad. Psychiatry & L. 69 (1987).

5. H.R. 372, 101st Cong., 1st Sess. (1989); H.R. 5275, 100th Cong., 2d Sess. (1988); H.R. 5266, 100th Cong., 2d Sess. (1988).

6. S. Brakel, J. Parry & B. Weiner, The Mentally Disabled and the Law 371 (3d ed. 1985).

7. National Conference of Commissioners on Uniform State Law, U.P.C. section 5-101(1) (1975).

reconsider the Uniform Probate Code definition for incapacity and recognize the need for a functional definition for incapacity.[8]

Associated Press Investigation

Basic quantitative knowledge about guardianship is limited. The recent national investigation by the Associated Press, using sixty-seven Associated Press reporters and editors in fifty states and the District of Columbia, estimated that there are 300,000 to 400,000 elderly people under guardianship nationally.[9] From its review of 2,200 randomly[10] selected guardianship court files, the investigation found that the average length of time for each guardianship is 3.4 years.[11] When causes of incompetence were listed in the files, the most reported reasons were:

- 19 percent: inability to care for self or finances;
- 16 percent: senility or dementia;
- 11 percent: organic or chronic brain syndrome;
- 8 percent: old or advanced age;
- 8 percent: mental illness;
- 6 percent: stroke;
- 2 percent: Alzheimer's disease;
- 1 percent: forgetfulness;
- 1 percent: alcoholism.[12]

The average age of wards reported was seventy-nine; 67% were female.[13]

---

8. *Guardianship: An Agenda for Reform: Recommendations for the National Guardianship Symposium and Policy of the American Bar Association*, 13 Mental & Physical Disability L. Rep. 271, 288 (1989). The recommendation was approved by the American Bar Association Board of Delegates on February 7, 1989.

This revisionism in the definition for incompetence and incapacity may be misplaced to the extent it concentrates on functioning rather than decisional capacity. A guardian is a substitute decisionmaker or services broker, not a social worker or human crutch.

9. Guardians of the Elderly: An Ailing System, Associated Press Special Report, Sept. 1987, at 1, 5 (hereinafter AP Report). The Ontario Public Trustee's Office manages the financial affairs of 6,000 people over 65 who have been declared "financially incompetent." Sweden has an estimated 15,000 people under guardianship. In Japan, 600,000 senior citizens are estimated to be "dependent on others in daily life." *Id.* at 10.

10. There may be some controversy concerning the actual randomness of the review. Discussion with Honorable Kenneth Pat Gregory, Probate Court Judge, Houston, Texas, in Cambridge, Massachusetts (Apr. 21, 1989).

11. AP Report, *supra* note 9, at 14.

12. *Id.* at 13.

13. *Id.*

The guardian was a family member 70% of the time, an outsider 25% of the time, and unknown 4% of the time. The investigation reported a further breakdown for the guardian:

  35% were children of wards;
  6% were spouses of wards;
  8% were siblings of wards;
  20% were other relatives, including nieces, nephews, grandchildren, etc;
  5% were attorneys;
  7% were friends;
  7% were agencies;
  2% were public guardians;
  4% were banks;
  3% were unknown.[14]

Thirty-five percent of the wards lived at home before guardianship.[15] After they became wards, 33% were moved, and 64% were placed in a nursing home at some point.[16] Most wards lived no more than two years.[17] Concerning estate size, the Associated Press reported:

  $97,551 was the average size of estates at opening;
  $85,545 was the average size at closing;
  $24,353 was the average annual expenditure when indicated;
  11% of the estates were depleted during guardianship;
  2.9 was the average number of years it took to deplete an estate;
  55% had estates below $50,000 at opening;
  7% had estates above $250,000 at opening.[18]

Alexander and Lewin Study

Other available guardianship studies are more local in scope. Alexander and Lewin investigated the management of the estates of 400 legal

---

14. *Id.* at 15. Percentages are rounded.
15. *Id.* at 4, 13.
16. *Id.* at 13.
17. *Id.* at 6.
18. *Id.* at 13.

incompetents in New York.[19] They reported that they found no benefit that could not have been achieved without an adjudication of incompetence, and that in almost every case the elderly ward was in a worse position after the finding of incompetence than they were before. They concluded:

> Under the present system of "Estate Management by Preemption" we divest the incompetent of control of his property upon the finding of the existence of serious mental illness whenever divestiture is in the interest of some third person or institution. The theory of incompetency is to protect the debilitated from their own financial foolishness or from the fraud of others who would prey upon their mental weaknesses. In practice, however, we seek to protect the interests of others. The state hospital commences incompetency proceedings to facilitate reimbursement for costs incurred in the care, treatment and maintenance of its patients. Dependents institute proceedings to secure their needs. Co-owners of property find incompetency proceedings convenient ways to secure the sale of realty. Heirs institute actions to preserve their dwindling inheritances. Beneficiaries of trusts or estates seek incompetency as an expedient method of removing as trustee one who is managing the trust or estate in a manner adverse to their interests. All of these motives may be honest and without any intent to cheat the aged, but none of the proceedings are commenced to assist the debilitated.[20]

Benjamin Rose Institute Study

A frequently cited study which illustrates the high risks of intervention was conducted with a quasi-experimental design by Blenkner and associates through the Benjamin Rose Institute in Cleveland.[21] The provision of enriched protective services, including guardianship, to the experimental group failed to prevent or slow the ward's deterioration or death. Instead, the experimental group had a higher rate of institutionalization and death than the control group who received referral agency services or no services. Reanalysis of the data by other investigators suggested that the death rate findings were a consequence of initial group differences in survival-related characteristics not controlled by random sampling tech-

---

19. G. Alexander & T. Lewin, The Aged and the Need for Surrogate Management (1972).
20. *Id.* at 135.
21. M. Blenkner, M. Bloom, M. Nielson & R. Weber, Final Report—Protective Services for Older People: Findings from the Benjamin Rose Institute Study (1974). *See also* Blenkner, Bloom & Nielson, *A Research and Demonstration Project of Protective Services*, 52 Soc. Casework 483 (1971).

niques, but this did not mitigate the strong effect of experimental group membership on the tendency to be institutionalized.[22]

National Public Guardianship Study

In 1979, the United States Administration on Aging funded a national study of public guardianship.[23] The purpose of the study was to assess the extent to which public guardianship assisted and hindered the elderly in securing access to their rights, benefits, and entitlements.[24] The study design included a review of the literature and the existing and proposed public guardianship laws in all states; a telephone survey of the thirty-four states with some statutory provision for public guardianship to determine the extent of public guardianship operations; site visits to five states[25] representative of organizational model,[26] statutory provisions, program size, geographic region, and services provided; comparison site visits within a state[27] without a public guardianship law; and development of recommendations, and a model public guardianship statute.

The public guardianship study found a 1977 per capita guardianship filing rate in Florida of .056% (one of every 1,785; 4,724 guardianships opened in a population of 8,432,927)[28] that corresponded interestingly to the filing rate of .059% (one of every 1,706; 17,000 guardianship petitions filed from a population of twenty-nine million) reported in another study of six states.[29] The Associated Press used the Florida annual filing rate, with adjustment for the two-year ward lifespan, to estimate the 15,000 to 25,000 current guardianships in Florida.[30] Other single state estimates include 30,000 conservatorships in California, 25,000 guardian-

---

22. Berger & Piliavin, *The Effect of Casework: A Research Note*, 21 Soc. Work 205 (1976).

23. W. Schmidt, K. Miller, W. Bell & E. New, Public Guardianship and the Elderly (1981).

24. Public guardianship is appointment and responsibility of a pubic official to serve as legal guardian.

25. Arizona, California, Delaware, Illinois, and Maryland.

26. The organizational models were: court model, independent state office, division of social service agency, county agency.

27. Fort Lauderdale, Jacksonville, Miami, Tampa/St. Petersburg, and West Palm Beach, Florida.

28. Schmidt, *Guardianship of the Elderly in Florida: Social Bankruptcy and the Need for Reform*, 55 Fla. B. J. 189 (1981).

29. ABA Commission on the Mentally Disabled, Executive Summary 21 (1979), studying Delaware, Minnesota, North Carolina, Ohio, Washington and Wisconsin.

30. AP Report, *supra* note 9, at 6.

ships and conservatorships in Michigan, and 9,000 conservatorships in New York.[31]

The public guardianship study reported certain demographic characteristics for the public guardian wards in the thirty-four identified states. The main referral source was social services. The great majority of public guardian wards were over age sixty-five, female, low income, and institutionalized in a nursing home or mental hospital. The proportion of minorities varied. There were very few restorations of legal competency.[32]

Based on the six-state field research, the study found that public guardian wards received very little personal attention (many only a few hours per year); partial, limited, and voluntary guardianships were rarely established; court review of guardianships was perfunctory at best; guardianship was frequently sought for management and paper purposes of medical consent rather than out of concern for the ward; and a significant number of private individuals each held guardianships for dozens of wards.[33] Confidence was expressed in knowledge of the context for guardianship and the perceived reality, but the study identified significant information gaps. For example, the incidence and type of victimization reportedly generating a need for guardianship were unknown, with an implication "that alternatives short of guardianship might be found appropriate."[34] Other missing information included the proportion of wards who are severely confused and disturbed compared with those who appear intact and competent to make decisions; the extent to which expert evaluative findings and recommendations about wards are "related to individual needs and conditions"; the real interests served by guardianship; the extent to which strong protective services constitute a guardianship alternative; the frequency with which guardianship is established solely because of inability to care for medical needs; and the feasibility of civil commitment or "other mechanisms" as an alternative to guardianship.[35]

The study identified these practices as alternatives to public guardianship:

1. (Benign) neglect; no action;
2. Individuals assuming the function of guardianship without the legal status;

---

31. *Id.* at 5–6.
32. W. Schmidt, K. Miller, W. Bell & E. New, *supra* note 23, at 67–70, 168. See Bell, Schmidt & Miller, *Public Guardianship and the Elderly: Findings from a National Study*, 21 Gerontologist 194 (1981).
33. W. Schmidt, K. Miller, W. Bell & E. New, *supra* note 23, at 172–73.
34. *Id.* at 175.
35. *Id.* at 175–77.

3. The assignment of a relative or friend;
4. Commitment to a state mental hospital;
5. Private attorneys;
6. Banks, trust companies;
7. Nonprofit organizations, usually with a religious affiliation;
8. County level social service programs utilizing volunteers;
9. Citizen groups serving as guardian bank.[36]

These alternatives to public guardianship are behavioral and descriptive, rather than necessarily appropriate or sufficient. There is a difference between alternatives to guardianship as a substitute for guardianship, and alternatives to guardianship that are preventive or diversionary.[37] Each of these two sets of guardianship alternatives is presumably appropriate at different times in a life history.

The public guardianship study concluded that services could be successful if several basic maxims are honored.[38] The public guardian should be independent of any service-providing entity; that is, there should be no conflict of interest in consenting to one's own services for a ward. The public guardian should not have the authority both to serve as guardian and to petition for adjudication of incompetence; that is, there should be no opportunity for self-aggrandizement. The public guardian should be adequately staffed and funded so that no office is responsible for more than 500 wards, and no staff professional is responsible for more than thirty wards (i.e., size limit and staffing ratio). Finally, the guardianship statute governing public guardianship should have strict criteria and procedures.

States such as New Hampshire and Tennessee used the public guardianship study as assistance to their statutes and programs. Subsequent conferences and professionals have cited and adopted findings and recommendations from the study.[39]

---

36. *Id.* at 149. *See* Schmidt, Miller, Bell & New, *Alternatives to Public Guardianship*, 14 State & Loc. Gov't Rev. 128 (1982).

37. Guardianship, An Agenda for Reform, *supra* note 8, at 277, 279, 292–94 (recommendations to explore alternatives, screen and divert inappropriate guardianship cases, use limited guardianship and other less restrictive alternatives).

38. W. Schmidt, K. Miller, W. Bell & E. New, *supra* note 23.

39. *See, e.g.,* E. Wood (ed.), Statement of Recommended Judicial Practices Adopted by the National Conference of the Judiciary on Guardianship Proceedings for the Elderly, Washington, D.C.: ABA Commission on Legal Problems of the Elderly and The National Judicial College (June 1986) (adopted as policy resolutions by the 1988 American Bar Association Annual Meeting); Guidelines for Guardianship Service Programs: Preliminary Guidelines for Development and Operation of Three Program Models—Public, Corporate, and

Dade County (Florida) Grand Jury Investigation

One of the next reported empirical studies of guardianship was accomplished by the Dade County (Miami, Florida) Grand Jury for the 1982 Spring Term.[40] The grand jury supervised a review of two hundred random guardianship cases opened between 1979 and 1981.

> Eight-five percent of the wards in our study were over the age of sixty and fifty-eight percent were over seventy-five years of age. Six of every ten were women. In seven of every ten cases the guardian appointed was a relative of the ward and in two of the cases a nonrelative. In the remaining ten percent of cases the guardian was a bank or a lawyer. In 46% of the cases the assets of the ward (control of which, of course, is vested in the guardian) were in excess of $50,000. In 39% of the cases the assets were below $50,000 with 15% of the wards being insolvent.
>
> These statistics clearly suggest the basis for concern: elderly persons being divested of control of their assets by a process in which they cannot, or do not, participate, with control of their assets being given to another individual who will, hopefully, act in the ward's interest and not in their own.[41]

The grand jury then cited such cases as a ward "living in squalor" in an adult congregate living facility owned by her guardian, despite having a $150,000 bank account.[42] Another ward's attorney was appointed guardian and submitted identical billings for the same work, including $1,018 for three hours spent purchasing a $200 clock. The grand jury found 87% of the two hundred random cases were not up to date in statutorily mandated annual reports of ward personal status, 75% of the cases were incomplete in financial reports, and 91% were not timely in physical examination reports.[43] A systematic assessment of the consequences

---

Volunteer, Ann Arbor, Michigan: Center for Social Gerontology (1987); Guardianship, An Agenda for Reform, *supra* note 8.

40. Grand juries in Florida have certain civil, as well as criminal, jurisdiction.

41. Final Report of the Grand Jury, Dade County, Fla., p.29 (Nov. 9, 1982). See also Schmidt, *The Evolution of a Public Guardianship Program*, 12 J. Psychiatry & L. 349, 355 (1984).

42. Final Report, *supra* note 41, at 29. See also Schmidt, *supra* note 41, at 355.

43. Final Report, *supra* note 41, at 30–32. See also Schmidt, *supra* note 41, at 356. The same problem with annual reports was reported nationally by the Associated Press, AP Report, *supra* note 9, at 1 (money accountings missing in 48% of examined files); in Leon County (Tallahassee) Florida for 1977 to 1982, Peters, Schmidt & Miller, *Guardianship of the Elderly in Tallahassee, Florida*, 25 Gerontologist 532, 536 (1985); and in Connecticut, Connecticut Probate Administration, Report on Guardianship Accounting, p. 12 (1985), *cited* in E. Wood (ed.), *supra* note 39, at 52.

to people who become wards is very difficult with such an inadequate base of information.

Leon County (Florida) Study

The next reported empirical study examined probate court records in Leon County (Tallahassee), Florida for 1977–1982.[44] For the forty-two incompetency/guardianship cases during that period, the average age of the ward was seventy-three, 75% were age seventy or older, two-thirds were female, 67% lived in private homes at the time of the incompetency/guardianship hearing, 31% resided in a nursing home or hospital, and relatives were available and willing to serve as guardians 70% of the time. The reported diagnosis of the alleged incompetent by the petitioner, and by the examining committee, is summarized below.[45]

Diagnosis	(at time of petition)		(of examining committee)	
	n	%	n	%
Age related (Organic brain syndrome, senility, Alzheimer's Disease)	16	38	30	71
Reference to simple "medical" or "physical" incapacity	16	38	0	0
Medical disorders (stroke, brain damage, epilepsy)	6	14	10	24
Retardation	0	0	2	5
Unknown	4	10	0	0

The distribution of estate size was reported as follows:

Size of estate	n	%
Greater than $100,000	9	21
$50–$100,000	11	26
$25–$50,000	5	12
Less than $25,000	13	31
Unknown	4	10

When estate size was greater than $50,000, relatives were significantly more likely to assume guardianships.[46]

---

44. Peters, Schmidt & Miller, *supra* note 43, at 534.
45. *Id.* at 535.
46. *Id.* at 536.

Pennsylvania State University Study

At the 1989 guardianship reform conference on the role of counsel,[47] some attention was paid to a 1983 study of the adult guardianship process in three Pennsylvania counties.[48] While there was representation at the conference that this study favors guardianship, a close reading finds the analysis generally consistent with other available guardianship research.[49]

Cohen obtained a 45% sample of 124 guardianship cases for the period February 24, 1978 to January 31, 1979 from three Pennsylvania counties: Chester, Montgomery, and Philadelphia. He reviewed court records and other documents; interviewed lawyers, judges, court personnel, petitioners, and guardians;[50] and observed hearings. The persons most likely subject to guardianship of the estate were elderly, single, or female (40% of the time all three), and needed institutional medical care paid for from the liquidation of real property. Petitions for guardianship of the person were brought to address such immediate problems as placement and medical procedures. "The subject's refusal to cooperate was a significant contributing factor, and some variety of institutional placement or residence contributed to the need to bring the petition."[51] The guardians were most often family members, friends, or the petitioner.

---

47. Sponsored by the Task Force on Guardianship Reform, American Bar Association Section of Real Property, Probate and Trust Law, Cambridge, Massachusetts (Apr. 21–23. 1989).

48. M. Cohen, An Analysis of the Dynamics of the Adult Guardianship Process (1983) (unpublished political science thesis, Pennsylvania State University).

49. Cohen's literature review includes a summary of the legal research and social service research as of 1983, in addition to a review of the older empirical research. Id. at 16–40 (citing, e.g., R. Allen, E. Ferster & H. Weihofen, Mental Impairment and Legal Incompetency (1968); Ferster, *The Law in Transition: Civil Incompetency in the District of Columbia*, 16 Am. U. L. Rev. 236 (1967); Levy, *Protecting the Mentally Retarded: An Empirical Survey and Evaluation of the Establishment of State Guardianship in Minnesota*, 49 Minn. L. Rev. 821 (1967); Mesibov, Conover & Saur, *Limited Guardianship Laws and Developmentally Disabled Adults: Needs and Obstacles*, 18 Mental Retardation 221 (1980); Zenoff, *Civil Incompetency in the District of Columbia*, 32 Geo. Wash. L. Rev. 243 (1963)).

[Cf. Keith & Wacker, *Guardianship Reform: Does Revised Legislation Make a Difference in Outcomes for Proposed Wards?*, 4 J. Aging & Soc. Pol'y 139 (No. 3/4, 1992) (in Iowa and Missouri, least restrictive alternatives seldom employed and few petitions denied before or after legislative changes, but guardianships significantly longer before changes); H. Kritzer, Adult Guardianships in Wisconsin: An Empirical Study, Madison, Wis.: Elder Law Center (Jan. 1992) (describes implementation problems).]

[The opposition to guardianship reform by Real Property, Probate and Trust groups is well known. See, e.g., Barnes, *Florida Guardianship and the Elderly: The Paradoxical Right to Unwanted Assistance*, 40 U. Fla. L. Rev. 949, 952 n.10 (1988).]

50. Wards and medical experts were not interviewed.

51. M. Cohen, *supra* note 48, at 145.

Cohen concluded: "Though guardianship in and of itself does not have significant positive impacts on the alleged incompetent, neither are there many of the horror stories frequently found in previous guardianship research."[52] Guardianship's impact was positive on both the people closest to the ward and the institution treating the ward. Cohen suggested that reforms aimed at the guardianship weaknesses of questionable hearings, all-or-nothing judgment, and lack of concern for small estates, "may not be able to overcome ongoing workgroup dynamics"[53] determined by organizational factors (e.g, "doing justice, disposing of caseload, maintaining group cohesion, and reducing uncertainty").[54] He recommended prescreening to increase visibility, adding new workgroup participants, and providing expertise. He advocated more extensive use of trusts and avoidance of institutionalization. He suggested that courts should ask: "What is the person's situation and will guardianship enhance and protect him from a real danger?"[55] Finally, "In the end, we must be careful to have a system ... which does not necessarily interfere in people's lives but which makes certain that if such a need exists, alternatives will be available and used."[56]

San Mateo County (California) Study

A study of probate conservatorship court records for San Mateo County, California analyzed a sample of 178 proposed wards over age sixty from petitions filed in March, June, September, and December of 1982 and 1984 and between January and August, 1986.[57] The researchers estimated that a probate conservatorship petition was filed for approximately one third of one percent of the persons over age sixty-five in San Mateo County annually.[58] Those over age sixty accounted for 84% of probate conservatorships; two-thirds were women; the median age was eighty (eighty-two for women, seventy-seven for men). The study concluded that probate conservatorship for nonminors was viewed "as a permanent, terminal arrangement."[59] The Public Guardian petitioned in forty-five of the 178 cases; private parties in 133. The mean amount of personal property in the public cases was $41,000; $122,000 in private cases.

---

52. *Id.* at iv.
53. *Id.* at 227.
54. *Id.* at 55.
55. *Id.* at 229.
56. *Id.* at 229–30.
57. Friedman & Savage, *Taking Care: The Law of Conservatorship in California*, 61 So. Cal. L. Rev. 273 (1988).
58. *Id.* at 279.
59. *Id.*

The cause for conservatorship included a variety of events: "In most cases, the ward is quite impaired and the need is obvious."[60] Business affairs frequently made conservatorship necessary. In private cases, the petitioner was usually a relative who proposed to be conservator of both person and estate. The petitioner asked for extra authority for the conservator, including power to give informed medical consent in 70% of the cases. In forty-nine of the 178 cases, the conservator requested authority to sell property, and some files indicated this authority as the trigger for conservatorship.[61]

All but nineteen of 135 files had wards who were single, divorced, or widowed (68%). The Court Investigator reported that 60% of the sample made "intelligible" responses to questions.[62] The research observed "a high mortality rate" of 26.14% (forty of 153) during the "short" study period. By the time of the first annual review, fifty-two of fifty-eight wards were institutionalized.[63] At least half of the wards were able to give "intelligible" responses at the time of the annual review. The Court Investigator identified fifty-one of fifty-eight wards lacking capacity to give informed medical consent, which the researchers assessed as "oddly discordant" with the intelligibility report; "it is likely that there were some whose degree of mental impairment fell short of incompetence."[64] While the researchers found no "gross abuse of the process," they did suggest "a more subtle form of discrimination" or "prejudice (probably, unconscious) against the elderly" in third parties like convalescent homes which refused to accept a solitary, unsupervised, and injured elderly person without a conservatorship.[65]

The study observed that it was difficult to say whether probate conservatorship is used too much or too little. Measurement of underuse, which is the failure to get protection and the subsequent victimization, was problematic. The San Mateo study concluded that, "Perhaps the more important danger is *overuse*."[66]

Needs Survey

In contrast to an overuse hypothesis, some commentary suggests that the aspect of guardianship most in need of reform is the supply of

---

60. *Id.* at 280.
61. *Id.* at 282.
62. *Id.* at 283.
63. *Id.*
64. *Id.* at 284 n.26.
65. *Id.* at 284, 286.
66. *Id.* at 285 (emphasis in original).

guardians.[67] The Florida Department of Health and Rehabilitative Services reportedly estimated that it would cost $7 million to $9 million a year to provide (public) guardians to meet the need for guardians in Florida, a state that with its high proportion of elderly, represents aging America's demographic future.[68]

The only published quantitative research on the need for guardianship assessed the need in Florida in February 1983.[69] The study surveyed Florida's eleven Aging and Adult district offices; seventy-four public receiving facilities, community mental health centers, and clinics; thirty private receiving facilities; six state mental hospitals; and Developmental Services institutional and residential placements. The survey found 11,147 identifiable persons in need of public guardianship services: 6,054 functional incompetents for whom a petition would be instituted if public guardianship services were available; 2,842 legal incompetents without guardians adjudicated incompetent under the pre-1972 civil commitment statute; 1,643 institutionalized Developmental Services clients; and 608 residential Developmental Services clients. The survey did not include private clients residing in nursing homes[70] and adult congregate living facilities, or transients not served by public health and social services. While documenting the "rather substantial" unmet need, the realistic necessity to reduce the need through the use of alternatives to guardianship was acknowledged and advocated.[71]

Florida Public Guardianship Pilot Study

As a continuation of the Florida guardianship research agenda, the Florida Office of the State Courts Administrator sponsored a 1983 evaluation of the Florida Public Guardianship Pilot Program.[72] The Florida legislature appropriated funds for the purpose of piloting and evaluating professional and volunteer models of providing public guardianship services. The data sources for the program evaluation included: (1) intake

---

67. *See* W. Schmidt, K. Miller, W. Bell & E. New, *supra* note 23. *See also* Schmidt, *supra* note 28, at 191.

68. Topolnicki, *The Gulag of Guardianship*, Money, Mar. 1989, at 140, 149.

69. Schmidt & Peters, *supra* note 4. [*See also* chap. 3, *supra*.]

70. A survey of the need for guardians in Tennessee's nursing homes was underway through the Memphis State University Center for Health Services Research. [*See* chap. 3, *supra*.]

71. Schmidt & Peters, *supra* note 4, at 81–82.

72. Schmidt, Miller, Peters & Loewenstein, *A Descriptive Analysis of Professional and Volunteer Programs for the Delivery of Public Guardianship Services*, 8 Prob. L. J. 125 (1988).

form; (2) the Department of Health and Rehabilitative Services Client Assessment Form measuring living situation, activities, functional status (daily skills), nutrition status, medical status, intellectual functioning and behavior, and services and social support, which was administered at the time of appointment of the guardian program, and during the 9 1/2 month project's final few weeks; (3) guardianship plans, modeled after mental disability treatment and habilitation plans; (4) guardian activity reports, similar to work chronology records,[73] and attorney timekeeping logs; and (5) site visit observations and interviews of significant actors, including wards.

One of the most important findings of the evaluation was that although the wards of both program models were the product of one state guardianship law, the wards in each model were demographically different.[74] The twenty-one wards of the Dade County professional model were younger, more acutely disturbed (half were diagnosed as psychotic), and more likely to reside in a psychiatric (29%) or general medical hospital (24%). The fifty-two wards of the volunteer model were older (average age seventy seven, median age eighty-two), 80% female (two-thirds female in the professional model), and all but two were white (74% white in the professional model), with 42% in nursing homes and 22% in hospitals. Similarities included highly reduced self-care capabilities, confusion, no family (30% in professional, 39% in volunteer), limited personal contact with the guardian program personnel, need for supervision, marginal financial situations dependent upon Social Security and public benefit programs, and passive, isolated lives limited to eating, sleeping, and watching television.

> The principal significance of this finding debates a perception that incompetent persons without resources to employ a private guardian, and without willing and responsible family members or friends to serve as guardian, are homogeneous. The data in this study [suggest] that wards of a public guardian may not be homogeneous.
>
> Such a finding would stimulate several questions. Are public guardian wards unique, or instead are they virtually indistinguishable from other classes of persons, except for the fact that public guardian wards have been identified and adjudicated incompetent? If public guardian wards are indistinguishable from other groups, what is the purpose of the legal label of incompetence?[75]

---

73. *See* H. Mintzberg. The Nature of Managerial Work 21–22 (1973).
74. Schmidt, Miller, Peters & Loewenstein, *supra* note 72, at 133–34, 148–49, 152.
75. *Id.* at 152 (citing Mitchell, *Involuntary Guardianship for Incompetents: A Strategy for Legal Services Advocates*, 12 Clearinghouse Rev. 451, 453 (1978) ("Benevolent motivations justify the use of amorphous incompetency standards...")).

The professional model wards were also compared with clients of the Cathedral Foundation in Jacksonville, a protective services and guardianship "alternative" or prevention program funded by the Area Agency on Aging with Older Americans Act funds.[76] The intention was to test change in the level of functioning without guardianship, but these two groups turned out demographically different (by age, race, independent living, and psychiatric condition) as well. While the professional model wards and protective services clients were comparable in many functional and behavioral variables, the protective services clients were five times as likely to live independently, and half as likely to reside in an institution.[77] Concerning demographic characteristics, the evaluation concluded:

> [W]hy are two groups, who have relevant functional and behavioral variables in common, legally incompetent on one hand (Dade), and mere protective services clients (Cathedral) on the other? One possibility suggested during interviews was that there are historical incidents that lead to legal incompetence that are not reflected in functional assessments after adjudication of incompetence. This matter of possibly unique case histories requires further study.[78]

Another significant finding of the evaluation was that the status of the professional and volunteer programs' wards at the time of the final assessment was equal to or better than at the outset of guardianship.[79] Restoration of legal competence was a very rare event. This suggests that guardianship neither rehabilitates nor necessarily slows natural deterioration. The questions of guardianship's real purpose, and the nature of wards' histories, seem reinforced.

A most important accomplishment of the pilot program was the empirical identification of the quantity and nature of (public) guardian work.[80] The professional program averaged 5.6 hours to each ward per month, the volunteer program ten hours. Both programs spent more time on their wards' medical status, services and social support, and financial status than on activities, self-care skills, nutrition, and behavior and orientation problems. "A major function of the guardian is that of procuring, as opposed to delivering direct services...."[81]

---

76. The Cathedral Foundation has enjoyed an excellent reputation. *See, e.g.*, W. Schmidt, K. Miller, W. Bell & E. New, supra note 23; AP Report, *supra* note 9, at 26; Topolnicki, *supra* note 68, at 144–45.
77. Schmidt, Miller, Peters & Loewenstein, *supra* note 72, at 151–52.
78. *Id.* at 152.
79. *Id.* at 136, 152–53.
80. *Id.* at 141–45, 149, 155.
81. *Id.* at 143.

The panacea of volunteers was sharply questioned. "Volunteers must be recruited, trained, professionally supported, monitored, and replaced. All of this activity is at the opportunity cost of the direct client services that recruiters, trainers, professionals, and monitors could be performing instead. In essence, volunteers are not truly cost-free...."[82]

The evaluation concluded that "[g]uardianship realistically is a legal, surrogate decisionmaking device to facilitate legal, social functioning concerning persons who are incapable—or perhaps unwilling—of making decisions."[83] As such, eligibility criteria should be tightened and procedures enhanced, and "much greater use" should be made of "legal alternatives to guardianship."[84]

Andrus Gerontology Center Study

The purpose of a recent study, funded by the U.S. Department of Health and Human Services "Social Services Policy Research" initiative, was to examine the 270 cases of vulnerable elders referred to the Los Angeles County Public Guardian in the first quarter of 1985 "in order to identify service system and policy gaps which may impede the use of less restrictive alternatives."[85] Representatives of thirty-seven organizations participated in weekly case conferences and bi-monthly technical and policy assistance group meetings to analyze the content of cases and to recommend courses of action. In 1983 and 1984, 10% of the ninety referrals per month resulted in probate conservatorships that were recommended by the public guardian and approved by the court. In the first quarter of 1985, 20% of referrals were appropriate for public probate conservatorship.

Eighty percent of referrals were over age sixty from a Los Angeles population of 7 ½ million, with ¾ million over age sixty-five. "The most prevalent presenting problems [of all referrals] were needs for money management or protection of assets, chronic or acute physical illness, chronic or new mental impairments, and lack of family supports."[86] "Gap in social service" cases were 14.1% (thirty-eight) of the 270 referrals and con-

---

82. *Id.* at 155. *See also id.* at 146.
83. *Id.* at 153.
84. *Id.*
85. R. Steinburg, Alternative Approaches to Conservatorship and Protection of Older Adults Referred to Public Guardian, Sept. 1985, p. 1 (Institute for Policy and Program Development, Los Angeles, CA).
86. *Id.* at "Summary."

tributed to "inappropriate referrals for conservatorship and premature institutionalization."[87] The project experience suggested that case management programs had "a tendency to refer the case to PG [the Public Guardian] when the client is unpleasant, has threatening or indifferent relatives, needs help with money or property management, needs a new placement, or has behavior patterns such as substance abuse which interfere with 'cost effectiveness.'"[88]

Lawyers constituted the fifth largest referral source (twenty-two referrals, 8%) and had the highest acceptance rate (33.3%). Fifty-one of the referrals (18.9%) were examples of referral sources using conservatorship as a threat to noncompliant clients or client family members. The study found that numerous nursing home residents did not have family or family surrogates to act as the responsible party; unverified labels of mental or physical impairment led to inappropriate care and inattention to rehabilitation; assistance with money management was a major service gap; transitional decisions required moderate use of temporary conservatorships; many persons not meeting conservatorship criteria were new residents of skilled nursing facilities needing case advocacy; appropriate placement was impeded by nonmedical intermediate care service shortages and gaps; inappropriate referrals often needed on-going case management; more extensive monitoring and technical assistance was required for conservatorships; skillful casework could have addressed service and medical treatment refusals; and a potential conservatorship alternative was the Durable Power of Attorney for Health Care.[89] Three "cross-cutting" obstacles for the agency representatives were inadequate levels of public guardian staffing, inadequate practitioner knowledge about alternative community resources, and inadequate client communication.[90]

Ethnographic Illinois Study

One of the most recently published accounts of guardianship research was a six month ethnographic study of judicial decisionmaking in three Illinois counties (Cook, Lake, and Du Page) involving fourteen courtroom observations and interviews with eleven attorneys or program administrators.[91] The only quantitative information from the published study was

---

87. *Id.* at 47, 49.
88. *Id.* at 49.
89. *Id.* at "Summary."
90. *Id.* at 82–83.
91. Iris, *Guardianship and the Elderly: A Multi-Perspective View of the Decisionmaking Process*, 28 Gerontologist 40 (June Supp. 1988). [At least one case does not consider ethnography to be science for judicial purposes. United States v. Pryba, 678 F.Supp. 1225

that in thirty-eight (49%) of seventy-seven cases from Lake County, an adult child was appointed guardian of a parent; other relatives (spouses, siblings) were the guardians in 25% of the cases. In Du Page County, adult children were guardians of parents in fifty (47%) of 106 cases; other relatives in 35%. The study found that the guardianship proceedings drew upon medical and legal standards in determining individual need for surrogate decisionmaking, and recommended explication of the link between these standards. Legal and medical practitioners' failure to distinguish between transitory mental status and permanent change inhibited imposition of limited guardian powers. Beliefs and attitudes about aging had great impact on the guardianship process, resulting in some unnecessary restrictions on autonomy.

Summary

Guardianship research has reached the point of providing some descriptive and quantitative information about numbers of wards in particular places at certain times. Information about what causes people to be brought into the court system is limited to some data about general disabilities, the facilitation of third party interests, particular triggering incidents in case histories, lack of family supports, and needs for money management and assets protection. Older people under guardianship do not seem particularly homogeneous; or at least, common predictive characteristics are as yet unidentified.

The guardians are frequently relatives, with some tendency to a correlation between the size of the estate and availability of relatives. Incompetents without willing and responsible family members or friends, and without resources to secure professional guardianship services, are eligible for public guardianship.

After persons become wards, there is some evidence of home selling, institutionalization, and possibly death, as well as unprofessional guardianship service. The guardianship information about low income and minority elderly wards is fairly preliminary and geographically limited. Knowledge about the guardianship system in varied communities (e.g, urban, rural) is almost nonexistent.

(E.D. Va. 1988), *aff'd*, 900 F.2d 748 (4th Cir. 1990).]

[*See also* Bulcroft, Kielkopf & Tripp, *Elderly Wards and Their Legal Guardians: Analysis of County Probate Records in Ohio and Washington*, 31 Gerontologist 156 (1991) (standardized and reliable competency assessments lacking; family member petition for guardianship seldom challenged; goal of most guardianships is to preserve the estate).]

Assessment

While there is widespread advocacy of alternatives to guardianship, relatively little attention has been paid to the distinction between alternatives to guardianship for persons who are incompetent, and (preventive or diversionary) alternatives to guardianship for persons who are not incompetent (and for whom guardianship is inappropriate). In order for a preventive or diversionary alternatives strategy to be successful, there should be evidence to support the Administration on Aging's hypothesis that "assistance and education, before the issue reaches the crisis stage, might reduce the level of service required, delay the need for the service or even make the service unnecessary."[92]

Future Research

The ideal approach for proving preventability would be to randomly assign older persons to experimental groups receiving diversionary alternatives, and to control groups receiving either traditional services or nothing, and to track the groups over time with the anticipation that the rate of guardianship would be lower for the experimental group than the control group. This ideal approach is problematic because of the very low base rate of guardianship, the limited time period for most projects, the likely high cost, the ethical risks of bad outcomes for the experimental group, and service deprivation for the control group.

A variation of this design might utilize a competence assessment instrument[93] to focus the groupings on the most vulnerable elderly. One of the difficulties is that while such instruments can discriminate institutional from non-institutional populations, no available instrument has been val-

---

92. 53 Fed. Reg. 50, 166 (1988). [*But see* Wilber, *Alternatives to Conservatorship: The Role of Daily Money Management Services,* 31 Gerontologist 150 (1991) (quasi-experimental design used to show no significant difference in rates of conservatorship between those offered daily money management service and those not; daily money management does not seem to divert from conservatorship).]

93. *E.g.*, G. Fillenbaum, Multidimensional, Functional Assessment of Older Adults: The Duke Older American Resources and Services Procedures (1988); Reisberg, Ferris & Transsen, *An Ordinal Functional Assessment Tool for Alzheimer's—Type Dementia,* 36 Hosp. & Community Psychiatry 593 (1985); Saunders & Simon, *Individual Functional Assessment: An Instruction Manual,* 11 Mental & Physical Disability L. Rep. 60 (1987); P. Loeb, Validity of the Community Competency Scale with the Elderly (1983) (unpublished Saint Louis University dissertation).

idated for identifying and predicting legal incompetence and guardianship.[94]

The best viable approach may be a retrospective analysis of a population of wards, and a population of persons receiving guardianship alternatives, in order to identify common and distinguishing characteristics, as well as to determine causation on a case history basis, and outcomes.

---

94. *See, e.g.*, Hafemeister & Sales, *Interdisciplinary Evaluations for Guardianships and Conservatorships*, 8 Hum. Behav. Nos. 3 & 4, 335 (1984); Nolan, *Functional Evaluation of the Elderly in Guardianship Proceedings*, 17 L. Med. & Health Care 210 (1984); Scogin & Perry, *Guardianship Proceedings with Older Adults: The Role of Functional Assessment and Gerontologists*, 10 L. & Psychology Rev. 123 (1986).

Part VII

Beyond the Court of Last Resort: Involuntary Adult Protective Services

Chapter 13

Improving the Social Treatment Model in Protective Services for the Elderly: False Needs in the Therapeutic State

Winsor C. Schmidt, Jr.
Kent S. Miller

>   Abstract. With the aging of the population bulge and legal reform of the civil commitment and guardianship processes, greater use of adult protective services can be anticipated. Adult protective services are subject to the same therapeutic state exploitation and abuse as civil commitment and guardianship. The pure social treatment model of protective services seems to do more harm than good. The necessary improvement to the social treatment model is concentration on a new and more sophisticated legal intervention approach. In a time of scarce resources and cutback, imposition of legal model improvements also carries economic and efficiency imperatives.

About 23.5 million people (one of every nine) in the United States were over age sixty-five in 1977, and in excess of thirty-two million were over age sixty.[1] The aging of the population bulge is going to cause even higher elderly proportions in the future.

Assessments of older people in Cleveland, Ohio and Durham, North Carolina indicate that only one of every five over age sixty-five is not impaired, with twenty-three percent generally impaired.[2] An assumption that individuals "greatly impaired" or worse need some form of protective services means that fourteen percent of the over age sixty-five population, or 3.3 million people, require protective care or assistance. This is close to Regan and Springer's estimates, without the functional assess-

---

1. J. Regan & G. Springer, Protective Services for the Elderly: A Working Paper, Washington, D.C.: U.S. Government Printing Office (1977).
2. Comptroller General, The Well-Being of Older People in Cleveland, Ohio, Washington, D.C.: General Accounting Office (1977).

ments, that ten to fifteen percent, or three to four million, over age sixty need protective services, and another three to four million may be in need if existing forms of support from family, friends, and special services cease.

The social cost of neglect to older individuals has been reviewed elsewhere.[3] While there are at least 134 federally sponsored or supported programs providing assistance to older people, and while persons over age sixty-five receive over $90 million in retirement funds from pension and disability programs like Social Security, Supplement Security Income, Railroad Retirement, and Federal Employee Retirement, public policy still relies primarily on institutional care as the principal service to disabled older persons.[4] But there is the beginning of a structure to provide alternatives.

The provision of protective services under Title XX of the Social Security Act has the following specific goals:

(1) Achieving or maintaining economic self-support to prevent, reduce, or eliminate dependency;

(2) Achieving or maintaining self-sufficiency, including reduction or prevention of dependency;

(3) Preventing or remedying neglect, abuse, or exploitation of children and adults unable to protect their own interests, or preserving, rehabilitating, or reuniting families.

(4) Preventing or reducing inappropriate institutional care by providing for community-based care, home-based care, or other forms of less intensive care;

(5) Securing referral or admission for institutional care when other forms of care are not appropriate, or providing services to individuals in institutions.[5]

Virtually every state in the United States has a statutory or regulatory provision for adult protective services, and some services are offered under private auspices.[6] A majority of the clients of these program are elderly. However, the concept of protective services is not uniformly or well developed.[7]

---

3. *See, e.g.*, J. Regan & G. Springer, *supra* note 1; W. Schmidt, K. Miller, W. Bell & E. New, Public Guardianship and the Elderly (1981).

4. Comptroller General, *supra* note 2; J. Regan & G. Springer, *supra* note 1.

5. 45 C.F.R. section 228 (a).

6. Regan, *Adult Protective Services: An Appraisal and a Prospectus*, in National Law & Social Work Seminar: Proceedings and Prospects 12–19 (1982).

7. M. Axilbund, Exercising Judgment for the Disabled: Report of an Inquiry into Limited Guardianship, Public Guardianship and Adult Protective Services in Six States, Washington, D.C.: American Bar Association Commission on the Mentally Disabled (1979).

The extent of provision for adult protective services internationally is unclear. Forty-three countries have general mental health legislation, and some countries have specific laws providing for guardianship or foster-home care that facilitate payments for such care, or protect property rights.[8] Quebec and other provinces in Canada provide the services of a public trustee, in Alberta under the auspices of a Dependent Adults Act.[9] England,[10] the Netherlands,[11] and Poland[12] address protective services clients in the context of guardianship. The international experience with protective services seems otherwise undocumented.

The services provided to achieve the goals outlined in the Social Security Act may include supportive care in the home, diagnosis and treatment of health problems (including mental health), placement in a variety of institutional settings, and a range of legal interventions (e.g., powers of attorney, guardianship, civil commitment).

Protective services, in contrast to social services, should only occur on a surrogate basis either at "the request of a vulnerable, dependent person or ordered by the court."[13]

> The surrogate function is the heart and soul of a protective service program. It can be defined as the delegation by the client, or the substitution through legal means, of the client's decision-making power to another person, or persons, professionally responsible and legally accountable for the purposes of assuring that the client receives the necessary protection, whatever services this may require.[14]

It is the potential misuse of this "authority to intervene" and the assumption of the surrogate function that is the major focus of this chapter. The

---

8. Curran, *Comparative Analysis of Mental Health Legislation in Forty-three Countries: A Discussion of Historical Trends*, 1 Int'l J. L. & Psychiatry 79 (1978).

9. Bergeron, *The Legal Status of a Person Under the Jurisdiction of the Public Trustee: Quebec Law with Comparisons to that of Other Provinces of Canada*, 5 Int'l J. L. & Psychiatry 355 (1982).

10. Gostin, *The Merger of Incompetency and Certification: The Illustration of Unauthorized Medical Contact in the Psychiatric Context*, 2 Int'l J. L. & Psychiatry 127 (1979). [See also Barnes, *Beyond Guardianship Reform: A Reevaluation of Autonomy and Beneficence for a System of Principled Decision-making in Long Term Care*, 41 Emory L. J. 633, 660–62 (1992) (protective services in England).]

11. Dekker, *Mental Health Legislation in the Netherlands: Civil and Administrative Law*, 2 Int'l J. L. & Psychiatry 469 (1979).

12. Gostin, *supra* note 10.

13. E. Ferguson, Protecting the Vulnerable Adult: A Perspective on Policy and Program Issues in Adult Protective Services, Ann Arbor, MI: Institute of Gerontology, p. 39 (1978).

14. G. Hall & G. Mathiason, Overcoming Barriers to Protective Services for the Aged, New York: National Council on Aging (1968).

"readiness to use professional authority" is said to be central to a successful program, but it is this authority that is now being brought into question.

Some states authorize involuntary protective services court intervention merely upon a showing of physically caused functional disorders. Such provisions raise questions concerning informed consent and privacy. There seems to be a shift in protective services legislation from mental capacity to make decisions, to capacity to care and protect oneself, a trend toward possibly excessive and paternalistic protectionism. This may be particularly inappropriate in light of recent understandings. There is a general popular premise that old age is necessarily equated with deterioration, usually of an irreversible nature. The literature indicates, however, that variation in function increases as the age of people studied increases, and that any generalization about "the aged" may be unsound.[15] The observed decline in intellectual functioning among older persons is not intrinsically related to the aging process. Several studies indicate that the elderly as a class are "treatable" and much more capable of independent functioning than is generally assumed.[16]

Criteria permitting protective services intervention can be vague, including justification like "advanced age," "the infirmities of aging," and senility." Such court experts as mental health professionals too frequently have the responsibility of discretion, at least by default, to determine the applicability of these vague but seemingly therapeutic labels. Old age can begin statutorily at age sixty in one state or age seventy in another. Involuntary placement on an "emergency" basis without a formal hearing can last for six days in Florida, or three or four weeks in Alabama. In short, safeguards against inappropriate placement and procedural abuse seem inadequate.

Background

The traditional approach to protective services in the late 1960s and the 1970s was the "social treatment model",[17] as epitomized by the Benjamin Rose Institute of Cleveland and United Charities of Chicago.[18] While

---

15. Horstman, *Protective Services for the Elderly: The Limits of Parens Patriae*, 40 Mo. L. Rev. 215 (1975).

16. R. Glasscote, Old Folks at Home, Washington, D.C.: Joint Information Service of the American Psychiatric Association and the National Association for Mental Health (1977); Horstman, *supra* note 15.

17. Siporin, *Social Treatment: A New-Old Helping Method*, 15 Soc. Work 13 (1970).

18. Blenkner, Bloom & Nielson, *A Research and Demonstration Project of Protective Services*, 52 Soc. Casework 483 (1971); W. Schmidt, K. Miller, W. Bell & E. New, *supra* note 3.

there have been other demonstration protective service projects,[19] the Benjamin Rose Institute study is one of the most frequently cited, and uniquely, involved an experimental design.

The Benjamin Rose study casts grave doubt on the efficacy of the social treatment model.[20] Not only did the provision of state-of-the-art protective services fail to prevent or slow deterioration or death, but the experimental group had a higher rate of institutionalization and death than did the control group receiving referral agency services or no services, an outcome inconsistent with the Title XX goals of preventing or reducing institutionalization, reuniting families, or preventing dependency.

A subsequent reanalysis by other investigators suggested that the findings on death were a result of initial group differences in survival-related characteristics not controlled by the random sampling techniques; but the reanalysis did not mitigate the strong effect of experimental group membership on the tendency to be institutionalized.[21] Furthermore, there is considerable evidence that mortality is higher to a staggering degree in institutional populations than in the general population.[22] The higher mortality rate among protectively placed elderly applies to nursing homes as well as mental institutions.[23] After a certain period of time, institution staff spend more time treating the effects of "institutionalization syndrome"[24] than the original disability.[25]

The lack of credibility for social treatment model protective services correlatives with a growing disenchantment for the "therapeutic state"

---

19. G. Hall & G. Mathiasen, Guide to the Development of Protective Services for Older People, Springfield, IL: Charles C. Thomas (1973); Report of the National Protective Services Project for Older Adults, OHEW Publication No. 585 72-23008 (1971). [The National Committee for the Prevention of Elder Abuse and the San Francisco Consortium for Elder Abuse Prevention are compiling findings from U.S. Administration on Aging Title IV research and demonstration projects on elder abuse, protective services, and guardianship for a 1994 grant from the Administrative on Aging.]

20. Blenkner, Bloom & Nielson, *supra* note 18; M. Blenkner, M. Bloom, M. Nielson & R. Weber, Final Report—Protective Services for the Elderly: Finding from the Benjamin Rose Institute Study, Cleveland, OH: Benjamin Rose Institute (1974).

21. Berger & Pillavin *The Effect of Casework: A Research Note*, 21 Soc. Work 105 (1976).

22. Special Senate Committee on Aging, Mental Health Care and the Elderly: Shortcomings in Public Policy, Washington, D.C.: S. Rep. No. 38-596, 92nd Cong., 2d Sess. (1970).

23. Subcommittee on Long-Term Care of the Senate Special Committee on Aging, Nursing Home Care in the United States: Failure in Public Policy—Introductory Report (1974).

24. E. Goffman, Asylums: Essays on the Social Situation of Mental Patients and Other Inmates, Garden City, NY: Anchor Books (1961).

25. Deposition of Dr. Israel Zwerling, *Wyatt v. Stickney*, in Legal Rights of the Mentally Handicapped, New York, NY: Practicing Law Institute (1973).

generally.[26] In 1971, Kittrie identified the growth of a "new system of social controls" designated as "the therapeutic state".[27] Clients of the therapeutic state include such "deviants" as criminals, the mentally ill and retarded, juvenile and defective delinquents, alcoholics, drug offenders, sex offenders, wards of the public guardian, and the protectively serviced elderly.[28] The danger of the therapeutic state lies in the conditioning of society to consider those with any label of deviance as "'different', rarely considering the possibility that deviance could easily be broadened to encompass many unsuspecting conditions."[29]

Congruent with the Benjamin Rose study, there is some evidence that involuntary treatment for dangerousness to self increases the rate of suicide.[30] A long term major delinquency program found no significant difference between treatment and control groups; in fact, the longer and more intensive the treatment, the more negative eventual outcomes.[31] A study of mental patients released from Alabama mental institutions by court order concluded that "family members adjusted expectations and accepted the patient home" when the state did not provide the alternative of a mental hospital.[32] Currently there seems to be a widespread belief that there is a large number of frail older people in the United States who are in need of protection and treatment, and who are not in a position to make competent judgments about these needs. In order to provide this care and treatment, several mechanisms have been employed — civil commitment, guardianship, the appointment of a representative payee, and the like. The attention formerly focused on civil commitment shifts to guardianship as commitment criteria and procedures are tightened and a legal

---

26. W. Gaylin, I. Glasser, S. Marcus & D. Rothman, Doing Good: The Limits of Benevolence, New York, NY: Pantheon Books (1978); N. Kittrie The Right to Be Different: Deviance and Enforced Therapy, Baltimore: Johns Hopkins Press (1971); K. Miller, Managing Madness: The Case Against Civil Commitment, New York: Free Press (1976)); K. Miller, The Criminal Justice and Mental Health Systems: Conflict and Collusion, Cambridge, MA: Oelgeschlager, Gunn & Hain (1980); T. Szasz, Law, Liberty, and Psychiatry: An Inquiry into the Social Uses of Mental Health Practices, New York: Macmillan (1963). [P. Conrad & J. Schneider, *Deviance and Medicalization: From Badness to Sickness*, Philadelphia: Temple Univ. Press (1992).]

27. N. Kittrie, *supra* note 26, at 41.

28. Horstman, *supra* note 15; N. Kittrie, *supra* note 26; W. Schmidt, K. Miller, W. Bell & E. New, *supra* note 3.

29. N. Kittrie, *supra* note 26, at 361.

30. Greenberg, *Involuntary Psychiatric Commitments to Prevent Suicide*, 49 N. Y. U. L. Rev. 227 (1974).

31. *See, e.g.*, McCord, *A Thirty-Year Follow-up of Treatment Effects*, 33 Am. Psychologist 284 (1978).

32. Leaf, *Patients Released After Wyatt: Where Did They Go?*, 28 Hospital & Community Psychiatry 366 (1977).

model is implemented. In turn, as the therapeutic model in guardianship is balanced by a more formal legal model, it can be expected that the therapeutic model will prosper is newer areas, such as "protective" or supportive services.

While generalizability, and applicability to protective services, must necessarily be limited, we believe services findings from Benjamin Rose, and similar findings for analogous treatment efforts, are clear enough that consideration of an alternative, and comparatively innovative, approach to protective services is warranted.

Proposed Problem Resolving Approach

Legal intervention generally cannot be claimed as a new approach to protective services, as it was the mode for delivering protective services in the late 1950s and early 1960s, "reaching tidal wave proportions by the mid-1960s."[33] Protective services during this period were a response to the 1962 and 1965 amendments to the Social Security Act, and the Older Americans Act of 1965, and consisted of particular "protective" legal proceedings, primarily guardianships of the estate and commitment to mental institutions. The outcomes for protective services at this time included disproportionate invocation of such proceedings against the elderly, at the initiation and for the principal benefit of persons other than the client.[34]

The revitalization of protective services followed the 1974 social services amendments to the Social Security Act. The new definition and goals for protective services expanded eligibility criteria in an effort to get the elderly out of the courts, but retained "the concept of impairment from the previous legalistic definition without recognizing the source of the concept."[35] The result has been a notion of protective services that is so broad, almost any social services constitutes a protective services, and almost any adult client, especially the elderly, qualifies.[36]

Given the inevitable frustration from such a vagueness that is manifest in the Benjamin Rose outcomes, we propose that adult protective service programs be improved by overtly recognizing the significance of legal interventions for protective services through identification and imple-

---

33. Hobbs, *Adult Protective Services: A New Program Approach*, 34 Pub. Welfare 28, 30 (Summer 1976).
34. *See, e.g.*, Note, *The Disguised Oppression of Involuntary Guardianships: Have the Elderly Freedom to Spend?*, 73 Yale L. J. 676 (1964).
35. Hobbs, *supra* note 33, at 30.
36. Hobbs, *supra* note 33.

mentation of a state-of-the-art continuum of legal interventions for elderly clients.

What distinguishes the new legal intervention approach from the 1960s legal intervention approach is the expansion and sophistication of the legal interventions available on behalf of a client. The inappropriate use of guardianship and civil commitment proceedings has continued under the 1970s social treatment model of protective services, and has been sharply criticized.[37] It is not widely appreciated, for example, that an adjudication of incompetence in guardianship restricts or takes away "the right to: make contracts; sell, purchase, mortgage, or lease property; make gifts; travel, or decide where to live; vote, or hold elected office; initiate or defend against suits; make a will, or revoke one; engage in certain professions; lend or borrow money; appoint agents; divorce or marry; refuse medical treatment; keep and care for children; serve on jury; be a witness to any legal document; drive a car; pay or collect debts; and manage or run a business."[38] Just not being able to drive a car can have a devastating, domino effect on the life of an older person in today's mobile society.

The social treatment model has dealt with authority,[39] and the seeking and exercise of authority over an older person, by denying its use and utility.[40] We propose the approach of limiting protective services to the surrogate function encompassing either requests for protective services by older persons, or services ordered by court.

There is a wider range of legal intervention approaches available than just guardianship and civil commitment. These interventions extend on an intrusiveness continuum from less restrictive and drastic, and compatible with a client's wishes, to more restrictive and drastic, and less compatible with a client who considers him- or herself unworthy, wishes to harm oneself, or is incapable of indicating volition.

One legal intervention that can be utilized is power of attorney, and its close namesake, the durable family power of attorney. A power of attorney involves one person (the "principal") giving another person (the "attor-

---

37. *See, e.g.*, G. Alexander & T. Lewin, The Aged and the Need for Surrogate Management, Syracuse, NY: Syracuse University Press (1972); Mitchell, *Involuntary Guardianship for Incompetence: A Strategy for Legal Services Advocates*, 12 Clearinghouse Rev. 451 (1978); Parmalee, *Protective Services for the Elderly: Do We Deal Competently with Incompetence?*, 2 L.& Pol'y Q. 387 (1980); Regan, *Protective Services for the Elderly: Commitment, Guardianship and Alternatives*, 13 Wm. & Mary L. Rev. 569 (1972); Regan, *supra* note 6; W. Schmidt, K. Miller, W. Bell & E. New, *supra* note 3.

38. R. Brown, The Rights of Older Persons, New York, NY: Avon Books, p. 286 (1979).

39. G. Mathiasen, Guardianships and Protective Service for Older People, Albany, NY: Fort Orange Press (1963).

40. Hobbs, *supra* note 33.

ney in fact") the written authority to do some act in the name of the principal.[41] The durable family power of attorney device designates a close relative (spouse, parent, child, or sibling) to handle one's affairs. A regular power of attorney is terminated by any incompetency, whereas a durable family power of attorney remains valid unless there is a formal adjudication of incompetency in a guardianship proceeding. The power of attorney can be used to eliminate dependency, maintain self-sufficiency, and prevent exploitation. It is not usually necessary to involve a court to give power of attorney. The durable family power of attorney is an effective substitute for guardianship.[42] It can be used to plan for incapacity, and can alleviate the need for guardianship, civil commitment, or the problems of mechanical life-supporting measures when terminally ill.[43] Attorneys in the New York and New Jersey metropolitan area utilize living wills in the mental hospital discharge planning and aftercare process.

Other ways, short of guardianship, by which economic self-sufficiency can be achieved, dependency minimized, and exploitation prevented, include single transaction court ratification of a particular action, custodianship and gifts to minors, joint ownership, inter vivos transfers of property, deeds of guardianship, and trusts. There is a detailed literature[44] for each of these measures. It is sufficient to say at this point that the proper legal alternative for protective services clients will reduce or eliminate the need to take legal action against a client, while increasing the array of legal interventions that secure social services for the client and protect the client's interests and resources. This is nothing less than personal and estate planning for low and middle income elderly persons (who frequently have hidden or undiscovered assets merely requiring discovery, rather than a presumption of poverty). (This presumption of poverty may be another manifestation of the sort of ageism that discriminates against older persons and treats them as less than whole persons.)

One task of another legal intervention, public guardianship, and its private sector equivalent, corporate guardianship, is to discover hidden assets

---

41. See, e.g., Regan, *supra* note 37.

42. *Legal Problems of the Aged and Infirm—The Durable Power of Attorney—Planned Protective Services—The Living Will*, 13 Real Prop. Prob. & Tr. J. 321 (1975). [But cf. J. Federman & M. Reed, *Abuse and the Durable Power of Attorney: Options for Reform*, Albany, NY: Gov't Law Center of Albany Law School (1984) (nat'l survey of 410 responding attorneys, social service providers, and NY surrogate court judges, of 7,000 surveys distributed, found that 94% believed durable power of attorney abuse occurs at least occasionally; provides 15 legislative reform options).]

43. Alexander, *Premature Probate: A Different Perspective on Guardianship for the Elderly*, 31 Stan. L. Rev. 1003 (1979).

44. See, e.g., R. Brown, *supra* note 38; Regan, *supra* note 37; Schlesinger, *Deeds of Guardianship*, 8 Prob. & Prop. 4 (1979).

and to secure access to government benefits, and the like, that are forthcoming to an older person who may appear to be indigent.[45] The public fiduciary, conservator, and public trustee[46] are all similar approaches and potential legal interventions on behalf of protective service clients.

Another legal intervention is substitute or representative payee. Recipients of funds from several government agencies (Social Security Administration, Veterans Administration, Department of Defense, Railroad Retirement Board, Civil Service) can have substitute payees appointed if an individual meets a test of incapacity that varies from agency to agency.[47] Use of this intervention could reduce inappropriate guardianship, prevent or remedy exploitation, and assist with economic self-support.

Much has been written about the traditional legal interventions of guardianship and civil commitment. Protective services itself has acquired its own legal criteria and procedures.[48] The state-of-the-art concerning guardianship and civil commitment has become more sophisticated; better criteria and procedures have been identified for successful employment of these interventions, and their inappropriate use can be reduced.[49] The President's Commission on Mental Health suggests one further approach for improvement:

> Unfortunately, many state protective services laws provide for involuntary protective services without the same due process procedural protections which are required by State . . . involuntary commitment laws. These proceedings should not be used as a method of avoiding the constitutionally required procedures.
>
> Additionally, a State's involuntary commitment, guardianship and protective service laws should interrelate to each other in a rational manner and definitions should be consistent.[50]

Guardianship, for example, is more appropriate than civil commitment for an individual who needs treatment but is not aware of that need. Civil commitment should only be utilized in the event of: severe mental disorder, overt dangerous acts, absence of capacity, and treatability.[51]

---

45. W. Schmidt, K. Miller, W. Bell & E. New, *supra* note 3.

46. *The Public Trustee—Is it the Answer for Modest Sized Estates, Trusts and Conservatorships?*, 10 Real Prop. Prob. & Tr. J. 321 (1975).

47. R. Brown, *supra* note 38; Regan, *supra* note 37.

48. Regan, *Protecting the Elderly: The New Paternalism*, 32 Hastings L. J. 1111 (1981).

49. *See, e.g.. Guardianship and Conservatorship Act*, 3 Mental Disability L. Rep. 264 (1979); *Legal Issues in State Mental Health Care: Proposals for Change—Civil Commitment, Guardianship*, 2 Mental Disability L. Rep. 75, 443 (1977).

50. Report of the Task Panel on Legal and Ethical Issues, in President's Commission on Mental Health, Vol IV, Washington, D.C.: U.S. Government Printing Office (1978).

51. *Legal Issues in State Mental Health Care: Proposals for Change—Civil Commitment, Guardianship*, *supra* note 49.

Conclusion

Mental health programming is the grist for the mill of the therapeutic state. Unlike the welfare state, the therapeutic state assumes that its clients are too mentally incompetent to be voluntary, or to realize the beneficence of preferred assistance, and therefore attempts to administer its services involuntarily.[52] Involuntary civil commitment of alcoholics, drug abusers, juveniles, the mentally ill, and the mentally retarded, and involuntary guardianship, are the legal means by which this is carried out.

To these processes may be added involuntary protective services. With the same avowedly benign and ever humanitarian purpose (e.g., treatment, prevention of neglect and abuse), and with the same vague mental health criteria (e.g., mental or emotional dysfunctioning), adults, and especially the elderly, are subject to removal from their homes (why does the victim get displaced, and the abuser remain, as the means of protecting the victim?), placement in an institution, subversion of volition, and adoption of the state's wishes regarding the disposition of one's life. Accused criminals are subject to stricter eligibility criteria (definitions of crime), and far more rights and due process.

We suggest that there are less restrictive and more appropriate legal alternatives to protective services,[53] and that the criteria and procedures for imposing protective services can be strengthened. We do not deny that there is a real, desperate, and growing need for services to older persons, but we do not believe that such services should be imposed at the discretion of a mental health professional. Matters of free will and responsibility are the appropriate subject of law. Enhancing the legal model for service delivery will restore the existing imbalance.

Improving protective services through enhancement of a legal model is even more imperative in view of national cut-backs in health and social services. In order for limited resources to be expanded efficiently, over-protectionism, inappropriate services, and services that cause more harm than good must be reduced. Appropriate legal safeguards will furnish far more benefits in efficiency than costs. Limiting the proliferation of the therapeutic state becomes almost an afterthought.

Finally, a question only preliminarily examined in the literature, but appropriate for further research, involves a cross-cultural analysis of the issues raised here. What is done about individuals appropriate for pro-

---

52. N. Kittrie, *supra* note 26; T. Szasz, *supra* note 26.
53. [*Cf.* K. Wilber & J. Reynolds, Rethinking Alternatives to Guardianship (1994) (unpublished manuscript) (proposes analytical framework "comprised of capacity, risk, complexity, and support...to assess performance expectations and identify limitations" in four decision-making interventions: supportive, shared, delegated, and surrogate).]

tective services in West Germany with its concept of limited guardianship (*Pflegschaft*), in England where the civil commitment experience is similar, in Scandinavia with its tradition of social welfare, and in the Orient where the elderly have traditionally been so revered?

Chapter 14

Adult Protective Services and the Therapeutic State

Winsor C. Schmidt, Jr.

Introduction

In 1971, Nicholas Kittrie identified a growing "new hybrid system of social controls" and designated it as "the therapeutic state".[1] Clients of the therapeutic state include such "deviants" as the mentally ill and retarded, juvenile and defective delinquents, drug abusers, alcoholics, sex offenders and wards of the public guardian.[2] Unlike the welfare state, the therapeutic state assumes that its clients are too mentally incompetent to seek the "beneficial" services offered on a voluntary basis, and therefore the therapeutic state attempts to administer its services involuntarily.[3] The danger posed by the therapeutic state lies in the fact that society has been conditioned to consider those labelled "deviant" as 'different', rarely considering the possibility that deviance could easily be broadened to include many unsuspecting conditions.[4] This chapter reviews the extension of the therapeutic state into the unsuspecting area of adult protective services.

---

1. N. Kittrie, The Right to be Different: Deviance and Enforced Therapy 40 (1971). *See generally* [P. Conrad & W. Schneider, Deviance and Medicalization from Badness to Sickness (1992);] R. Singer & W. Statsky, *The Therapeutic State*, in Rights of the Imprisoned (Cases, Materials and Directions) 13–268 (1974); T. Szasz, Law, Liberty and Psychiatry: An Inquiry into the Social Uses of Mental Health Practices (1963).
2. N. Kittrie, *supra* note 1; W. Schmidt, K. Miller, W. Bell & E. New, Public Guardianship and the Elderly (1981) [hereinafter cited as Public Guardianship]; R. Singer and W. Statsky, *supra* note 1, at 1–268.
3. N. Kittrie, *supra* note 1, at 40–41; T. Szasz, *supra* note 1, at 212–22.
4. N. Kittrie, *supra* note 1, at 361.

Background

Adult protective services are defined as "a system of preventive, supportive, and surrogate services for the elderly living in the community to enable them to maintain independent living and avoid abuse and exploitation."[5] Protective services, in contrast to social services, should only occur on a surrogate basis, either at "the request of a vulnerable, dependent person or ordered by the court."[6]

> [T]he surrogate function is the heart and soul of a protective service program. It can be defined as the delegation by the client, or the substitution through legal means, of the client's decision-making power to another person, or persons, professionally responsible and legally accountable for the purposes of assuring that the client receives the necessary protection, whatever services this may require.[7]

"Adult protective services" has been a generic term, encompassing guardianship and civil commitment.[8]

Estimates of the number of states that have created adult protective services programs range from "almost half"[9] to "virtually every state."[10] State adult abuse programs enacted by statute or regulation can include mandatory reporting laws modeled after child abuse reporting laws,[11] as

---

5. Regan, *Intervention Through Adult Protective Services Programs*, 18 Gerontologist 250, 251 (1978).

6. E. Ferguson, Protecting the Vulnerable Adult: A Perspective on Policy and Program Issues in Adult Protective Services 39 (1978).

7. Overcoming Barriers to Protective Services for the Aged 11 (G. Hall and G. Mathiasen eds. 1968).

8. *See* Horstman, *Protective Services for the Elderly: The Limits of Parens Patriae*, 40 Mo. L. Rev. 215 (1975). Horstman considers the distinction between civil commitment and guardianship to be that the former is primarily a police power activity, while the latter is a *parens patriae* activity. Regan, *Protective Services for the Elderly: Commitment, Guardianship and Alternatives*, 13 Wm. & Mary L. Rev. 569 (1972).

9. Kapp, *Adult Protective Services: Convincing the Patient to Consent*, 11 L. Med. & Health Care 163, 163 (1983).

10. Regan, *Adult Protective Services: An Appraisal and a Prospectus*, in National Law & Social Work Seminar: Proceedings and Prospects 12 (1982) [hereinafter cited as Law & Social Work].

Provisions for adult protective services are reported for the following 30 states: Alabama, Arizona, Arkansas, California, Colorado, Connecticut, Florida, Georgia, Kentucky, Maine, Maryland, Michigan, Minnesota, Montana, Nebraska, New Hampshire, New York, North Carolina, North Dakota, Oklahoma, Oregon, South Carolina, Tennessee, Utah, Vermont, Virginia, Washington, Wisconsin, and Wyoming.

11. Dalend, Kane, Satz & Pynoos, *Elder Abuse Reporting: Limitations of Statutes*, 24 Gerontologist 61 (1984) [hereinafter cited as *Elder Abuse*] (comparison and analysis of elder abuse statutes passed between 1973 and 1980 in 16 states: Alabama, Arkansas,

well as special involuntary intervention proceedings as an alternative to civil commitment and guardianship.[12] The special, involuntary, adult protective services are the focus of this chapter.

Involuntary Protective Services Statutes

The rationale for involuntary protective services statutes is unclear. The introduction to a "Model Adult Protective Services Act" suggests an intention to provide legal authority for involuntary intervention in situations requiring less drastic interference than civil commitment or guardianship.[13] A New York group cites the lack of right of access to victims, and the unavailability of involuntary procedures to a majority who might benefit.[14] One commentator endorses adult protective services simply because older persons often accept such services voluntarily after being encouraged to do so by health care professionals.[15] But the President's Commission on Mental Health concludes:

> Unfortunately, many State protective services laws provide for involuntary protective services without the same due process procedural protections which are required by State guardianship or involuntary commitment laws. These proceedings should not be used as a method of avoiding the constitutionally required procedures.
>
> Additionally, a State's involuntary commitment, guardianship and protective services laws should interrelate to each other in a rational manner and definitions should be consistent.[16]

Connecticut, Florida, Kentucky, Minnesota, Missouri, Nebraska, New Hampshire, North Carolina, Oklahoma, South Carolina, Tennessee, Utah, Vermont, and Virginia). *See also* K. Meyers & J. Bergman, An Analysis of Elder Abuse Laws in Massachusetts and Other States (1979); I. Sloan, The Law and Legislation of Elderly Abuse (1983); Faulkner, *Mandating the Reporting of Suspected Cases of Elder Abuse: An Inappropriate, Ineffective and Ageist Response to the Abuse of Older Adults*, 16 Fam. L. Q. 69 (1982); Katz, *Elder Abuse*, 18 J. Fam. L. 695 (1979–80). *See generally* McDougal, Lasswell & Chen, *The Human Rights of the Aged: An Application of the General Norm of Nondiscrimination*, 28 U. Fla. L. Rev. 639 (1976).

    12. Regan, *Protecting the Elderly: The New Paternalism*, 32 Hastings L. J. 1111, 1117 (1981).

    13. J. Regan & G. Springer, Protective Services for the Elderly (a working paper prepared for the Special Committee on Aging, U.S. Senate), p. 56 (1977).

    14. Ad hoc Committee on Adult Homes, Nassau Division National Association of Social Workers, Model Adult Protective Services Law (1982).

    15. Kapp, *supra* note 9.

    16. *Report of the Task Panel on Legal and Ethical Issues* in Report to the President from the President's Commission on Mental Health Vol. IV (1978), p. 1397 n.15. *Accord* M. Axilbund, Exercising Judgment for the Disabled: Report of an Inquiry into Limited Guardianship, Public Guardianship and Adult Protective Services in Six States (Executive Summary) (1979) (concept of protective services is not uniformly or well developed).

One analysis of involuntary adult protective services statutes finds eleven states that have established such intervention procedures since 1973.[17] The analysis concludes:

> Serious procedural flaws [deficiencies in notice, client presence at the hearing, right to counsel, standard of proof] exist in the laws of Alabama, Florida, Oklahoma, and South Carolina, and lesser weaknesses exist in several other states. The standards for intervention are...vague and conclusory. Finally, the intervenor, even a public agency, is rarely accountable to anyone, including the court, once the court has signed the order. The result has been that protective services, especially when provided by a public agency, are becoming in many states a mechanism to allow the public agency to assume total dominion over elderly clients.[18]

A more recent analysis identifies four other states with provisions for involuntary service.[19] The analysis observes that such provisions vary widely. Some statutes require a determination of mental incapacity to consent before services can be rendered. Some provide for emergency service, protective placement, or guardianship. Some require a petition for the right to enter a home to investigate, or to prevent a caretaker from interfering with service. Due process safeguards such as the right to a hearing, the right to have representation, and the right to present one's own evidence are included only in varying degrees.[20] The analysis concludes that such special procedures accentuate a tendency to infantilize the elderly, and imply a failure of preexisting criminal and civil law. Studies of the effects and consequences of these statutes are encouraged by the authors so that a thorough conceptualization of the law can be realized.[21]

While the statutory experience with involuntary protective services has been analyzed, the judicial experience with these services has not been examined up to this point.

---

17. Regan, *supra* note 12, at 1116 n.30, 1117 (Alabama, Connecticut, Florida, Maryland, New Hampshire, North Carolina, Oklahoma, South Carolina, Tennessee, Utah, and Wisconsin).

18. *Id.* at 1127. Accord In re Boyer, 636 P.2d 1085 (Utah 1981) (guardianship criteria unconstitutionally vague).

19. *Elder Abuse, supra* note 11 (Arkansas, Kentucky, Missouri, Virginia). *See* Ark. Stat. Ann. sections 59-1301–59-1314 (1983 Supp.); Ky. Rev. Stat. sections 209.010–209.160 (1982); Mo. Ann. Stat. sections 455.010–455.085 (Vernon 1984 Supp.); Va. Code sections 63.1-55.1–63.1-55.7 (1983 Supp.); Brown, *Remaining Problems with the Adult Abuse Act*, 38 J. Mo. B. 582 (1982); Quarm & Schwartz, *Legal Reform and the Criminal Court: The Case of Domestic Violence*, 10 N. Ky. L. Rev. 199 (1983); Comment, *Governmental Services and Social Welfare*, 63 Va. L. Rev. 1440, 1441–42 (1977).

20. *Elder Abuse, supra* note 11, at 62.

21. *Id.* at 66.

Mary Northern—"In Pari Materia" With Mental Health Law

The first involuntary protective services case in an appellate court involved Mary Northern in Tennessee.[22] The Tennessee Department of Human Services brought a proceeding under the "Protective Services for Elderly Persons" statute alleging that 72-year old recluse, Mary Northern, suffered from gangrene of both feet, that amputation of both feet was necessary to save her life, and that she lacked capacity to appreciate her condition or to consent to surgery.[23] This kind of case has traditionally been handled as a single transaction with court ratification of a particular act or as a (limited) guardianship situation.[24]

The Tennessee protective services statute authorized the chancellor of the chancery court to enter an order designating "'an individual or organization to be responsible for the personal welfare of the elderly person and for consenting to protective services'" if the chancellor found "'that the elderly person is in imminent danger of death if he does not receive protective services and lacks capacity to consent to protective services.'"[25] The chancellor granted an order designating the petitioning Department of Human Services as the entity responsible for the patient's welfare, and also designating that Department as the entity responsible for consenting to protective services on behalf of the patient. This dual designation is inherently self-aggrandizing and represents a conflict of interest.[26]

On appeal, there were numerous assignments of error, and the Tennessee Court of Appeals made several holdings in deciding the case. The court found that the Tennessee adult protective services statute "properly and constitutionally recognizes and utilizes the inherent power of a court of equity to act in a preliminary, ex parte, manner to preserve the status quo and integrity of the subject matter of the suit."[27] The court also stated that such action is appropriate "in emergency cases" where there is inadequate time for a notice and hearing, but any "[a]ffirmative steps producing an injury or irreversible condition (such as amputation)" do not

---

22. State Dep't of Human Serv. v. Northern, 563 S.W.2d 197 (Tenn. Ct. App. 1978), aff'd, 575 S.W.2d 946 (Tenn. 1978).
23. Tenn. Code Ann. sections 14-25-102—14-25-107.
24. *See, e.g.*, Lane v. Candura, 6 Mass. App. Ct. 377 (1978); Public Guardianship, *supra* note 2.
25. 563 S.W.2d at 202, *citing* Tenn. Code Ann. section 14-2306(a).
26. *Cf.* Public Guardianship, *supra* note 2 (social service agency should not be public guardian because of self-aggrandizement and conflict of interest possibilities).
27. 563 S.W.2d at 206.

lie within inherent powers of equity and are not authorized under the statute, without notice and a hearing.[28]

Miss Northern indicated that she would "possibly" prefer to die rather than lose her feet, but in evidencing a strong desire both to live, and to keep her dead feet, she allegedly refused to make a choice. This is not a "'right to die'" case because, "If the patient would assume and exercise her rightful control over her own destiny by stating that she prefers death to the loss of her feet, her wish would be respected."[29] The court did not explain why verbalization was necessary in order for her choice of refusing to choose to be respected.

The court found that failure to give the statutorily required forty-eight hours' notice to the patient and her guardian ad litem was cured with an unusual rehearing by the court of appeals. The court also declined to require the guardian or "quasi-guardian" to post bond in the absence of statutory mention. The alleged error in designating a department of the government to make a treatment decision was corrected by the designation of the department commissioner, individually, in a modification of the chancellor's order. While "[a]n organization might properly be designated to provide or make available the necessities of the elderly person,...where the fiduciary function involves decision-making on behalf of or control of the elderly person, it would be more appropriate to designate a particular individual to assume direct and specific responsibility and accountability."[30]

The statutory use of the words "imminent danger of death" and "capacity to consent" was rescued from unconstitutional vagueness by judicial definition. "The words 'imminent danger of death' mean conditions calculated to and capable of producing within a short period of time a reasonably strong possibility of resultant cessation of life if such conditions are not removed or alleviated."[31] The court of appeals also articulated a calculus of, for example, a "mild imminence of danger of death" authorizing only a mild encroachment on the individual's freedom. This seems as ill-considered as the slippery slope of increased (inappropriate) guardianships anticipated with the provision of limited guardians for limited incompetents.[32]

---

28. *Id.*
29. *Id.* at 207.
30. *Id.* at 208. *But see* In re Kaufman, 114 Misc. 2d 1078, 453 N.Y.S.2d 304 (N.Y. Sup. Ct. 1982).
31. 563 S.W.2d at 209.
32. *Cf.* Public Guardianship, *supra* note 2 (judges are to some extent deterred in marginal cases by the all or nothing approach of plenary guardianship; limited guardianship would facilitate adjudication).

Regarding "'capacity to consent,'" the court ruled that "Capacity means mental ability to make a rationale decision, which includes the ability to perceive, appreciate all relevant facts and to reach a rational judgment upon such facts."[33] But, "A person may have 'capacity' as to some matters and may lack 'capacity' as to others."[34] Miss Northern's "mind or emotions have resorted to the device of denying the unpleasant reality" that the flesh of her feet are "dead, shriveled, rotting and stinking."[35] This "'delusion'" rendered her incapable of making a rational decision about lifesaving surgery. If Miss Northern comprehended "the facts of her condition" and expressed an "Unequivocal desire," that decision would be honored.[36] But she could not or would not.

The court leaves little room for the possibilities of one's competent refusal to comprehend, or to express an "unequivocal" choice. The court defines capacity as (rational) communication rather than "ability" or potential. Miss Northern faced a ninety to ninety-five percent probability of death without surgery, and a fifty-fifty probability with surgery, plus inability to walk and the "immense—chances" of suffering severe mental and emotional problems.[37] She wanted to live and keep her dead feet, and "'possibly'" preferred to die rather than lose her feet. If we are unable to do any better when we either deny the unpleasant reality of death, or go crazy, why did the court expect any more of Miss Northern?

In response to an assignment of error alleging that the chancellor failed to comply with the requirements of the Tennessee Mental Health Act, the court held that the protective services statute "may properly be considered an amendment of or addition to the Mental Health Law or in pari materia therewith."[38] The court of appeals concluded that Miss Northern was "incompetent on the subject of feet, amputation and death."[39]

---

33. 563 S.W.2d at 209.
34. Id.
35. Id.
36. Id. Her guardian ad litem has pointed out that "they questioned her competence only because she refused amputation." Mary Northern Revisited: Case Study in Protective Policy, in Law & Social Work, supra note 10, at 88.
37. Id. at 204, 209.
38. Id. at 211.
39. Id. In a separate concurring opinion, Judge Drowota stated: "Though Miss Northern's case is, to me, undoubtedly close to the constitutional limits of the state's power over an individual, it is within those limits." Id. at 215 (Drowota, J., concurring).

The Tennessee Attorney General's Office suggests that Northern implicitly recognizes a right to be free from nonconsensual invasion of bodily integrity. Office of the Att'y Gen. of Tenn. 82–314, slip op. at n.1 (June 23, 1982).

Surgery was never performed on Miss Northern because complications increased the danger. She died 2-1/2 months after the Tennessee Supreme Court affirmed the court of appeal's decision. A blood clot from the gangrenous tissue migrated to a vital organ. Id.

Herbert Byrne and Norma Turner—Civil Commitment Requirements "Inapplicable"?

The Florida case involving Herbert Byrne and Norma Turner concerned another situation common in the area of guardianship and adult protective services.[40] Herbert Byrne, age 79, called for help on June 5, 1979, because his niece, Norma Turner, had fallen, and he was unable to get her up. The visiting social worker found the two completely naked, surrounded by excrement and debris, plumbing not working, and a falling ceiling from which wires were dangling. A police officer took both to a hospital.

On June 6, 1979, the social worker filed petitions for emergency custody orders under Florida's Adult Protective Services Act.[41] The court immediately issued ex parte emergency custody orders. The court appointed counsel for Herbert Byrne and Norma Turner on the following day.

The appointed attorneys filed motions to dismiss the petitions on June 8, 1979, on the ground that the statutory emergency procedures were unconstitutional. The court immediately held a hearing and denied the motion to dismiss, but found sufficient evidence to justify continued services. An order denying the motion and "'acquitting'" Herbert Byrne and Norma Turner "from further involuntary custody" was issued on June 13, 1979.[42]

The issue on appeal was whether section 410.104, authorizing the Department of Health and Rehabilitative Services to take elderly persons into custody and transport them to a protective service or medical facility in an emergency without their consent, comports with due process and is constitutional.[43] The Florida Supreme Court held that the statutory procedures comported with constitutional due process requirements.[44]

The court observed that relocation without consent is limited to elderly persons "who are 'likely to incur a substantial risk of life-threatening

---

at 212.

Mary Northern's case was the occasion for the "most exciting" session of a law and social work conference on protective services. *Mary Northern Revisited: Case Study in Protective Policy*, in Law & Social Work, *supra* note 10, at 90. Eli Cohen concluded that the court "'chose to waffle or muddle through' rather than find either for or against the rights of Mary Northern or the state." *Id.*

40. *In re Byrne*, 402 So. 2d 383 (Fla. 1981), *appeal dismissed for want of jurisdiction*, 455 U.S. 1009 (1982).

41. Fla. Stat. sections 410.10–410.11 (1979). Florida's involuntary protective services statute has been criticized as one of the most procedurally deficient in the country. See text accompanying note 18, *supra*.

42. 400 So. 2d at 384.

43. *Id.*

44. *Id.* at 385.

physical harm or deterioration if not immediately removed from the premises....'"⁴⁵ The subsection also provides "two procedural safeguards:" (1) the emergency situation must be personally observed by both a representative of the Department of Health and Rehabilitative Services and a law enforcement officer; and (2) the relocation may occur only when authorized by court order. Emergency relocation without consent is limited to no more than forty-eight hours, within which time a preliminary hearing must be held to determine probable cause for temporary protective placement for up to four days, pending a hearing on the need for continuing services.⁴⁶

Appellants' attorney argued that due process requires notice, an opportunity to be heard, and effective assistance of counsel.⁴⁷ The court found "civil commitment" proceeding requirements "inapplicable," reasoning that the purpose of the protective services statute is "to free persons suffering from infirmities of aging from dangerous or oppressive conditions," rather than to confine or incarcerate mentally incompetent persons.⁴⁸ The court concluded that relocating elderly persons "held hostage by others or by their own environment," who "may not know what is best for them or even know what they want after living under such conditions," and providing them with "medication" and proper nourishment, "is necessary to help them to regain a proper perspective on life so they can make a deliberate and unconstrained decision on whether to return."⁴⁹

Appellants' attorney argued that the judicial authority to order continuing services might lead to indefinite involuntary commitment.⁵⁰ The supreme court ruled that services not voluntarily received could be ordered

---

45. *Id. citing* Fla. Stat. section 410.104(2).
46. Fla. Stat. sections 410.102(6), 410.104(3) (1979).
47. 402 So. 2d at 385, *citing* Specht v. Patterson, 386 U.S. 605 (1967); In re Beverly, 342 So. 2d 481 (Fla. 1977).
48. 402 So. 2d at 385. The statutory purpose "to protect the elderly" is genuine rather than a euphemism for punishment. *Id. citing In re* Gault, 387 U.S. 1 (1967).

The court also observed that the protective services statute is limited to an "emergency" situation wherein due process is not offended by a "temporary" loss of liberty in a life-threatening situation. 402 So. 2d at 385–86 *citing* Fhagen v. Miller, 29 N.Y.2d 348, 328 N.Y.S.2d 393, 278 N.E.2d 615 (1972), *cert. denied*, 409 U.S. 845 (1972) (a civil commitment case allowing 15 days loss of liberty).

49. 402 So. 2d at 386.
50. *Id. Cf.* Hobbs, *Adult Protective Services: A New Program Approach*, Pub. Welfare 28, 33–34 (Summer 1976) (less than 10% of generic protective services cases in San Diego were treated for over six months, 70% were closed in three months or less; the National Council on Aging and the U.S.Dept. of Health, Education and Welfare demonstrated "that protective cases could be stabilized in six months or less"); Regan, *supra* note 12, at 1120 *citing* M. Axilbund, *supra* note 16 (entire Wisconsin protective services system is in reality a protective placement system).

"only until the person is no longer facing a substantial risk of life-threatening harm or deterioration."[51]

Finally, appellants' attorney argued that the parens patriae doctrine did not authorize the state to "impose services, treatment, and confinement upon competent elderly persons."[52] The court noted that the statute prohibited forced medical care or treatment "'in contravention of the stated or implied objection of such person,'" but concluded that "[p]eople whose mental and physical capabilities are deteriorating because of old age may be approximating mental incompetency," and "the state has the authority to exercise its parens patriae power when it appears such persons are incapable of caring for themselves."[53]

The Florida Adult Protective Services Act has subsequently been combined with Florida's abuse statute, also a subject of criticism.[54]

Missouri—Restraining the Abuser

Unlike the guardianship and civil commitment approaches to adult protection exemplified in the Tennessee and Florida situations, Missouri's "Adult Abuse" statute[55] provides involuntary remedies against the vic-

---

51. 402 So. 2d at 386.
52. Id.
53. Id. citing In re Beverly, 342 So. 2d at 485 (upholding the constitutionality of Florida's civil commitment statute); Fla. Stat. section 410.101.
Cf. R. Glasscote, Old Folks at Home 68 (1977); Horstman, *supra* note 8, at 263, 273 (variation in function increases as age of people studied increases and any generalization about "the aged" may be unsound; decline in intellectual functioning among older persons not intrinsically related to the aging process; the elderly as a class are more capable of independent functioning than is generally assumed).
Herbert Byrne died after the notices of appeal were filed, and Norma Turner was adjudicated incompetent, 402 So. 2d at 384.
For the "checkered career" of the parens patriae doctrine, *see generally* Bartol, *"Parens Patriae": Poltergeist of Mental Health Law*, 3 L. & Pol'y Q. 191 (1981); Coleman & Solomon, *Parens Patriae "Treatment": Legal Punishment in Disguise*, 3 Hastings Const. L. Q. 345 (1976); Curtis, *The Checkered Career of "Parens Patriae": The State as Parent or Tyrant?*, 25 DePaul L. Q. Rev. 895 (1976); Custer, *Origins of the Doctrine of "Parens Patriae"*, 27 Emory L. J. 195 (1978); Horstman, *supra* note 8.
54. Fla. Stat. Ann. sections 415.101–415.112 (West 1983 Supp.) (formerly sections 410.10–410.11, 827.09). See Shinholster v. Graham, 527 F. Supp. 1318, 1320–27 (N.D. Fla. 1981) (abuse reporting system does not constitute an administrative scheme with an orderly system of review and appeal sufficiently adequate to trigger the requirement of exhaustion of state administrative remedies prior to maintenance of section 1983 suit in federal court).
55. Mo. Ann. Stat. sections 455.010–455.085 (Vernon 1984 Supp.). Cf. Note, *Domestic Relations: Oklahoma's Protection from Domestic Abuse Act*, 36 Okla. L. Rev. 349 (1983).

timizer rather than the victim. Any adult who is subject to the actual or attempted physical injury by a present or former adult household member may petition for an ex parte order of protection issued without notice or a hearing, and for a full order of protection issued after notice and a hearing on the record.[56] An ex parte order may restrain the respondent from "abusing, threatening to abuse, molesting or disturbing the peace of the petitioner"; and from entering the petitioner's premises where the petitioner has a property interest, even if the petitioner is a spouse with no formal property interest in the marital dwelling unit.[57] A full order of protection may temporarily enjoin the same behavior, as well as award child custody, support, maintenance, and visitation.[58] Missouri's adult abuse statute makes "[v]iolation of the terms and conditions of an ex parte order of protection of which the respondent has notice," a class C misdemeanor, as is violation of a full order of protection.[59]

A trial court found the statute unconstitutional, and thus unenforceable against a 230 pound, former Golden Gloves boxer, who on numerous previous occasions, and on November 13, 1983, "'intentionally, knowingly and willfully beat petitioner...causing...serious physical injury...requiring petitioner to be hospitalized...' for 12 days."[60] The trial court found that the statute permitted the deprivation of constitutionally protected interests by allowing someone to be excluded from one's home or kept away from one's children for fifteen days prior to notice and a hearing.[61]

> In resolving the statute's constitutionality, the Missouri Supreme Court used the analysis and balancing of interests formula adopted by the United States Supreme Court in *Mathews v. Eldridge*.[62] Under this formula, a court looks at three specific factors identifying the interests represented by each factor in the case at hand, and then it balances the factors against each other to determine which is the most important. In analyzing the first factor, the private interest affected by the statute, the Missouri Supreme Court recog-

---

56. Mo. Ann. Stat. sections 455.010, 455.020.
57. Mo. Ann. Stat. section 455.045. The ex parte order may also include a temporary child custody order. *Id.*
58. Mo. Ann. Stat. section 455.050.
59. Mo. Ann. Stat. section 455.085. For a discussion of problems regarding notice, *see* Brown, *supra* note 19.
60. State *ex rel.* Williams v. Marah, 626 S.W.2d 223, 226 (Mo. en banc 1982).
61. *See* 626 S.W.2d at 229; Mo. Ann. Stat. section 455.040.
The Missouri Supreme Court also noted a liberty interest in one's reputation. 626 S.W.2d at 230 n.8 citing Taub, *Ex parte Proceedings in Domestic Violence Situations: Alternative Frameworks for Constitutional Scrutiny*, 9 Hofstra L. Rev. 95, 104–06 (1980).
62. Mathews v. Eldridge, 424 U.S. 319 (1976).

nized the property interest a person has in his home and the liberty interest he has in the custody of his children.[63]

In analyzing the second factor, the extent of the governmental interest involved, the Missouri court characterized the Adult Abuse Act as an exercise of the state's broad police power to protect and promote the general health, welfare, and safety of its citizens, and noted that states are given deference in adopting reasonable summary procedures when implementing the police power.[64] The court observed that the choice in adult abuse cases "is reduced to the victim of the abuse leaving or the court ordering the abuser to leave."[65]

The third factor of the *Eldridge* test is "'the fairness and reliability of the existing pretermination procedures, and the probable value, if any, of additional procedural safeguards.'"[66] In analyzing this factor, the Missouri Supreme Court drew an analogy between an ex parte order of protection issued upon a showing of "'an immediate and present danger of abuse to the petitioner,'" and a temporary restraining order.[67] For a petitioner to obtain an ex parte order of protection (or any other restraining order), the petitioner must satisfy the court that grounds exist to justify granting this order. The petitioner will usually be required to appear before the court personally in order for the court to test the petitioner's credibility and see "first hand" any manifest evidence of physical abuse. If the petitioner cannot appear before the court because of her injuries, the very fact that she is unable to appear, if proven, will allow the court to determine that there is an immediate and present danger of abuse. Once granted, an ex parte order for protection remains effective until a hearing is held, which must occur within fifteen days after the petition is filed. The statute requires that the respondent (abuser) be personally served with a copy of the petition at least five days before the hearing and that it must state the date of the hearing and any ex parte order of protection granted.[68] Even though the ex parte order is effective for fifteen days, noth-

---

63. 626 S.W.2d at 230.
64. *Id.* at 230–31 *citing* Mackey v. Montrym, 443 U.S. 1 (1979); Day-Brite Lighting, Inc. v. Missouri, 342 U.S. 421 (1952).
65. *Id.* at 230.
66. *Id.* at 231 *citing* 424 U.S. at 343.
67. *Id. citing* Mo. Ann. Stat. section 455.035.
The court also noted an analogy to a probable cause requirement for issuance of a warrant. *Id.* at 231 n.11.
68. *Id.* at 231 *citing* Mo. Ann. Stat. section 455.040(2).
The supreme court suggested that the trial court could include information about the procedure for an earlier hearing in the notice. *Id.*

ing in the statute suggests that the respondent (abuser) could not obtain an earlier hearing.

The court compares the Missouri statute with categories of cases allowing outright seizures, and concludes that the statute is directly necessary to secure important governmental interests in preventing abuse and protecting abuse victims. The court also concluded that the statute was applied to a situation necessitating prompt action, ("'immediate and present danger of abuse'") and that the government kept strict control over its powers by giving judges discretionary power to issue ex parte orders.[69] The provisions concerning ex parte orders granted against abusers "comply with due process requirements because they are a reasonable means to achieve the state's legitimate goal of preventing domestic violence, and afford adequate procedural safeguards, prior to and after any deprivation occurs."[70]

The court, in conclusion, also faced the issue of whether a misdemeanor conviction for violating the ex parte protection order or the full protection order is void for vagueness. It was argued that such a conviction is void because it violates the prior notice of prohibited conduct and because it is an impermissible delegation of basic policy matters to the judiciary. In upholding the statute, the court said that 'abuse' was defined, that orders could issue only upon immediate and present danger of abuse, and that the trial court's discretion was limited in that it could only determine whether the situation warranted the issuance of "all or less than all of the two or three restraining orders expressly available."[71]

Statistics Show That the Statute is Already Frequently Being Used

Jackson County, Missouri, reported that seventy-four ex parte protection orders were issued in 1981 while *Williams* was on appeal from the Jackson County Circuit.[72] Greene County reported ninety orders, St. Louis

---

69. *Id.* at 232 *citing* Fuentes v. Shevin, 407 U.S. 67, 91–93 (1972) (disapproving private parties from invoking state power to unilaterally replevy goods).

70. *Id.* at 232.

71. *See id.* at 232–35.

Judge Bardgett suggested that contempt proceedings might be more appropriate than making violation of an order a crime. *Id.* at 236–37 (Bardgett, J., concurring).

Judge Welliver concluded that the Adult Abuse Act "exhibits the fullest potential for creating nine new evils for every evil it would seek by its terms to correct." *Id.* at 237 (Welliver, J., dissenting).

72. Brown, *supra* note 19, at 588 n.3.

County reported 575, and the City of St. Louis Circuit reported 1,438 ex parte protection orders.[73] One observer suggests that with this volume of cases, the *Williams* decision, and the promulgation of forms and rules by the Supreme Court, the Adult Abuse Act is fully implemented "and accomplishing its purpose of preventing incidents of domestic violence."[74]

West Virginia—Compelling the State to Help

West Virginia also attempts to provide involuntary injunctive remedies against caretakers who abuse or neglect an "incapacitated adult," defined as "any person who by reason of physical, mental or other infirmity is unable to independently carry on the daily activities of life necessary to sustaining life and reasonable health."[75] The "Social Services for Adults" statute prohibits compulsory assistance except in an emergency or emergency situation, defined as "a situation or set of circumstances which presents a substantial and immediate risk of death or serious permanent injury to an incapacitated adult."[76]

In *Hodge v. Ginsberg*, six homeless Charleston residents lacking the means to maintain a permanent residence and "forced to spend their days and nights on public streets, alleys, riverbanks and other various outdoor locations," sought through a proceeding in mandamus to compel the Commissioner of the West Virginia Department of Public Welfare to provide adult protective services for themselves and others similarly situated.[77] The West Virginia Supreme Court of Appeals focused its inquiry on whether petitioners were entitled to relief under the Social Services for Adults Act. The respondent contended that petitioners were not "incapacitated adults" under the Act, and that providing protective services under the Act was discretionary and thus precluded relief by mandamus.

---

73. *Id.*
74. *Id.* at 583.
75. W.Va. Code sections 9-6-1(4), 9-6-4 (1984).
"The department or any reputable person may bring and maintain an action against any person having actual care, custody or control of an incapacitated adult, for injunctive relief, including a preliminary injunction, to restrain and abate any abuse of neglect of an incapacitated adult or to abate an emergency situation." W. Va. Code section 9-6-4.
76. W. Va. Code sections 9-6-1(5), 9-6-7.
77. Hodge v. Ginsberg, 303 S.E.2d 245, 247 (W. Va. 1983), The Association of Retarded Citizens in Kanawha and Putnam Counties, and the Coalition on Alternative Residential Emergency Shelter, intervened as parties petitioner, and Community Kitchen, Inc. and Romero House, Inc. participated as *amicus curiae*. *Id.* at 247 n.1.

In its analysis, the West Virginia Supreme Court first cited regulation 29010 of the West Virginia Social Services Manual. The regulation states that a goal of adult protective services is to remedy "neglect," defined as "'the failure to provide adequate food,...shelter or medical care.'"[78] The respondent contended that only clients with "a serious impairment in physical or mental functioning" qualified as physically or mentally infirm under the Act.[79] The court pointed out that the statutory definition of "incapacitated adult" included "'other infirmity,'" and that a commonly accepted dictionary definition of "infirmity" includes more than the serious physical or mental impairment limitation of department regulations.[80] The court concluded that the term "incapacitated adult" was intended "to encompass indigent persons like the petitioners, who, by reason of the recurring misfortunes of life, are unable to independently carry on the daily activities of life necessary to sustaining life and reasonable health."[81]

On the issue of administrative discretion, the court pointed out that the statute says that the department "'may develop a plan for a comprehensive system of adult protective services,'" but that the department "'shall offer such services as are available and appropriate in the circumstances...to adults who may request and be entitled to such protective services.'"[82] The court also stated that once the department had exercised its statutory discretion to promulgate regulations establishing a duty to provide assistance, then the Commissioner has a duty to provide such assistance to eligible petitioners.[83]

The supreme court granted the writ of mandamus directing the Commissioner to provide "emergency shelter, food and medical care to the petitioners and other similarly situated persons" as required by the Social Services for Adults Act and the applicable regulations.[84]

---

78. Id. at 248–49.
79. Id. at 249 (citing Social Services Manual, Regulation 29100(A)).
80. Id. at 249–50.
81. Id. at 250. A primary goal of the Department of Welfare is to provide aid to indigents. Id. at 248 citing W. Va. Code section 9-1-2(g) (1979), relating to definition of "indigent person".
82. Id. at 250 citing W. Va. Code section 9-6-7.
83. Id. at 251.
84. Id. Justice Neely concluded that the majority opinion, "though woofed with dreams, is warped with folly." Id. (Neely, J., dissenting). He argued that the majority has read a "new entitlement" into the statute, that there is no guidance or limitation in the opinion, that the burden will fall on the "traditional clients" of the department, and "that the sense and realism of the majority opinion are entirely inadequate." Id. at 252–53 (Neely, J., dissenting).

The State of Protective Services Advocacy

At least two of the most prominent advocates of involuntary protective services legislation and mandatory reporting of elder abuse, John Regan[85] and James Bergman,[86] have reportedly altered their views.[87]

In 1977, Professor Regan advocated a model protective services act; a model guardianship, conservatorship, and power of attorney statute; and a model public guardianship act.[88] By 1981, he was suggesting a moratorium on public agency use of involuntary orders for emergency services, protective services, protective placements, and guardianships.[89] In 1982, he adopted a "middle ground" of "minimal intervention"[90] between the "largely ignored"[91] due process approach of his model legislation and "'abolitionist'" views.[92] Regarding protective services, Professor Regan suggested the following:

> Public agencies should be limited to providing services willingly accepted by clients and to seeking court authorization for providing specific services to individual clients in emergency and high-risk situations, but not in the role of guardian.
> ...Basic procedural safeguards for the client must be provided as an essential part of any protective services program.
> ...The ethical responsibilities of the social worker toward protective services clients need to be better defined.
> ...Steps should be taken [trusts, joint accounts, joint tenancies, durable family power of attorney, expanded living will] both by state legislatures and by state and local service agencies to emphasize and promote client control of intervention decisions.[93]

Meanwhile, Professor Bergman, an advocate of protective services legislation especially as it concerns elder abuse and mandatory reporting, has recently acknowledged that the child abuse model was a poor precedent

---

85. *See* Regan, *supra* notes 5, 8, 10, 12.
86. *See, e.g.*, J. Bergman & E. Villmoare, Abuse and Neglect: A Guide for Practitioners and Policy Makers (1981). Mr. Bergman has been with Legal Research and Services for the Elderly, Inc., Boston, Massachusetts.
87. Law & Social Work, *supra* note 10, at 80.
88. J. Regan & G. Springer, *supra* note 13.
89. Regan, *supra* note 12, at 1131.
90. Regan, *supra* note 10, at 14, 18.
91. Regan, *supra* note 12, at 1131.
92. Regan, *supra* note 10, at 14 citing Mitchell, *The Objects of Our Wisdom and Our Coercion: Guardianships for Incompetents*, 52 S. Cal. L. Rev. 1405 (1979).
93. Regan, *supra* note 10, at 17–18 *citing* Alexander, *Premature Probate: A Different Perspective on Guardianship of the Elderly*, 31 Stan. L. Rev. 1008 (1979) (proposing expanded living will).

and that "'we made some wrong decisions.'"[94] Bergman brands the definitions of 'abuse,' 'neglect,' 'exploitation,' and 'abandonment' as overbroad. He also says that mandatory reporting laws create a presumption of wrongdoing that is stigmatic, that money and resources do not follow the enactment of such statutes, and that absence of services results in unnecessary institutionalization, that guardianship laws are not easily changed because of the attitudes of judges and the private bar who prefer a known evil, and that the inability to reform guardianship makes the lowered standards for involuntary protective services a more attractive and abused option.[95] Bergman concludes that "no help and much harm can be done if we provide intrusive laws and no money."[96] He suggests forgetting "about mandatory reporting and finding shortcuts around guardianship laws."[97]

Conclusion

Adult protective services have proceeded in the well intended but tainted tradition of the therapeutic state. Elderly citizens have been added to the list of deviant client groups who are too readily identifiable as being somehow different and therefore deserving of the state's clumsy, conforming attention.

Special adult protective services statutes have proliferated. As with concerns in guardianship and the therapeutic state's civil commitment statutes for mentally ill and retarded persons, alcoholics, drug abusers, juvenile delinquents, and sex offenders; involuntary protective services statutes suffer from vague, categorical, stigmatic, and overinclusive eligibility criteria and from deficient or nonexistent procedural protections. As one social control mechanism is reformed, the action seems only to shift to another.

Perhaps adult protective services would be acceptable if they helped. What discourages dedicated protective services proponents so much is that protective services may not help. In the classic Benjamin Rose Institute study, not only did providing state-of-the-art protective services fail to prevent or slow deterioration or death, but the experimental group had

---

94. Law & Social Work, *supra* note 10, at 80.
95. *Id.* at 81 (*citing* Elder Abuse: The Hidden Problem, Joint Hearing before the Senate Special Comm. on Aging and the House Select Comm. on Aging, 96th Cong., 2d Sess. (1980) (identifying unnecessary institutionalization of abuse and neglect cases). *Cf., e.g.,* Harris, *The Utah Child Protective System: Analysis and Proposals for Change,* 1983 Utah L. Rev. 1.
96. *Id.* at 81.
97. *Id.*

a higher rate of institutionalization and death than did the control group receiving referral agency services or no services.[98]

The limited judicial experiences with adult protective services seems as problematic as the legislative experience. The judiciary defers to legislative identification of governmental interests in attempting to protect older persons. The judiciary is understandably unable to distinguish adult protective services from civil commitment law and guardianship functions. The *Mathews v. Eldridge*[99] calculus allows the judiciary to invent new means of appellate tolerance for legislative prerogative against individual rights at each opportunity. Adult protective services were unable to keep the client from dying in both the Tennessee and Florida cases.

Coincidentally, exploiting this judicial reticence is a possible legislative trend away from the well-intentioned, but poorly performing and paternalistic parens patriae approach of older protective services statutes in Tennessee and Florida and toward the restrain-the-victimizer-not-the-victim police power approach seen in Missouri and West Virginia. A thorough conceptualization for adult protective services may be evolving under judicial aegis.

One should not be required to choose between a due process model and an abolitionist approach to adult protection services. No matter the extent to which procedural protections are judicially out of fashion, one may safely err on the side of procedure when the other choice is unbridled discretion in the legislative or rulemaking processes. Those deterred by procedures probably should be deterred. There is ample authority in the law for addressing true emergencies; other situations can await the proper process.

---

98. *See* M. Blenkner, M. Bloom, M. Nielsen & R. Weber, Final Report—Protective Services for the Elderly: Findings from the Benjamin Rose Institute Study (1974); Blenkner, Bloom & Nielsen, *A Research and Demonstration Project of Protective Services*, 52 Soc. Casework 483 (Oct. 1971).

A subsequent reanalysis by other investigators suggested that the findings on death were a result of initial group differences in survival-related characteristics not controlled by the random sampling techniques; but the reanalysis did not mitigate the strong effect of experimental group membership on the tendency to be institutionalized. Berger & Piliavin, *The Effect of Casework: A Research Note*, 21 Soc. Work 205 (1976).

Furthermore, there has been considerable evidence that mortality is higher to a staggering degree in institutional populations than in the general population. Special Senate Committee on Aging, Mental Health Care and the Elderly: Shortcomings in Public Policy, 92d Cong., 2d Sess. 139–40 (1970).

The higher mortality rate among protectively placed elderly has applied to nursing homes as well as mental institutions. Subcomm. on Long-term Care of the Senate Special Comm. on Aging, Nursing Home Care in the United States: Failure in Public Policy—Introductory Report, 93d Cong., 2d Sess. 6 (1974).

99. 424 U.S. 319 (1976).

As for the abolition of special legal mechanisms such as involuntary adult protective services, few should lament the limitations placed on their legal proliferation since no one can prove that they do more good than harm. Involuntary adult protective services duplicate and confuse civil commitment and guardianship even more than involuntary civil commitment duplicates and confuses preventive detention and mental health care.

Adult abuse, neglect, and exploitation are arguably functions of both criminal justice deficiencies in catching abusers and exploiters and of poor distribution of resources to those in need. Such problems should be addressed in the context of the criminal and civil justice systems and the economic system, and not with statutory systems for every new and "different" "client" group. We should identify, segregate, and victimize the victimizer, rather than the victim, especially when the victimizer may be the therapeutic state.

Part VIII

Conclusions and Recommendations

The purpose of the Model Public Guardianship Statute that constitutes the conclusions and recommendations for this book is to provide a tool for use in guardianship and public guardianship reform. While the Model Statute does not directly address private guardianship, or adult protective services, it does serve as a model for private guardianship as well as for involuntary adult protective services.

The Model Public Guardianship statute has been criticized as not going far enough.[1] But, given the opposition to guardianship reform by Real Property, Probate, and Trust Sections and Committees in such states as California and Florida,[2] as well as the still limited number of states that have accomplished reform, the Public Guardianship Statute remains a viable model.

The most recent research on guardianship processes in ten states suggests that problems with guardianship continue.[3] For example, several states requiring legal representation of alleged incompetents (Florida, Kansas, Minnesota) have only a 75% to 90% actual representation rate. The rate in Michigan is 8%. In cases where there was evidence of a respondent objection, there was no legal representation 26% of the time. Only 12% of studied cases had independent evaluations ordered. Presence of

---

1. National Senior Citizens Law Center Washington Weekly (April 18, 1980), pp. 4-5.
2. *See, e.g.*, Barnes, *Florida Guardianship and the Elderly: The Paradoxical Right to Unwanted Assistance*, 40 U. Fla. L. Rev. 949, 952 n.10 (1988).
3. L. Lisi, A. Burns, P. Hommel, K. Baird, C. Lindgren, E. Roe & S. Brewster, Final Report: National Study of the Guardianship System and Feasibility of Implementing Expert Systems, Ann Arbor, MI: Center for Social Gerontology (1992). *See also* Bulcroft, Kielkopf & Tripp, *Elderly Wards and Their Legal Guardians: Analysis of County Probate Records in Ohio and Washington*, 31 Gerontologist 156 (1991) (standardized and reliable competency assessments lacking; family member petition for guardianship seldom challenged; goal of most guardianships is estate preservation) Keith & Wacker, *Guardianship Reform: Does Revised Legislation Make a Difference in Outcomes for Proposed Wards?*, 4 J. Aging & Soc. Pol'y 139 (1992) (least restrictive alternatives seldom employed; few petitions denied; guardianships significantly longer before legislative reform); H. Kritzer, Adult Guardianships in Wisconsin: An Empirical Assessment, Madison, Wis.: Elder Law Center (1992) (implementation shortcomings).

the respondent at guardianship hearings occurred in 28% of the cases. The incidence of limited guardianships in four states (California, Indiana, Kansas, and Michigan) is 3% or less.

Chapter 15

Model Public Guardianship Statute

Winsor C. Schmidt, Jr.
Kent S. Miller
William G. Bell
B. Elaine New

Introductory Comments

The intent of providing a model public guardianship statute with this book is to offer tangible and very specific recommendations regarding public guardianship that will improve present public guardianship laws, their administration, and the methods of operation for public guardian offices. To this extent the model statute should act as a guide. However, for those states without provisions for public guardianship and experiencing a need, the statute should also serve as a concrete model for legislation. To this extent, the model statute is intended to facilitate translating the findings and recommendations in this book into policy and law.

The public guardian, and the public guardian process, do not exist in isolation. It would be difficult, misleading, and unrealistic to draft a statute addressing only the office of the public guardian. The public guardian is an end point in the process of guardianship, which itself seems to exist in a continuum of protective services and civil commitment. In fact, the success of a public guardian seems to be quite dependent upon the quality of the state's guardianship statute.

The model public guardianship statute does not directly address guardianship and conservatorship procedures, but it does address the procedures that seem to be necessary for a public guardian to be appointed. In short, the problems with public guardianship nationally are serious enough, and the private guardianship market has enough potential, that we do not believe such an approach for elderly persons should be adopted more widely unless the procedures for appointing a public guardian are improved considerably and unless the office of public guardian and the public guardianship process are adequately funded. The public guardianship approach should not be adopted more widely without adoption of the provisions in the model public guardianship statute.

While the procedures by which a public guardian should be appointed are more stringent than most existing guardianship and conservatorship procedures, the model statute is drafted as an entity that could stand with existing procedures. Adoption of the model public guardianship statute could admittedly spark equal protection challenges to non-public guardianship procedures, but without directly addressing these procedures, such collateral change and benefit would seem to be appropriate, desirable, and timely.

Another threshold issue is the extent to which public guardianship is an approach for the elderly only. The public guardianship experience began with the mentally retarded. Other constituent groups, in addition to the elderly, have included the mentally ill, alcoholics, addicts, juveniles, and other traditional "incompetents". Because one complaint regarding guardianship is the discrimination, stigma, and labeling wrought by having such a vague triggering criterion as "advanced age" and because it seems more efficient and equitable to have one public guardianship statute, rather than one for each of several constituent groups, the model public guardianship statute utilizes a functional, as opposed to causal or categorical, definition of eligibility. This model public guardianship statute is intended for general use, including the elderly and disabled.

The model public guardianship statute reflects not only the findings and recommendations of this book, but also a distillation and compilation of existing state statutes and a series of model (public) guardianship statutes. No current state statute alone should be considered a model, although California, Arizona, and Maryland have statutes and programs that merit consultation. Our model statute utilizes Regan and Springer's Model Public Guardian Act as a base.[4] Their model act, in turn, is an elaboration of the model state statute on the public guardian proposed by Legal Research and Services for the Elderly.[5] The other model statutes consulted and borrowed from include the Suggested Statute on Guardianship,[6] the Optional Short Form Model Guardianship and Conservatorship Act,[7] and the Model (Guardianship and Conservatorship) Statute

---

4. J. Regan & G. Springer, Protective Services for the Elderly III (a working paper prepared for the Special Committee on Aging, U.S. Senate, July 1977).

5. Legal Research and Services for the Elderly, National Council of Senior Citizens, Inc., Legislative Approaches to the Problems of the Elderly: A Handbook of Model State Statutes (1971).

6. *Legal Issues in State Mental Health Care: Proposals for Change—Guardianship*, 2 Mental Disability L. Rep. 444 (1978).

7. *Guardianship and Conservatorship Act*, 3 Mental Disability L. Rep. 266 (1979); *also* Developmental Disabilities State Legislative Project, Guardianship and Conservator-

of the Developmental Disabilities State Legislative Project.[8] We can readily endorse any of these latter three models as improvements on existing state statutes if a more comprehensive statute is desired. Every model has its own introductory comment and annotations, which should be consulted.

Declaration of Policy and Legislative Intent

The first paragraph of this section of the model public guardianship statute is based on Regan and Springer's model, except that persons with grave disability are the subjects, rather than particular elderly citizens. This is functional, rather than causal or categorical, eligibility. The intent to provide for partial or limited guardianship, rather than the common all-or-nothing approach, is also expressed.

This model consciously avoids financing dependent upon fee generation because of the resulting inducements in such financing to serve wealthier clients at the expense of low income persons and to seek incompetence adjudication for wealthy individuals in less appropriate circumstances. At the same time, the model implicitly provides for services to moderate income persons who cannot afford private guardianship.

The second paragraph of this section is based on the Developmental Disabilities Project model. The intent is that the ward's volition be honored as much as possible, that the purpose of public guardianship is restoration or development of capacity, that public guardianship is not a life sentence or a facilitator of others' interests, and that these objectives should be achieved by the least drastic means.

Definitions

"Gravely disabled" is adopted from the Suggested Statute on Guardianship, is similar to California's criterion for conservatorship under the progressive Lanterman-Petris-Short Act,[9] and establishes a clear distinction between civil commitment and public guardianship. Nondangerous individuals who need treatment are more appropriately the subject of guardianship rather than civil commitment. "Lack of capacity to make informed decisions about care, treatment or management services" is also derived from the Suggested Statute and may be a "constitutional precondition"

---

ship 78 (1979).

8. Developmental Disabilities State Legislative Project, Guardianship and Conservatorship 78 (1979).

9. Cal. Welf. & Inst. Code sections 5008(h), 5350 (West 1972).

to intervention in an individual's life by court order.[10] The definition for "psychotropic medication" is taken from Florida Statutes §918.15(4)(b) (1979).[11]

The definition for "severe mental disorder" is taken, as conceived in the Suggested Statute on Guardianship, from the Suggested Statute on Civil Commitment.[12] Most guardianship statutes define "mental illness", "mental incompetence", "mental incapacity", "mental disability", "senility", "lunacy", "insanity", "imbecility", "idiocy", and the like in vague or tautological terms, if they provide any definition at all. This definition includes the emotional, volitional, and cognitive components of mental functioning in terms understandable to disability professionals, attorneys, and lay persons alike. Persons suffering from "advanced age", epilepsy, mental retardation, and acute intoxication or addiction would meet this definition if any such disability produced a severe mental function disorder. Such a definition, along with the other criteria, should reduce the inappropriate use of public guardianship and facilitate the more appropriate use of such alternatives as trusts, powers of attorney, living wills, gifts to minors and custodianship, single transaction court ratifications, private nonprofit corporations, volunteer services, supportive or protective services, and civil commitment.

The definition for "unable...to manage one's financial resources" is an adaptation of the definition for "unable to meet essential requirement for one's physical health or safety", which is taken from the Suggested Statute on Guardianship. The definitions should eliminate the possibility of preventive incompetence adjudication or detention and reduce the incidence of contradictory expert predictions and evaluations. The source for the stipulation that inability to manage one's financial resources may not be evidenced solely by isolated incidents of negligence or improvidence is California Probate Code §1460 (West 1977). Individuals who are disabled should have as much of a right to be wrong as those who are not disabled.[13]

Establishment of Office

Regan and Springer's Model Public Guardian Act offered four alternatives for location of the public guardian: (1) within each court having

---

10. *See Legal Issues in State Mental Health Care: Proposals for Change—Civil Commitment,* 2 Mental Disability L. Rep. 77, 89–93 (1977).

11. *See also* Winick, *Psychotropic Medication and Competency to Stand Trial,* Am. B. Foundation Research J. 769 (1977).

12. *Legal Issues...—Civil Commitment, supra* note 10 at 89, 113.

13. Developmental Disabilities Project, *supra* note 8 at 78.

guardianship jurisdiction, as originally provided in the model state statute on the public guardian proposed by Legal Research and Services for the Elderly; (2) within the state executive branch; (3) within the state's office on aging, department of social services, or department of health and mental hygiene; or (4) within each county.

The least attractive location is one of the state's social service agencies because of the serious conflict of interest. There could not be a worse location for the office of the public guardian than the very agency that often fosters the need for advocacy and protection of the ward. The courts are a tempting location, but the judges, who recognized a need for public guardianship, themselves voiced discomfort with the potential conflict of interest and responsibility for administrative activity. An independent state office under the governor is also tempting, especially considering the success enjoyed by such an analogous agency as New Jersey's Department of the Public Advocate.[14] However, the intent of the office of public guardian is to deliver individual, personalized guardianship services. This would be geographically precluded in all but the very smallest states, which could utilize a public guardian at least as effectively at our location choice, the county level.

The remaining parts of this section are intended to assure the independence of the public guardian, the aversion of any conflict of interest, and the limitation of the public guardian office's scope to a serviceable and manageable number of clients. It is vital for every ward that the public guardian not be part of any county social service-providing agency. The public guardian must be able to represent a ward as independently as a private guardian. In addition, the primary reason for problems in any public guardian office is because the office and professional staff members have responsibility for too many wards. The dynamics of a public guardian office are such that growth beyond 500 wards hinders access to rights, benefits, and entitlements and the provision of guardianship services. The best public guardian offices resist growth, but require and appreciate an explicit statutory limitation on size to forestall the inevitable pressure and inclination to aggrandize. The best offices are also staffed sufficiently to have a ratio of one professional staff member for every thirty wards. These considerations are so important that without them, proposed wards would be better off with no public guardianship.

---

14. Kannensohn & Kessler, *Representing the Public Interest: A Report on New Jersey's Department of the Public Advocate*, 48 St. Gov't. 252 (1975).

Powers and Duties

The model statute provides for appointment of the public guardian by the court pursuant to the guardianship and conservatorship law of the state, except that the proposed ward must have the opportunity for the hearing prescribed in a later section. Any contingencies for the public guardian or his or her ward not provided for in the model statute, such as notice requirements, should be considered by reference to the state's guardianship and conservatorship law.

The model statute provides for the additional responsibility, as suggested by Regan and Springer, of intervention by the public guardian in proceedings involving a ward or a proposed ward for nonfulfillment of guardian duties, disproportionate waste by costs or the ward's best interests. Public guardian offices with a high number of limited or partial guardianships would thus retain a full quota of duties. Such intervention should function as a necessary monitor and check on both the private guardianship market and other public guardian offices in the state.

The source for the other subsections is also Regan and Springer. However, the basis for the provision prohibiting the public guardian from committing a ward to a mental facility is Maryland Estates and Trusts Code Annotated § 13-706(b)(2) (1977).

Persons Eligible for Services

This section sets the criteria of eligibility for the service of the public guardian: (1) grave disability; (2) inability to compensate a private guardian; (3) no willing and responsible family member or friend to serve as guardian; and (4) the lack of capacity to make informed decisions about proposed care, treatment, or management services. These criteria are a composite from the Suggested Statute on Guardianship and from Legal Research and Services for the Elderly.[15] The services are limited to the needy in order to minimize the conflicts of fee generation schemes and incentives and to not discourage successful private guardianship alternatives such as social services by religious organizations.

A difficult issue is whether there should be provision for voluntary public guardianship, as suggested by Regan and Springer. Such an alternative is rarely utilized, and the abuse of analogous, well-intended, voluntary

---

15. *See also* O'Connor v. Donaldson, 422 U.S. 563, 576 (1975) ("In short, a state cannot constitutionally confine without more [than custodial care] a nondangerous individual who is capable of surviving safely in freedom by himself or with the help of willing and responsible family members or friends.")

civil commitment has been serious and widespread.[16] However, given that a purpose of the public guardianship scheme is to enhance and encourage individual autonomy and responsibility, the model statute provides for voluntary petitioning as an alternative of considerable positive potential and opportunity. The court must incorporate any requested limitations on public guardianship authority; the filing of such petition creates no inference regarding competence; and the court must ensure beyond a reasonable doubt that the voluntary petition is not the product of mistake, fraud, or duress.

Allocation of Costs

This section is adopted from Regan and Springer's Model Public Guardian Act. The financial ability test is intended to afford some flexibility in income or asset eligibility, inclusive of some moderate income persons who cannot afford private guardianship, but with encouragement of court zealousness in concern with asset depletion rather than short-run overprotection of public funds.

Explicit provision for a reimbursement claim upon the estate at death is not made, so as to avoid any express incentive to perpetuate the guardianship to death or to preserve assets for any other than the ward's benefit. It seems clear that the intended purpose of such a provision—to discourage courts from requiring immediate costs payment or reimbursement—is adequately addressed elsewhere.

Appointment and Hearing Procedure

The model statute departs, as recommended by all of these model guardianship statutes, from the traditional indefinite term for guardianship and places the burden on the petitioner to secure successive appointments at one year intervals or less after the initial appointment for six

---

16. Ennis, *Legal Rights of the Voluntary Patient*, J. Nat'l A. Private Psych. Hosp. 4 (Summer 1976); Gilboy & Schmidt, *"Voluntary" Hospitalization of the Mentally Ill*, 66 Nw. U. L. Rev. 429 (1971); [Lidz, Mulvey, Arnold, Bennett & Kirsch, *Coercive Interactions in a Psychiatric Emergency Room*, 11 Behavioral Sci. & L. 269 (1993);] Olin & Olin, *Informed Consent in Voluntary Mental Hospital Admissions*, 132 Am. J. Psych. 938 (1975); Palmer & Wohl, *Voluntary Admission Forms: Does the Patient Know What He's Signing?* 23 Hosp. & Community Psych. 250 (1972); Szasz, *Voluntary Mental Hospitalization: An Unacknowledged Practice of Medical Fraud*, 287 New Eng. J. Med. 277 (1972). *But see* McGarry & Greenblatt, *Conditional Voluntary Mental Hospital Admission*, 287 New Eng. J. Med. 279 (1972).

months or less. The criteria for appointment is stated, including a precondition that necessary, beneficial services are available. Such a precondition is the quid pro quo for the stigma, deprivation of liberty and autonomy, and exacerbation of disability that otherwise accompanies guardianship.

The suggested standard of proof is "clear, unequivocal, and convincing" evidence. Such a standard is intended to inform the fact-finder that the proof must be greater than for other civil cases. While it might be argued that an individual suffering from grave disability is not himself at liberty or free from stigma, we are quite comfortable with our assessment that it is much better at this time for a gravely disabled person to be free of public guardianship than for a person to be inappropriately adjudicated a ward of the public guardian. The provision of functional, rather than causal or categorical, criteria should facilitate the use of the standard. The clear, unequivocal, and convincing evidence standard is utilized in such analogous proceedings as deportation, denaturalization, and involuntary civil commitment.[17] Public guardianship is easily conceptualized as the denaturalization or deportation of an individual's legal autonomy as a citizen.

The provisions for accounting and review of the appointment are adopted from Regan and Springer. They incorporate by reference appropriate sections of the state's guardianship and conservatorship law.

The hearing subsection is a synthesis from Regan and Springer and the Suggested Statute on Guardianship. The provision requiring the presence of the proposed ward is taken from the California Probate Code § 1461 (1977). The subsections relating to counsel, trial by jury, and evaluation are from Regan and Springer. The public guardianship process is designed to be adversarial. The significance of effective, adversarial counsel for both the process and the proposed ward cannot therefore be overemphasized. Any failure of guardianship processes can be attributed in large measure to inappropriately paternalistic and condescendingly informal proceedings facilitated by counsel, whose real client is too seldom the proposed ward.

The second evaluation paragraph, relating to the rights of silence and of observers, is an adaptation from the Suggested Statute on Guardianship. The provisions for the right to present evidence and the duties of counsel are from Regan and Springer. The provisions for expert testimo-

---

17. Woodby v. INS, 385 U.S. 276, 285 (1967); Chaunt v. United States, 364 U.S. 350, 353 (1960); Schneiderman v. United States, 320 U.S. 118, 125, 159 (1943); Ala. Code section 22-52-10(a) (Supp. 1978); Tenn. Code Ann. section 33-604(d) (Supp. 1978). The U.S. Supreme Court has suggested that states would be "free to use that standard" of clear, unequivocal and convincing evidence. Addington v. Texas, 441 U.S. 418 (1979).

ny under the rules of evidence subsection and for psychotropic medication are from the Suggested Statute on Guardianship. The Developmental Disabilities Legislative Project is the source for the first rules of evidence paragraph and for the appeal provision.

Procedural safeguards are warranted in the public guardianship process because of the similarity and correlations with the civil commitment process. Such safeguards have sustained certain legal blows from the Supreme Court in cases involving the institutionalization of children by their parents and by state social workers.[18] However, any suggestion of unilateral deference to guardianship petitioners, psychiatrists, state social workers, and the like and any suggestion that such persons are necessarily acting in a proposed ward's best interests, should be taken with the equanimity demonstrated by Mr. Justice Brennan dissenting in part: "I find this reasoning particularly unpersuasive. With equal logic it could be argued that criminal trials are unnecessary since prosecutors are not supposed to prosecute innocent persons."[19] Even the majority indicated certain discomfort with their nonadversarial position, when they provided: "Of course, a state may elect to provide such adversary hearings in situations where it perceives that parents and a child may be at odds..."[20] The model public guardianship statute perceives and anticipates many situations where petitioner and proposed ward are "at odds" and accordingly elects procedural safeguards proportionate to the identified risks.

Public Guardianship Order

The provision for the order is an adaptation of the Suggested Statute on Guardianship. The intent is to depart from the traditional all or nothing approach that is so inconsistent with an individual's needs. The court should discriminate authorities over person and property, the extent to which such authorities are partial or limited, and the term of appointment appropriate for the ward's disability and restoration or development of capacity. The least restrictive alternative is a concept borrowed from the Developmental Disabilities Model Statute, but it is also a fundamental constitutional principle.[21]

---

18. Parham v. J.R., 442 U.S. 584 (1979); Institutionalized Juveniles v. Secretary, Public Welfare, 442 U.S. 640 (1979). [*See, e.g.,* Schmidt, *Considerations of Social Science in a Reconsideration of Parham v. J.R. and the Commitment of Children to Public Mental Institutions,* 13 J. Psychiatry & L. 339 (1985).]

19. Parham v. J.R., *supra* note 18, at 637.

20. *Id.* at 610–611 n.18.

21. *See, e.g.,* O'Connor v. Donaldson, 422 U.S. 563, 575 (1975); Shelton v. Tucker, 364 U.S. 479, 488 (1960); Dean Milk Co. v. City of Madison, 340 U.S. 349 (1951).

The medical consent provision is a derivation of common law that is designed as a substitute for provisions relating to temporary guardians, emergency guardianship powers, and the like. The primary purpose for temporary guardianship and emergency guardianship powers seems to be the provision of medical consent in an emergency. Indeed, this phenomenon accounts for considerable demand that public guardianship exist. Such provisions, as enumerated in the Suggested Statute on Guardianship, seem ultimately cumbersome and unsuccessful in actual emergency situations. The medical consent provision addresses the problem from the other perspective in relieving physicians of liability for failure to obtain consent from a ward or proposed ward of the public guardian in an emergency.[22] Situations of proposed public guardian wards not involving medical emergencies can be adequately handled through the regular public guardianship process or single transaction court ratification if necessary.

Right to Services

The source for the right to services subsection is the Suggested Statute on Guardianship. The subsection codifies the constitutional right justified either as a quid pro quo for the loss of autonomy and freedom, as a fulfillment of the state purposes in public guardianship (protection, restoration or development of capacity), or as the less restrictive alternative to indefinite or unnecessarily long guardianship.[23] Furthermore, *Parham v. J.R.*, viewed with *Addington v. Texas*, "seems to be signalling...a new awareness of the right to treatment in a broad medical as well as legal sense."[24]

Termination et al.

The remaining subsections are taken from either Regan and Springer or the Developmental Disabilities Model Statute and are self-explanatory for the most part.

A word should be said about appropriations. The funding source, whether county, state, or even federal, is kept deliberately flexible. County funding might be appropriate considering the location of the office, is

---

22. An emergency is *not* jeopardy to "emotional well-being" as ridiculously provided in Florida. Fla. Admin. Code section 10E-5.09(10) (1981).
23. *See* Wyatt v. Aderholt, 503 F.2d 1305 (5th Cir. 1974); Developments in the Law, *Civil Commitment of the Mentally Ill*, 87 Harv. L. Rev. 1190, 1245–53 (1974).
24. *Historic Supreme Court Decision on the Voluntary Admission of Minors Issue*, 3 Mental Disability L. Rep. 231, 234 (1979).

precedented in several of the better public guardian programs, and might facilitate enactment by state legislatures. Programs that are funded at the county level, on the other hand, are uniformly, and probably understandably, desirous of state funding. Other possibilities include federal reimbursement as contemplated for crime victim compensation (conceptualize public guardianship as social victim compensation), an increase in costs to private guardianship for the purpose of funding public guardianship, or some match of county and state, and perhaps federal funding. The principal concern should be that there is a need for public guardianship, if done correctly, and that it can be done in a cost-effective manner, even when done correctly. The economic, social, and opportunity costs of not meeting the need, or of not meeting the need properly, far outweigh actual expenses.

Volunteer Public Guardian Alternative

An alterative to public guardianship as proposed in this model statute has been suggested by the Developmental Disabilities State Legislative Project.

> In order to provide a close one-to-one relationship between the individual serving in a guardianship or conservatorship capacity and the person being served and to eliminate the inherent conflicts of interest which occur when the responsibility for public guardianship is placed in the agency providing services to minors and partially disabled or disabled persons, the act proposes that state funds be allocated to compensate private citizens who volunteer to serve as the limited personal guardian, personal guardian, limited conservator or conservator for a partially disabled or disabled person or a minor.[25]

The citizen volunteer model suggested by the Developmental Disabilities Project anticipates that its stated objectives can be accomplished with greater assurance while avoiding the cost of another social service bureaucracy. Yet their model statute also "provides for a 5 person, gubernatorially appointed oversight commission to assist in encouraging individuals to volunteer, providing information and training, and monitoring the appointment process,"[26] for which "a multifaceted staff will be necessary."[27] Volunteers may not serve as a limited guardian or guardian for more than

---

25. Development Disabilities Project, *supra* note 8, at 76.
26. *Id.* at 77, 86.
27. *Id.* at 90.

two individuals or as a limited conservator or conservator for more than four individuals.[28]

A one-to-one relationship is a desirable objective that is diluted by such statutory quotas. Expertise and continuity are also sacrificed with a system of part-time volunteers. Our research regarding volunteer guardianship programs suggests that qualified "volunteers" are difficult to recruit, train, and retain and that compensated "volunteers" may lack the motivation and dedication of volunteers who are functioning without necessity of recruitment.

The costs of both compensating the "volunteer" public guardians and financing the oversight commission with its multifaceted staff seem no less than compensation of decentralized public guardian offices. In fact, a cost analysis should reveal that a system of many fully compensated part-time volunteer public guardians with a limited quota of wards per guardian is more expensive and less efficient than a system of full-time public guardians for providing public guardianship services.[29] The primary problem is a lack of guardians for persons who cannot afford a private guardian, not identification of people who will serve if compensated.

In comparing these two alternatives, and assuming the need for public guardianship, the Developmental Disabilities Project proposal might accomplish somewhat more personalized guardianship service. Our model public guardianship statute will accomplish expert, efficient, full-time, continuous guardianship service that is cost efficient.

Model Public Guardianship Statute

Section 1. Title.

This act shall be known as the Public Guardianship Act.

Section 2. Declaration of Policy and Legislative Intent.

The legislature of the state of _____ recognizes that some persons in the state, because of grave disability, are unable to meet vary-

---

28. *Id.* at 148.
29. *See* Scott, *The Mental Health Advocacy Service,* in Mental Health Advocacy: An Emerging Force in Consumers' Rights 42, 49–50 (L. Kopolow and H. Bloom eds. 1977); and *Mental Health Advocacy Service,* 2 Mental Disability L. Rep. 270, 277–78 (1977).

ing essential requirements for their physical health or to manage varying essential aspects of their financial resources. The legislature finds that private guardianship is inadequate where there are no willing and responsible family members or friends to serve as guardian and where the gravely disabled person does not have adequate income or wealth for the compensation of a private guardian. The legislature intends through this act to establish the office of public guardian for the purpose of furnishing guardianship services to gravely disabled persons at reduced or no cost, unless the gravely disabled person has adequate income or wealth to compensate a private guardian.

The legislature intends to promote the general welfare by establishing a public guardianship system that permits gravely disabled persons to determinatively participate as fully as possible in all decisions that affect them; that assists such persons to regain or develop their capacities to the maximum extent possible; and that accomplishes such objectives through the use of the least restrictive alternatives.

This act shall be liberally construed to accomplish these purposes.

Section 3. Definitions.

As used in this act:

(1) "Court" means the court or branch having jurisdiction in matters relating to the affairs of decedents; this court in this state is known as _____.

(2) "Gravely disabled" means unable to meet essential requirements for one's physical health or safety or to manage one's financial resources as a result of severe mental disorder.

(3) "Lack of capacity to make informed decisions about care, treatment, or management services" means the inability, by reason of mental condition, to achieve a rudimentary understanding, after conscientious efforts at explanation, of the purpose, nature, or possible significant benefits of care, treatment, or management services to be provided under public guardianship; provided that a person shall be deemed incapable of understanding such purpose if, due to impaired mental ability to perceive reality, he cannot realize that his recent behavior has caused or has created a clear and substantial risk of serious physical injury, illness, or disease or of gross financial mismanagement or manifest financial vulnerability to oneself; and provided further that a person shall be deemed to lack the capacity to make informed decisions about care, treat-

ment, or management services if the reason for refusing the same is expressly based on either the belief that he or she is unworthy of assistance or the desire to harm or punish oneself.

(4) "Psychotropic medication" means any drug or compound affecting the mind, behavior, intellectual functions, perception, moods, and emotion and includes antipsychotic, antidepressant, antimanic, and antianxiety drugs.

(5) "Public guardian" means the office of public guardian.

(6) "Severe mental disorder" means a severe impairment of emotional processes, ability to exercise conscious control of one's actions, or ability to perceive reality or to reason or understand, which impairment is manifested by instances of grossly disturbed behavior or faulty perceptions.

(7) "Unable...to manage one's financial resources" means unable to take those actions necessary to obtain, administer, or dispose of real or personal property, intangible property, business property, benefits, or income so that, in the absence of public guardianship, gross financial mismanagement or manifest financial vulnerability is likely to occur in the near future. For purposes of this act, any such inability must be evidenced by recent behaviors causing such harm or creating a clear and substantial risk thereof, and at least one incidence of such behavior must have occurred within twenty days of the filing of the petition for public guardianship, except that such inability shall not be evidenced solely by isolated incidents of negligence or improvidence. The requirement of the preceding sentence shall not apply in the case of a petition for renewal of public guardianship.

(8) "Unable to meet essential requirements for one's physical health or safety" means unable, through one's own efforts and through acceptance of assistance from family, friends, and other available private and public sources, to meet one's needs for medical care, nutrition, clothing, shelter, hygiene, or safety so that, in the absence of public guardianship, serious physical injury, illness, or disease is likely to occur in the near future. For purposes of this act, any such inability must be evidenced by recent behaviors causing such harm or creating a clear and substantial risk thereof, and at least one incidence of such behavior must have occurred within twenty days of the filing of the petition for public guardianship. The requirement of the preceding sentence shall not apply in the case of a petition for renewal of public guardianship.

Section 4. Establishment of Office.

(a) Establishment of office.—Each county within the state shall establish the office of public guardian for disabled persons.

(b) Appointment.—The head of the office shall be the public guardian, who shall be appointed by the county (board of supervisors; council), upon consultation with appropriate advocacy agencies and individuals for disabled persons, for a term of five years from the time of appointment.

(c) Part-time appointments.—If the needs of the county do not require that a person hold only the position of public guardian, the county (board of supervisors; council) may appoint an individual as public guardian on a part-time basis with appropriate compensation, provided that no other part-time position occupied by such individual may present any conflict of interest.

(d) Compensation.—The compensation for the position of public guardian shall be fixed by the county (board of supervisors; council).

(e) Conflict of interest.—The office of public guardian shall be independent of any service-providing agency. The office of public guardian is authorized to take any actions on behalf of a ward that a private guardian is authorized to take, except as otherwise provided in this act.

(f) Effectiveness.—No office of public guardian shall be responsible for more than 500 wards. When an office of public guardian is responsible for 500 wards, another office of public guardian shall be established for additional wards.

No office of public guardian shall assume responsibility for any wards beyond a ratio of thirty wards per professional staff member.

Section 5. Powers and Duties.

(a) Appointment by court.—The public guardian may serve as guardian and/or conservator, after appointment by a court pursuant to the provisions of the (guardianship and conservatorship law of the state), provided that the proposed ward of the public guardian has had the opportunity for the hearing prescribed in Section 8 of this act.

(b) Same powers and duties.—The public guardian shall have the same powers and duties as a private guardian or conservator, except as otherwise limited by law or court order.

(c) Intervention.—The public guardian may, on his or her own motion, or at the request of the court, intervene at any time in any guardianship or conservatorship proceeding involving a ward by appropriate motion to the court, if the public guardian or the court deems such intervention to be justified because an appointed guardian or conservator is not fulfilling his or her duties, the estate is subject to disproportionate waste due to the costs of the guardianship or conservatorship, or the best interests of the ward require such intervention.

(d) Subordinates.—The public guardian may employ subordinates necessary for the proper performance of his or her duties, to the extent authorized in the budget for the office.

(c) Delegation of powers and duties.—The public guardian may delegate to members of his or her staff powers and duties as guardian or conservator and such other powers and duties as are created by this act, although the public guardian retains ultimate responsibility for the proper performance of these delegated functions.

(f) Other powers and duties.—The public guardian:

(1) may formulate and adopt such procedures as are necessary to promote the efficient conduct of the work and general administration of the office, its professional staff, and other employees;

(2) may contract for services necessary to carry out the duties of the office of public guardian;

(3) may accept the services of volunteer workers or consultants at no compensation or at nominal or token compensation and reimburse them for their proper and necessary expenses;

(4) shall keep and maintain proper financial and statistical records concerning all cases in which the public guardian provides guardianship or conservatorship services, provided that the privacy and confidentiality of such records for each ward are preserved; and

(5) may not commit a ward to a mental facility without an involuntary commitment proceeding as provided by law.

Section 6. Persons Eligible for Services; Petition by Gravely Disabled Person.

(a) Eligible persons.—Any gravely disabled person residing in the state who cannot afford to compensate a private guardian, who does not have a willing and responsible family member or friend to serve as guardian, and who lacks the capacity to make informed decisions about proposed care, treatment, or management services is eligible for the services of the public guardian.

(b) Petition by gravely disabled person.—A gravely disabled person may petition the court to have the public guardian appointed as his or her guardian or conservator with the powers and duties ordinarily conferred by law on guardians and conservators or for certain limited purposes described in the petition. If the petition requests that only limited powers be granted, the court shall incorporate such limitations into its order of appointment. The court shall ensure beyond a reasonable doubt that such petition is not the product of mistake, fraud, or duress. The filing of such a petition shall not be the basis for any inference concerning the competence of the petitioner or for any loss of civil rights or benefits.

Section 7. Allocation of Costs.

(a) Determination of costs.—If a public guardian is appointed guardian or conservator for a gravely disabled person, the administrative costs of the public guardian's services and the costs incurred in the appointment procedure shall not be charged against the income or the estate of the gravely disabled person, unless the court determines at any time that the person is financially able to pay all or part of such costs.

(b) Financial ability.—The ability of the income or estate of the gravely disabled person to pay for administrative costs of a public guardian or costs incurred in the appointment procedure shall be measured according to the person's financial ability to engage and compensate a private guardian. The ability is a variable dependent on the nature, extent, and liquidity of assets; the disposable net income of the person; the nature of the guardianship or conservatorship; the type, duration, and the complexity of the services required; and any other foreseeable expenses.

(c) Investigation of financial ability.—The public guardian shall investigate the financial status of a person who requests the appointment of the public guardian as his or her guardian or for whom a court is considering the appointment of the public guardian. In connection with such investigation, the public guardian shall have the authority to require the proposed ward to execute and deliver such written requests or authorizations as may be necessary under applicable law to provide the public guardian with access to records of public or private sources, otherwise confidential, as may be needed to evaluate eligibility. The public guardian is authorized to obtain information from any public record office of the state or of any subdivision or agency thereof upon request and without payment of any fees ordinarily required by law.

Section 8. Appointment; Accounting; Review of Appointment; Hearing Procedure.

(a) Appointment.—The initial appointment by a court of the public guardian as guardian or conservator shall be for no longer than six months, after the court determines by clear, unequivocal, and convincing evidence that the proposed ward of the public guardian is gravely disabled; cannot afford to compensate a private guardian; does not have willing and responsible family members or friends to serve as guardian; and lacks the capacity to make informed decisions about proposed care, treatment, or management services and that necessary services are available to protect the proposed ward from serious injury, illness, or disease or from gross financial mismanagement or manifest financial vulnerability. Successive appointments for a term no longer than one year may be made by the court after the same determinations.

(b) Accounting and review of appointment.—No later than thirty days prior to the expiration of his or her term as guardian or conservator, the public guardian shall file with the court an inventory and account in accord with the provisions of (section _____ of the guardianship and conservatorship law of the state), which shall be subject to examination pursuant to the provisions of (section of the guardianship or conservatorship law of the state). At the same time, the public guardian shall file a statement setting forth facts that indicate at least: (1) the present personal status of the gravely disabled person; (2) the public guardian's plan for regaining, developing, and preserving the well-being and capacity of the ward to make informed decisions about care and treatment services; and (3) the need for the continuance or discontinuance of the guardianship or conservatorship or for any alteration of the powers of the public guardian.

(c) Hearing.—The court shall hold a hearing to determine the findings set forth in subsection (a) above concerning the appointment, or renewal of the appointment of the public guardian, unless the court dismisses the petition for lack of substantial grounds.

(d) Presence of proposed ward.—The proposed ward of the public guardian shall be present at the hearing unless he or she is medically incapable of being present to the extent that attendance is likely to cause serious and immediate physiological damage to the proposed ward. Such waiver for medical incapability shall be determined on the basis of factual information supplied to the court by counsel, including at least the affidavit or certificate of a duly licensed medical practitioner.

(e) Counsel.—The proposed ward of the public guardian has the right to counsel whether or not the proposed ward is present at the hearing, unless the right to counsel is knowingly, intelligently, and voluntarily waived by the ward. If the proposed ward cannot afford counsel or lacks the capacity to waive counsel, the court shall appoint counsel who shall always be present at any hearing involving the proposed ward. Where the proposed ward cannot afford counsel, the state shall pay reasonable attorney's fees—that is, such compensation as is customarily charged by attorneys in this state for comparable services.

(f) Trial by jury.—The proposed ward of the public guardian shall have the right to trial by jury.

(g) Evaluation.—The proposed ward of the public guardian has the right to secure an independent medical and/or psychological examination relevant to the issues involved in the hearing at the expense of the state if the proposed ward is unable to afford such examination and to present a report of this independent evaluation or the evaluator's personal testimony as evidence at the hearing.

The proposed ward at any evaluation has the right to remain silent, the right to refuse to answer questions when the answers may tend to incriminate the proposed ward, the right to have counsel or any other mental health professional present, and the right to retain the privileged and confidential nature of the evaluation for all proceedings other than proceedings pursuant to this act; except that, after full explanation, the proposed ward may be required to submit to interviews for the purpose of ascertaining whether he or she lacks the capacity to make informed decisions about care and treatment services, and the proposed ward's failure to respond to questions relevant to that issue may be introduced as evidence of a lack of such capacity.

(h) Right to present evidence.—The proposed ward of the public guardian may present evidence and confront and cross-examine witnesses.

(i) Duties of counsel.—The duties of counsel representing a proposed ward of the public guardian at the hearing shall include at least: a personal interview with the proposed ward; counseling the proposed ward with respect to his or her rights; and arranging for an independent medical and/or psychological examination as provided in subsection (g) above.

(j) Rules of evidence.—Except where specified otherwise, the rules of evidence and rules of procedure, including those on discovery, that are applicable in civil matters shall govern all proceedings under this act.

Any psychiatrist or psychologist giving testimony or reports containing descriptions and opinions shall be required to provide a detailed explanation as to how such descriptions and opinions were reached and a specification of all behaviors and other factual information on which such descriptions and opinions are based. Such witnesses shall not be permitted to give opinion testimony stating the applicable diagnostic category unless the proposed ward of the public guardian raises the issue through cross-examination or the presentation of evidence.

(k) Psychotropic medication.—The proposed ward of the public guardian shall be entitled, upon the request of the proposed ward, to have the court and the jury, if any, informed regarding the influence of any psychotropic medication being taken by the proposed ward and its effect on the proposed ward's actions, demeanor, and participation at the hearing.

(l) Appeal.—The proposed ward of the public guardian shall have the right to appeal adverse orders and judgments in the manner prescribed in (the Rules of Civil Procedure), and the proposed ward shall have the right to appellate counsel, who shall be compensated as provided in subsection (e) above.

Section 9. Public Guardianship Order.

(a) Order.—If, pursuant to section 8 of this act, it is determined that the public guardian should be appointed for a proposed ward, the court shall enter an order that makes findings of fact on the basis of clear, unequivocal, and convincing evidence supporting each grant of authority to the public guardian and that

(1) establishes whether the public guardian has authority over the person, or the property, or both person and property, of the ward;

(2) establishes whether, and to what extent, the authority over person and/or property is partial; and

(3) sets the term of appointment, which shall be no longer than provided in section 8(a) above.

(b) Least restrictive alternative.—No grant of authority to the public guardian shall be more than the least restrictive alternative warranted under the facts, and the public guardian shall employ the form of assistance that least interferes with the capacity of a ward to act in his or her own behalf.

(c) Medical consent.—There shall be no liability by physicians for failure to obtain consent from a ward or proposed ward of the public guardian in an emergency that threatens death or serious bodily harm.

Section 10. Right to Services.

(a) Right to services.—Each ward of the public guardian shall have the right to prompt and adequate personal and medical care, treatment, and rehabilitative services for the purposes both of meeting needs for protection from physical injury, illness, or disease and of restoration to the abilities to care for oneself and to make one's own informed decisions about care and treatment services.

(b) Petition.—In the event that the public guardian is unable to provide such services out of funds available from the ward's estate and income and other private and governmental benefits to which the ward is entitled, the public guardian or ward may petition the court for an order requiring the (state and/or county) to provide such funds as are necessary to provide services that would implement the ward's right to services. Such petition shall provide complete details with regard to funds and other benefits at the public guardian's disposal and justification for the necessity and appropriateness of the services for which finances are unavailable. Upon receipt of the petition, the court shall schedule the matter for a hearing within twenty days and cause the petition and notice of the hearing to be served upon the public guardian, the ward, the ward's attorney, and (appropriate state and/or local officials). In preparation for the hearing, the (appropriate state-and/or local officials) shall have access to relevant care and treatment records of the ward. At the hearing, the burden of proof by a preponderance of the evidence shall be upon the petitioning party.

(c) Order.—At the conclusion of the hearing, the court shall enter an order dismissing the petition or requiring the (state and/or county) to provide the necessary funds for any services to which the ward has a right under subsection (a) of this section and from which there is at least a substantial probability of significant benefit to the ward.

Section 11. Termination.

The public guardian may be discharged by a court with respect to any of the authority granted over each ward upon petition of the gravely disabled person or any interested person or upon the court's own motion, when it appears that the services of the public guardian are no longer necessary.

Section 12. Succession to Position of Public Guardian; Vacancies.

(a) Succession in office.—When a person is appointed to the position of public guardian, he or she succeeds immediately to all rights, duties, responsibilities, powers, and authorities of the preceding public guardian.

(b) Continuation of subordinates' activities.—When the position of public guardian is vacant, subordinate personnel employed under section 5 of this act shall continue to act as if the position of public guardian was filled.

(c) Time limit to fill vacancy.—When the position of public guardian becomes vacant, a successor in office must be appointed within forty-five days.

Section 13. Court Costs.

In any proceeding for appointment of a public guardian, or in any proceeding involving the estate of a gravely disabled person for whom a public guardian has been appointed conservator or guardian, the court may waive any court costs or filing fees.

Section 14. Bond Required.

(a) General bond.—Upon taking office a public guardian shall file with the clerk of the court in which he or she is to serve a general bond in the amount of _____ dollars payable to the state or to people of the county in which the court is seated and issued by a surety company approved by the (chief judge; presiding judge) of the court. The bond shall be purchased with the (general funds of the state or county) and be conditioned upon the public guardian's faithful performance of his or her duties as conservator or guardian.

(b) Nature of bond.—The general bond and oath of a public guardian is in lieu of the bond and oath required of a private conservator or guardian.

Section 15. Authorization of Appropriations.

To carry out the purposes of this act, there is authorized to be appropriated $_____ for the fiscal year ending _____, $_____ for the fiscal year ending _____, and $_____ for the fiscal year ending_____.

Section 16. Severability of Sections.

If any section, subsection, paragraph, sentence, or any other part of this act is adjudged unconstitutional or invalid, such judgment shall not affect, impair, or invalidate the remainder of this act, but shall be confined to the section, subsection, paragraph, sentence, or any other part of this act directly involved in the controversy in which that judgment was rendered.

Section 17. Repeal. *(Insert repealer clause.)*

Section 18. Effective Date.

This act takes effect_____.

Contributors

Winsor C. Schmidt, J.D., LL.M., is Professor of Political Science and Director, Center for Health Services Research, University of Memphis.

William G. Bell, Ph.D., was Director of the Multi-Disciplinary Center of Gerontology and Professor of Urban and Regional Planning, Florida State University.

Robert Bickel, at the time of his contribution to the "Issues" article, was a graduate student at Florida State University.

Alex Heckert, Ph.D., is Assistant Professor of Sociology, Indiana University of Pennsylvania.

David Hightower, M.P.A., is a nurse administrator at the Memphis Veterans Administration Hospital.

David Loewenstein, Ph.D., is Associate Professor of Psychiatry, University of Miami School of Medicine.

Kent S. Miller, Ph.D., is Professor Emeritus of Psychology, Florida State University.

B. Elaine New, M.S.W., J.D., is General Counsel, Florida House of Representatives.

Roger Peters, Ph.D., is Associate Professor, Department of Mental Health Law and Policy, Florida Mental Health Institute, University of South Florida, Tampa.

Index

active public guardian programs, 65
adult protective services, 203–235
  abolition of, 232, 233, 234, 235
  accused criminals compared with, 215, 235
  and therapeutic state, 209–210, 215, 217, 233, 235
  capacity to consent and, 223, 226
  continuum of legal interventions and, 212–214
  defined, 218
  due process and, 227–229, 233, 234
  durable power of attorney and, 212–213
  emergency and, 230
  ex parte protection orders and, 229–230
  homelessness and, 230–231
  imminent danger of death and, 222
  in contrast to social services, 207, 218, 231
  in Florida, 224–226, 234
  in Missouri, 226–230, 234
  in Tennessee, 221–223, 234
  in West Virginia, 230–231, 234
  inapplicability of civil commitment requirements in, 224
  institutionalization in, 209, 233, 234
  institutionalization syndrome in, 209
  internationally, 207, 212, 215–216
  interrelationship with involuntary commitment and guardianship, 214, 219, 223, 225, 233, 234, 235
  involuntary protective services statutes, 219–220
  judicial experience with, 221–231, 232
  mandamus and, 230
  Mary Northern (Tennessee) and, 221–223, 234
  mortality in, 209, 234
  need for, 205–206
  parens patriae doctrine and, 226, 234
  police power and, 228, 234
  presumption of poverty and, 213
  preventing domestic violence and, 230
  refusing to choose and, 222
  representative payee and, 214
  restraining the abuser and, 226–229, 234
  social treatment model in, 208–209, 212
  specific goals of, 206, 231
  state of advocacy for, 232–233
  surrogate basis for, 207
alternatives to guardianship, 7–8, 174–175, 188, 199–200, 213
  constitutionally less restrictive, 7, 127–129, 247, 258
  diversion, 141, 170, 188, 199–201
alternatives to public guardianship, 79–88, 187–188
  banks and trust companies, 84
  benign neglect, 83, 187
  Broward County Gerontology

Program, 85–86
Cathedral Foundation (Jacksonville), 84–85, 172
Catholic Service Bureau (West Palm Beach), 86
Florida State Hospital Model Legal Services Program, 86
Guardian Association (Pinellas County), 86
informal guardianship, 83, 102
Jewish Children and Family Services (Miami Beach), 85
Leon-Wakulla Guardianship Services (Tallahassee), 86
mental hospitalization, 83
nonprofit corporations, 84–86
private attorneys, 74, 82–83
volunteer guardian bank, 85
guardianship
and aging, 63–64, 82, 87, 199, 240
and medical procedures, 191, 193
and need of institutional medical care, 191
and non-profit corporation, 66, 74, 84–86, 97, 171
appointment of counsel in, 100, 122–123
as last resort, 7, 8, 61, 73, 77, 84, 87, 147, 192, 193
as legal infantilization, 6, 220
Associated Press investigation of, 183–184
average length of, 183, 184, 191 n. 49
bifurcated process in, 91–92
bond differences in, 101
characteristics of guardians in, 184, 189, 190, 191, 198–199
computerization in, 138, 182

court monitoring in, 93–94, 97, 102–103, 105–106, 129, 137–138, 189
defined, 3, 91, 148, 174, 181–182
definition of incapacity in, 182–183
demographic findings about wards in, 97–99, 104, 153–154, 183–184, 189, 190, 191, 192, 193
depletion of estate in, 184
diagnoses in, 100–101, 124–125, 183, 190
diversion from, 141, 170, 188, 199–200
estate size and relatives in, 102, 190, 199
examining committees in, 99, 100–101, 125, 137
filing of annual reports in, 137–138
filing rate for, 3–4, 91, 183, 186–187, 192
grand jury investigation of, 136–138, 189–190
in Illinois, 198–199
in Pennsylvania, 191–192
in San Mateo County (California), 192–193
in Tallahassee (Florida), 91–106, 190
incompetency hearings in, 99–101, 104
institutionalization in, 185, 192, 193, 199
law in Florida, 96–97
legal representation in, 107–117, 122–124
mortality in, 184, 185, 193, 199
overuse of, 193
personal consequences of, 5–7,

81, 88, 93–94, 148–149, 184, 185
procedural and substantive issues in, 92, 104–106, 109–111
recommendations about, 104–106, 119–132
research about, 94, 109–111, 148–149, 181–200, 237–239
research questions about, 95–96, 151, 181
services broker role of, 183 n. 8, 196
size of estates in, 101, 102, 184, 189, 190, 192
third party interests served by, 185, 191, 192
time to adjudicate in, 103
guardianship statutory reform and procedure research, 9 n. 39
problems with statutory criteria and procedures, 8–10, 174
statutory remedies, 11–12, 61–62, 114–115, 128, 174, 191 n. 49
implicit public guardian states, 64–65, 69
judicial practices in guardianship proceedings
advanced age as a criterion, 126–127
ageism in, 127, 193, 213
court order maximizing autonomy, 127–129
investigative resources, 126
medical diagnosis as evidence, 124–125
notice to the alleged incompetent, 119–121
presence of the alleged incompetent at the hearing, 121–122
representation of alleged incompetent, 122–124
review of guardian reports, 129
right to independent evaluation, 125
training of guardians, 130
use of guardianship agencies, 130–131
lawyer representation of vulnerable clients
advocate role in, 113, 116, 117, 122, 123–124
client compensation funds for lawyer malpractice in, 115
ethical and professional standards for, 112–115
government intervention in, 112, 117
judicial remedies for, 115
legislative remedies for, 114–115
quality of, 108–111
recommendations about, 115–117, 122–124
right to effective assistance of counsel in, 116, 123–124
limited guardianship
by function, 58–59, 101–102, 104
by time, 58
in West Germany (Pflegschaft), 59, 216
participation by ward in, 59
problems with, 11 n. 52, 62, 74, 101–102, 199, 221, 222, 238
model public guardianship statute, 239–261
allocation of costs in, 245, 255
appointment and hearing procedure in, 245–247,

256–258
authorization of appropriations in, 260
bond required in, 260
clear, unequivocal, and convincing evidence in, 246
court costs in, 260
declaration of policy and legislative intent in, 241, 251
definitions in, 241, 251–253
establishment of office in, 242–243, 253
financing in, 241, 248–249
persons eligible for services in, 244, 254–255
powers and duties in, 244, 253–254
public guardianship order in, 247–248, 258
right to services in, 248, 258
severability of sections in, 260–261
succession in, 259–260
termination in, 248–249, 259
volunteer public guardian alternative in, 249–250

need for guardians
and consequences of legal incompetence, 32–34
and recommendations, 34–36, 138
as guardian advocates, 32, 86
by diagnosis, 31
by location, 31
Florida's approaches to, 139–141
in Aging and Adult Services (Florida), 29, 81
in Developmental Services (Florida), 29, 81
in nursing homes (Tennessee), 37–50
in private receiving facilities (Florida), 28
in public receiving and community facilities, 23–26
in state hospitals (Florida), 26–28, 81
needs assessment of (Florida), 20–21, 80–82, 138–139, 194
subjective reports of, 32, 73, 138

public guardianship
accomplished with award of money, 54
agent role of, 60, 196
and elder abuse, 146
and medical consent, 74, 187, 191, 193, 248, 258
and *parens patriae*, 146
and police power, 146
and securing access to rights, benefits, and entitlements, 55, 74, 186, 213, 243, 259
and social service providers, 147
and the "fox" model, 57
and the therapeutic state, 55–57
as institutionalized means for regulating poor, 64
as monarchical *parens patriae* power, 54
as product of private market failure, 53, 75
as social victim compensation, 249
case study findings about, 73, 187
change in guardianship plan needs in, 161
client assessment forms in, 140, 142, 151, 155–156

comparison of professional and
  volunteer models in,
  141–143, 145–177,
  195–197
conflicting perspectives about,
  75, 147–148
coordination role of, 60, 76
correlation between assessed
  needs and guardianship
  plans in, 159
correlation between guardianship plans and activities in,
  159–161
costs of, 142–143, 164–171,
  194
court cases involving, 72
court review of, 74
data sources about, 151–152,
  194–195
defined, 13, 19, 53, 79, 150,
  186
due process protections in, 72,
  74, 87, 95
duration of guardian activity
  in, 164–167
frequency of contact with
  wards in, 169
finding of programs in, 71, 76,
  77, 140, 194
guardian activities in, 162–164
guardian activity reports in,
  142, 152, 159–161,
  162–164
guardianship of person and
  property in 71, 247
Guardianship Oversight Commission and, 143
Guardianship Program of Dade
  County (Miami), 140–143,
  150–177
heterogeneity in, 70, 141,
  153–154, 172, 173, 195,
  199
historical incidents as independent variable in, 172, 177,
  196
in Arizona, 65–66, 92
in Chicago, 65, 80
in Florida, 140–141, 150–177
in Los Angeles, 65, 79–80, 197,
  198
in Maryland, 65
in Office of the State Courts
  Administrator, 140, 171,
  194–197
individual guardianship plans
  in, 140, 142, 152, 157–162
individuals served by, 70, 74,
  78, 141, 153–154, 187,
  195, 197, 240
information gaps about, 76–78,
  95–96, 187
legal considerations in,
  174–175
Lutheran Ministries of Florida
  and, 140, 143
minorities in, 74, 153, 172,
  187, 195, 199
ombudsman role of, 60
organizational models in, 70,
  140, 186, 242–243
problems of, 13–14, 65, 73–74,
  131, 174–175
professional literature about,
  148–150
program characteristics of, 71
proposed legislation for, 72,
  174–175, 239–261
recommendations about, 76,
  143, 161–162, 174–177,
  239–261
relationship in civil commitment, 74, 83–84, 87, 92,
  187, 210, 214, 239, 241,

247
relationship to protective services, 77–78, 81, 82, 85, 141, 170, 172, 174, 185–186, 187, 195–196
restoration of competency in, 73, 173–174, 187
role of family in, 154, 195
role of social casework in, 175
success factors in, 13–14, 66, 131, 188, 239, 243
Suncoast Area Public Guardianship Project (St. Petersburg), 140–143, 150–177

unique case histories as independent variable in, 172, 177, 196
volunteer program in, 167–169
volunteers in, 142–143, 162–171, 176–177, 196–197, 249–250
ward functioning changes in, 155–156
supply of guardians, 12–13, 138–139
Florida's approaches to, 14, 139–141